The CAHIMS Review Guide

The CAHIMS Review Guide

Second Edition

Preparing for Success in Healthcare Information and Management Systems

Edited by
Joanne Bartley
and Mara L. Daiker

HIMSS

Routledge
Taylor & Francis Group
A PRODUCTIVITY PRESS BOOK

HIMSS

350 N. Orleans St.
Suite S10000
Chicago, IL 60654

Attn: certification@himss.org

For more information about HIMSS, please visit www.himss.org

For more information about the CAHIMS program, please visit https://www.himss.org/resources-certification/cahims.

First published 2022
by Routledge
605 Third Avenue, New York, NY 10158

and by Routledge
4 Park Square, Milton Park, Abingdon, Oxon, OX14 4RN

Routledge is an imprint of the Taylor & Francis Group, an informa business

A catalog record for this title has been requested

ISBN: 9781138336568 (hbk)
ISBN: 9781138335295 (pbk)
ISBN: 9780429443862 (ebk)

DOI: 10.4324/9780429443862

Typeset in Garamond
by KnowledgeWorks Global Ltd.

First Edition published 2015
Printed in the U.S.A. 5 4 3 2 1

ISBN: 978-1-938904-88-2

Contents

Acknowledgments

HIMSS wishes to express gratitude to the contributing authors of the second edition:

Mohammad Bajwa, PhD, CPHIMS, CPHI, RHIA, MSCE
Anthony Blash, Pharm.D., BCompSc, CAHIMS, CPHIMS
Sophia Brown, PhD, DBA, RN-BC, CPHIMS, PMP
Stephanie H. Hoelscher, DNP, RN-BC, CPHIMS, CHISP, FHIMSS
Stephanie Koch, CPHIMS
Wil Limp, MS, RHIA, CHTS-TR
Susan McBride, PhD, RN-BC, CPHIMS, FAAN
Lori Richter, MA, RHIA, CPHIMS, CHPS
Susan Snedaker, MBA, CPHIMS, CISM, CHCIO, CHISL

Introduction

Congratulations! Your purchase of this book is one step in becoming a Certified Associate in Healthcare Information and Management Systems (CAHIMS)[SM] and being recognized for your specialized knowledge and skills.

This book is a comprehensive and timely introduction to healthcare information and management systems. We hope you find it extremely useful in preparing for the CAHIMS exam, and also as an invaluable resource for staying current in all aspects of our industry.

We invite you to apply for certification as a CAHIMS. This certification program, through the Healthcare Information and Management Systems Society (HIMSS), offers a unique opportunity for professional recognition and advancement. Achieving certification as a CAHIMS is a significant accomplishment that attests you have successfully met eligibility criteria and passed the examination.

This introduction provides an overview of the eligibility requirements, testing procedures, and the CAHIMS examination itself. Specific questions should be directed to certification@himss.org.

THE CERTIFIED ASSOCIATE IN HEALTHCARE INFORMATION AND MANAGEMENT SYSTEMS (CAHIMS) CERTIFICATION

HIMSS' CAHIMS certification program offers a pathway to careers in healthcare information technology (IT) for associate-level, emerging professionals, or those who would like to transition to health IT from another industry. CAHIMS is designed for individuals who may or may not have experience within the healthcare industry.

CAHIMS certification has three components:

- Eligibility requirements for participation in the program; to qualify to take the CAHIMS examination and earn CAHIMS certification, you must;
  - Hold a High School Diploma or equivalent **and**
  - Have at least 45 hours of continuing education in healthcare information technology, digital health or informatics, specifically covering content found on the CAHIMS Outline of Exam Topics **or** 150 hours experience in any type of IT and Healthcare setting or role (volunteer, practicum/internship, work)*.

  OR

  - Hold an associate, bachelor or advanced degree from an accredited college or university **and**
  - Have at least 25 hours of continuing education in healthcare information technology, digital health or informatics, specifically covering content found on the CAHIMS Outline of Exam Topics **or** 75 hours experience in any type of IT and Healthcare setting or role (volunteer, practicum/internship, work)*.

  **Candidates will be asked to submit a listing of courses taken or documentation of work experience to meet this requirement, which are subject to audit and verification.*

- A 100-question multiple-choice exam
- A renewal requirement. Certification is valid for three years, at which time it must be renewed through successful retest or documentation of participation in continuing professional education.

An individual who meets eligibility requirements and successfully completes the CAHIMS examination is awarded certification.

CAHIMS Exam

The CAHIMS Exam covers the following:

Section I: Healthcare and Technology Environments

- Healthcare Environment
- Technology Environment

Section II: Clinical Informatics

Section III: Healthcare Information and Systems Management

- Analysis
- Design
- Selection, Implementation, Support and Maintenance
- Testing and Evaluation
- Privacy and Security

Section IV: Management and Leadership

ADDITIONAL RESOURCES

It is recommended that review for the CAHIMS Exam focus on resources and programs that cover the tasks in the CAHIMS Outline of Exam Topics. It should not be inferred that questions on the CAHIMS Exam are selected from any single resource or set of resources or that study from this or other resources listed guarantees a passing score on the CAHIMS Exam.

- **CAHIMS Candidate Handbook:** A must for all CAHIMS Exam candidates, the candidate handbook provides information that is helpful when applying for and scheduling the CAHIMS Exam. The handbook includes the CAHIMS Outline of Exam Topics, directions on how to apply for the Exam and schedule your Exam appointment, what to expect on the day of the Exam as well as following the Exam. It is recommended that all CAHIMS candidates download a copy of the handbook from www.himss.org.
- **CAHIMS Practice Exam:** The practice exam simulates the CAHIMS Exam in content, cognitive level, difficulty, and format. After taking the practice exam, you will receive valuable, practical feedback in detailed score reports.

CAHIMS EXAM ADMINISTRATION

The CAHIMS Exam is delivered by computer at testing centers throughout the world. After applying and paying the exam fee through www.himss.org, candidates who meet the eligibility requirements will receive further instructions from HIMSS on how to schedule their exam through a testing center. The CAHIMS Exam is administered by appointment only, either Monday through Saturday (except major holidays) at a testing center, or through a virtual proctoring mechanism. As a candidate, you may test where you wish and when you feel you are prepared to take the CAHIMS Exam.

Special group administrations of the CAHIMS Exam may be scheduled with HIMSS chapters, corporate members, organizational affiliate members, nonprofit partners, regional extension centers, or other groups through arrangement with HIMSS. For more information on hosting an administration for your group, contact certification@himss.org.

The CAHIMS Exam is also administered at local, regional, domestic, or international HIMSS events. Special application and scheduling procedures may be in place for these events, so check with the event website to find out how to apply and schedule in conjunction with these events.

JoAnn W. Klinedinst, MEd, CPHIMS, PMP, DES, CPTD, LFHIMSS, FACHE, FCAHME

VP, HIMSS Professional Development

Editors

Joanne Bartley, CAE, is Program Manager, Professional Development for the Healthcare Information and Management Systems Society (HIMSS), a global advisor and thought leader supporting the transformation of health through information and technology.

With over 20 years of experience at HIMSS, Joanne has managed programs in North America, Asia, Europe, and the Middle East. Her passion is working with HIMSS members and has worked with hundreds of HIMSS volunteers across various content and program areas.

Joanne is a Certified Association Executive (CAE) and is a member of the American Society of Healthcare Executives and Association Forum.

Mara L. Daiker, MS, CPHIMS, RHIA, SHIMSS, is the Professional Development Program Director for the Healthcare Information and Management Systems Society (HIMSS), a global advisor and thought leader supporting the transformation of health through information and technology.

Ms. Daiker has served in various health information management and information technology roles and has almost 20 years combined HIMSS and industry experience. Ms. Daiker is a Registered Health Information Administrator (RHIA) and a Certified Professional in Healthcare Information and Management Systems (CPHIMS) with a bachelor's degree in Health Information Management from The College of St. Scholastica and a master's degree in Health Care Informatics from the University of Wisconsin-Milwaukee. She is an adjunct faculty member for Kent State University where she instructs coursework related to health records management. She is a senior member of HIMSS (SHIMSS) and an active member of the American Health Information Management Association (AHIMA) and its component state association, the Wisconsin Health Information Management Association (WHIMA).

Ms. Daiker lives in the Milwaukee, WI area with her husband and two children.

HEALTHCARE AND TECHNOLOGY ENVIRONMENTS

I

Chapter 1

Healthcare Environment

Learning Objectives

At the conclusion of this chapter, the reader will be able to:

- Recognize basic characteristics, interrelationships and services of different types of healthcare organizations (e.g., hospitals, clinics, physician practices, ambulatory centers, community health organizations, healthcare payers, regulators, research and academic)
- Identify and differentiate among major clinical and business departments and functions found in healthcare organizations
- Differentiate basic roles of healthcare information and management systems professionals.
- Identify and differentiate roles of governmental, regulatory, professional and accreditation agencies related to healthcare

Introduction

United States (U.S.) healthcare delivery systems have traditionally been viewed as a network of providers, payers and regulatory bodies dedicated to providing medical services to patients across the country and is the only industrialized country that does not have some form of universal health coverage (UHC) for all citizens. Other countries around the globe achieve this through single payer systems, socialized medicine, government mandates or a hybrid of approaches.

In recent years, however, the view of the U.S. healthcare delivery system has been expanded to reflect the growing belief that medicine is no longer simply the act of administering a cure to make sick people healthy. Rather, healthcare stakeholders now include all who have a vested interest in ensuring that healthy citizens remain that way and that those who are ill have access to the best care possible, in multiple avenues including non-traditional care settings.

As a result, patients, for example, are no longer considered passive recipients of care. Rather, they are increasingly viewed as partners in the development of care strategies that will address both their immediate health conditions and their long-term prospects for leading healthy lives.

Research has shown that patients who engage with their healthcare providers have better clinical outcomes and that healthcare organizations (HCOs) that emphasize patient engagement can improve productivity and patient satisfaction.[1]

In other words, the patient now constitutes the focus of the healthcare system, so any individual, profession or organization whose work supports that focus is part of the healthcare network. From providers and payers, to life science and technology firms, to pharmacists, nonprofit advocates and government policymakers, the healthcare sector includes a growing array of parties dedicated to the development, delivery and management of patient care techniques.

Underlying – and, indeed, fueling – these developments have been the advance of health information technology (health IT). While healthcare stakeholders have been working to integrate IT with medicine since the late 1950s, the past decade has brought an explosion of interest and support for implementing health IT tools from policymakers, providers and patients alike. As new ways of documenting, storing, sharing and analyzing health data have evolved and accelerated, efforts to integrate those tools and methods across the healthcare sector have similarly intensified.

DOI: 10.4324/9780429443862-2

Finally, concurrent with the development of new technology has come a more sustained focus on getting skyrocketing healthcare costs under control, worldwide. In order to develop a comprehensive understanding of the role health IT is playing, it's important to be able to recognize, at least in broad terms, the general structure of the healthcare sector, the countless methods being used to pay for healthcare services, the regulatory context and the specific clinical and administrative health technology applications and how they fit into the overall health IT landscape.

Healthcare Delivery

UHC is defined by the World Health Organization (WHO) as "all people and communities can use the promotive, preventive, curative, rehabilitative and palliative health services they need, of sufficient quality to be effective, while also ensuring that the use of these services does not expose the user to financial hardship".[2] UHC is typically achieved through four models; single payer systems, socialized medicine, government mandates or a hybrid approach. In a single payer system, the government pays for medical care and restricts alternative payment mechanisms for the services that it covers. Taiwan and Canada are the only two countries that have true single payer systems.[2] In the U.S., traditional Medicare is an example of a single payer system. In socialized medicine in addition to paying for healthcare, the government owns the facilities and employs the professionals. This is not the case in Taiwan or Canada, but is the case in the United Kingdom. In the U.S., the Veterans Health Administration (VHA) is an example of a socialized healthcare system. Most countries don't have either of these models. Rather they have either insurance mandates or they take a hybrid approach. For insurance mandates the government mandates that all citizens purchase health insurance from private or public health insurers. This often includes a requirement for a standard minimum coverage across all insurers, subsidies for low-income individuals and forbids underwriting and for-profit insurance. Some countries with insurance mandates include Germany, Japan, the Netherlands and Switzerland. Hybrid systems combine elements of single payer systems with private insurance mandates. Government provides a standard set of care for all citizens, with options to supplement with private insurance. Some countries with hybrid systems include Australia, France, Singapore, Sweden and the United Kingdom.[2] The healthcare industry in the U.S. is patterned after a mixed healthcare model that offers both public and private healthcare services. Public options include systems that are managed by the local, state or federal government bodies and publicly funded, while private options, which can be either nonprofit or for-profit, include systems that are privately owned and funded.

California-based Kaiser Permanente, for example, is a private, not-for-profit health plan consisting of 39 hospitals, 734 medical offices and other outpatient facilities and over 23,000 physicians as of 2022. On the public side, the federal VHA manages the U.S. largest integrated healthcare system that, as of this writing, consists of 170 medical centers, over 1,100 community-based outpatient clinics, community living centers, Vet Centers and other supportive care. Together, these healthcare facilities provide comprehensive care to more than nine million veterans each year.

Regardless of whether it is public or private, or how many facilities it encompasses, a healthcare system is an organization that delivers healthcare to individuals while promoting good health in populations.

Types of Healthcare

Healthcare is delivered in many different places, ranging from inpatient facilities to nursing and residential care facilities and outpatient facilities. But before looking at the various settings, all healthcare can be divided into one of three types of general care:

- **Primary care** addresses the majority of a patient's healthcare needs, is often the entry point into healthcare and includes screening, prevention, diagnosis and treatment for acute and chronic health problems.
- **Secondary care** is generally more specialized care and can include surgery, cardiology and other care provided by specialists.
- **Tertiary care** is complex and highly specialized healthcare. Tertiary care is provided in "tertiary care centers", often university hospitals, as it requires sophisticated technology, multiple specialists and subspecialists, a diagnostic support group and intensive care facilities. Often these are regional or national centers of excellence that are affiliated with medical schools and teaching hospitals. Examples of tertiary care include trauma centers, burn centers and neonatal care.

Places Where Care Is Provided

Healthcare is provided in an array of settings, ranging from hospitals and physicians' offices to community health clinics in both urban and rural settings.

Inpatient Healthcare Services

Inpatient Hospital-Based Healthcare Services

Acute care hospital facilities provide healthcare when a patient has been admitted to the facility to receive inpatient care.

Hospitals. Hospitals are physical structures that house patients who are sick or injured. Most acute care hospitals provide general, medical and surgical care. A person may be admitted to a hospital in one of two ways:

- A patient may go to an emergency department (ED) and be evaluated by a team of clinicians. If the clinicians feel a patient is sick enough and meet medical necessity for inpatient criteria, he or she may be admitted to the hospital for care.
- A patient may also be directly admitted to a hospital from a physician's office if they meet predefined medical necessity criteria.

A physician oversees the patient's hospitalization, orders diagnostic testing and coordinates and/or performs the specialized treatment required. Nurses attend to the hospitalized patient 24 hours a day with assistance from a wide variety of hospital staff including medical assistants, laboratory and radiology technicians and numerous others.

In the U.S., hospitals may be publicly or privately owned. Public hospitals may be administered by the city, county, state or at a federal level. Privately owned hospitals may be not-for- profit or for-profit, in which case they pursue profits like any other business and have tax obligations. Practically all European Union (EU) health systems contract both public and private providers. In some countries, such as the Nordic countries, hospital ownership is predominantly public, while in other countries, such as the Netherlands, public ownership is nonexistent.[3]

Another type of hospital is an academic medical center, which serves as a hands-on classroom for medical students, nursing students, resident physicians, fellows and other trainees. Usually at the leading edge of medical knowledge, teaching hospitals provide an essential training ground for physicians and other healthcare professionals and clinicians who care for patients under the supervision of senior medical personnel.

Non-Hospital Inpatient Facilities

U.S. nursing homes grew in number after a 1965 amendment to the Social Security Act provided government funding for nursing home costs. Originally part of the welfare system, nursing homes gradually became part of the current healthcare system. During that transition, nursing and residential care evolved into several levels of care.

Today's nursing and residential care facilities can be short-term facilities, where patients can receive intensive therapy and it is anticipated that patients will stay for a brief period of time before returning home, or long-term facilities, where patients may stay for an extended or indefinite period of time.

The facilities listed below provide post-acute inpatient care:

- **Rehabilitative facilities or acute rehabilitation hospitals** provide care for patients needing comprehensive rehabilitation and medical management often associated with stroke, joint replacement or other serious injury. After surgery or acute illness, a patient may be too frail to return home and may need to spend time in a rehabilitation center for specialized speech, physical and occupational therapy.
- **Skilled nursing facilities (SNFs, sometimes called nursing homes)** are establishments that provide full medical care after a hospitalization. They also provide assistance with activities of daily living, such as meals, personal care, housekeeping and laundry, while the patient is recovering. These facilities manage the transition of acute illness or injury to return to home. The average patient's stay in an SNF is greater than 25 days. SNFs may also provide long-term care for patients needing residential nursing services for an extended period of time.
- **Long-term acute care hospitals** are specialized hospitals designed for patients who need intensive, hospital-level care for weeks or months.

In long-term adult care, a range of services and support is provided – both medical care and assistance with basic, everyday personal tasks.

- **Adult day care** provides meals and activities during the day.
- **Independent living** typically takes the form of retirement communities consisting of condominiums or apartments. Residents can usually purchase added services such as meals or housekeeping.
- **Assisted living** facilities may take the form of separate apartments or private rooms in a common building where a number of services, such as personal care, medication administration, meals and housekeeping are provided by the facility.

Hospice Care

Hospice is specialized healthcare designed to serve patients with a terminal illness respecting a patient's wishes. Hospice care offers personalized care and support focusing on maximizing the quality of life and providing palliative care including pain control. Families are typically involved in the hospice care of their loved ones, and services such as grief counseling and help with managing the patient's final affairs are often provided to them. Hospice care can be provided in a variety of settings. Hospice programs can involve both inpatient care as well as hospice care provided in ambulatory environments, including the home.

Outpatient Healthcare Services

Healthcare is classified as outpatient care if a facility, physician or other clinical healthcare provider treats a patient who is sick or injured, but the patient has not been admitted to a hospital. Outpatient healthcare (also known as ambulatory healthcare) encompasses a wide range of services, including primary care, often provided in a doctor's office or a clinic.

Outpatient providers, also called ambulatory providers, may be EDs, surgical centers, clinics, physician offices, dental offices, medical and diagnostic laboratories, pharmacies or any other form of health service not provided as part of an inpatient stay. In the past decade some of these services have migrated from traditional locations to adding convenient care locations, such as grocery stores, airports and virtually via phone calls where patients can talk to and even see their provider on phone, skype or other technology.

Physician offices focus on primary, family or specialty care. Primary care physicians typically specialize in family care, internal medicine, obstetrics/gynecology (OB/GYN) and pediatrics. Physicians who specialize may concentrate on particular areas of medicine, such as gastroenterology or cardiology, or on surgical specialties, such as orthopedics or neurosurgery.

Some physicians work in a hospital setting, and some work in a separate medical office. Some physicians do both.

Other Outpatient Providers

There are other settings in which outpatient healthcare services are provided.

Ambulatory surgery centers (ASC). These are medical facilities equipped to handle surgery, pain management and certain diagnostic procedures that do not require overnight hospitalization. The centers may be part of a community general hospital, a specialty hospital or an independent medical facility with a prearranged hospital. The centers are staffed with health professionals as in conventional surgery departments. Common procedures performed in ASCs include lens and cataract procedures, tonsillectomies and hernia repairs.

Emergency department. This department of a hospital is responsible for the provision of medical and surgical care to patients arriving at the hospital in need of immediate care. Emergency department (ED personnel may also respond to certain situations within the hospital, such as cardiac arrests. If the patient is discharged directly from the ED, without being admitted, the episode is considered an outpatient event. While the patient is being evaluated in the ED, he/she is considered an observation patient. If admitted, the patient becomes an inpatient and ED services are normally bundled with the inpatient stay for reimbursement purposes.

Outpatient specialty medicine. Outpatient specialty medicine, such as sports medicine and rehabilitation, is provided in outpatient settings, including hospital-based clinics, physician offices or non-hospital clinic settings.

Diagnostic services. Diagnostic services refer to clinical services such as pathology and laboratory medicine, radiology and nuclear medicine.

- **Diagnostic imaging facilities** typically perform tests such as x-rays, computerized tomography (CT) scans (also called computerized axial tomography (CAT) scan), magnetic resonance imaging (MRI), mammograms and position emission tomography (PET) scans.
- **Medical laboratories** primarily evaluate biological specimens including blood. Divisions of a laboratory include chemistry, hematology, microbiology and toxicology.
- **Specialized medical laboratories** are dedicated to a particular type of testing. These types of testing include DNA testing, medical pathology, parasitology and mycology and toxicology. Specialized labs also provide non-radiologic testing services.

Community health clinics. Community health clinics, which provide care to underserved populations, are run by nonprofit organizations or state and local governments.

Home healthcare. Home healthcare is treatment provided to patients in their home by a skilled nursing professional. Home healthcare is usually prescribed by the patient's primary care providers (PCP) or general practitioner (GP) under certain circumstances:

- For patients who are disabled or who suffer chronic debilitating illness
- For seniors who are still able to live at home but require regular health oversight
- For patients who might otherwise require a stay in a more expensive long-term care hospital or rehabilitation facility
- For post-hospitalization recovery for patients just released from a long-term care hospital or rehabilitation center who require a few weeks of regular health oversight

Home healthcare typically includes a combination of professional healthcare services and life assistance services, such as medical or psychological assessment, nursing care, wound care, medication oversight or teaching, pain management, disease education and management and therapy and/or rehabilitation, which might include physical therapy, speech therapy or occupational therapy.

Home healthcare is often provided by a home health agency that employs or contracts with the various healthcare professionals and/or clinicians trained to address the diverse needs of this patient population.

School-based health centers. School-based health centers are located in schools and offer a wide range of services depending on state and local policy. They often provide screening and preventive care and treat minor illnesses. In addition, they may offer behavioral and other forms of counseling.

Employer-based health clinics. Employer-based health clinics may be located at an employment facility or they may be a mobile clinic that can serve several facilities. Their original focus was on occupational health and injury prevention, but in recent years, these clinics have expanded into providing preventive care, screening and chronic disease management. For the employer, these types of clinics provide the advantage of providing control over healthcare costs by emphasizing wellness care. Additionally, they allow employees to receive healthcare without having to take time off from work. Employee health is generally not considered a part of the patient medical record and should not be combined with a hospital or clinic's patient records.

Other ambulatory care for an employee might include use of an urgent care center, retail pharmacy, ambulance service, home healthcare, hearing and vision screening or participation in a wellness program like smoking cessation.

Healthcare Services Provided at the Federal Level

Within the U.S. healthcare system, care at the federal level is provided through both inpatient and outpatient services. This concept of an integrated healthcare delivery system (IHDS) is particularly applicable to government-funded systems, where services for targeted patients (veterans, for example) are provided at governmental hospital systems and outpatient service providers within the community.

The federal government provides healthcare in its own facilities to four major sectors of the U.S. population. They include:

- **Veterans Health Administration (VHA)** provides healthcare for veterans through a series of outpatient and inpatient facilities run by the U.S. Department of Veterans Affairs (VA). The VHA operates one of the largest healthcare systems in the world and provides training for a majority of America's medical, nursing and allied health professionals.

- **Military Health System (MHS)** is part of the U.S. Department of Defense and provides healthcare to service members, retirees and their families. Each branch of the armed forces has its own network of hospitals and healthcare facilities.
- **Indian Health Service (IHS)** is part of the U.S. Department of Health and Human Services (HHS). IHS provides healthcare to more than two million American Indians and Alaska natives.
- **Federal Bureau of Prisons** provides essential medical, dental and mental health services to the more than 200,000 inmates in federal prisons.[4]

Networks

Most U.S. hospitals are associated with a healthcare delivery system or network, which is an organization that owns and operates multiple hospitals and/or ambulatory facilities. Networks can be either horizontal or vertical:

- **Horizontal network** consists of multiple institutions of the same type. Examples are cancer treatment centers or dialysis centers owned by a single company.
- **Vertical network** provides different types of services, usually across the continuum of care. In a vertical network, the patient might receive primary care service, secondary care service, inpatient service, rehabilitative service and home health. A vertical network is positioned to manage and coordinate patient care across various providers.

Managing Care Across the Continuum of Care

The continuum of care is the provision of care from the entry of the patient into the healthcare system until care is no longer needed. Managing the patient across the continuum of care involves providing comprehensive care, coordinated over time and across services. For instance, a patient who needs hip surgery requires coordination among a variety of providers including services prior to surgery, the hospitalization and inpatient surgery, services in a rehabilitative facility and home health. An electronic health record (EHR) with comprehensive information about a patient's medical history supports coordination of care across the continuum. Although there has been significant progress in the use of EHRs, a complete longitudinal record remains a goal but not a reality. A longitudinal health record is a record organized and based on a patient's comprehensive clinical summary of a patient experience rather than visit-by-visit (or encounter) based.

Interdisciplinary Care

The use of interdisciplinary care has gained attention and has grown significantly, especially as disease management options have increased in complexity. With interdisciplinary care, the various types of physicians, specialists, nurses, clinicians and other care providers work together in treating the patient. The team of care providers exchanges information with each other, coordinating the care. The shift toward team-based care has led to the growing use of the patient-centered medical home (PCMH). This is a term introduced by the American Academy of Pediatrics in 1967 and now endorsed by multiple physician organizations. The PCMH is characterized by physician-directed medical care; a primary care physician leads a team of individuals who collectively take responsibility for the care of the patient.

Public Health

Ultimately, healthcare exists to improve the health of an entire population. According to Charles Edward Winslow, a famous American bacteriologist and public health expert during the first half of the 20th century, public health is the science and art of preventing disease, prolonging life and promoting health through the organized efforts and informed choices of society, organizations both public and private, communities and individuals.[5]

Public health has had a significant impact on the control of infectious diseases, such as typhoid, smallpox and goiter, and has helped identify nutritional deficiencies and contributed to a greater understanding of diseases. It has also supported improvements in data collection, healthcare training and infrastructure.

Recent improvements in data collection and analysis have aided epidemiologists who look at the patterns, causes and effects of health and disease conditions in defined populations. Data from health IT systems can inform policy decision and evidence-based practice by identifying risk factors[6] for disease and targets for preventive healthcare.[7]

Positions and Departments within Healthcare Organizations

Healthcare delivery is a complex endeavor that relies on the skills of multiple healthcare professionals and workers to provide quality care to patients. To coordinate the services of its multiple workers, adhere to professional standards and legal requirements, and ensure that its business objectives are met, an HCO must be carefully administered.

Like other businesses, HCOs follow an organizational structure that distributes responsibilities among departments, divisions and personnel. The size of the HCO and the services it offers influence its organizational structure and how its departments interact. Figure 1.1 presents one example of a hospital's organizational structure.

Departments in the Healthcare Field

All HCOs have certain core functions required for delivering healthcare. These include management, medical staff, nursing, clinical support, ancillary support, finance, information services and facilities management. How these functions are manifested have to do with the size and type of the organization.

Management: Board of Directors

The Board of Directors authorizes actions and oversees all business affairs of the hospital or HCO. The board meets several times a year to discuss the entity's current and future state. The board's primary role is to ensure the entity's mission, vision and values are carried out. Duties of the Board of Directors include establishing broad policies and objectives, selecting a chief executive officer (CEO) and reviewing his or her performance, approving annual budgets and ensuring the hospital's financial resources are sufficient and in order.

Management: Officers

The highest-ranking officers in the management division deal primarily with the business concerns of the HCO. These officers include:

- **Chief Executive Officer.** The CEO leads an HCO and may report to a board of directors or board of trustees.
- **Chief Operating Officer (COO).** The COO reports directly to the CEO and is responsible for the day-to-day operations of the HCO.
- **Chief Financial Officer (CFO).** The CFO manages the fiscal aspects of the organization, including the operating budget, contracts, income, expenditures, billing and compensation.

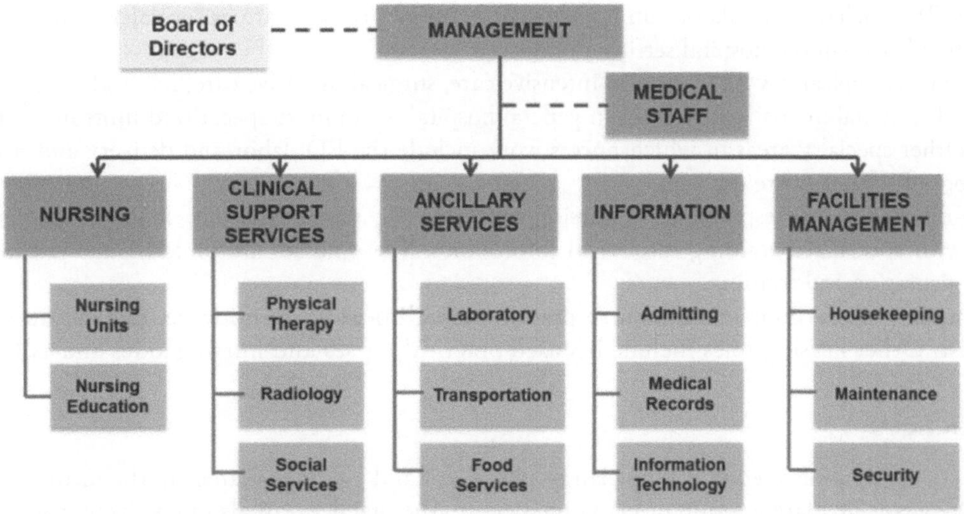

Figure 1.1 Typical hospital organizational structure.

Source: CC-BY by Jan Jraus.

Management: Patient Care and Information

In addition to the top business-oriented officers, other key positions include the chief medical officer (CMO), chief information officer (CIO), chief medical information officer (CMIO) and chief nursing officer (CNO) and chief nursing informatics officer (CNIO).

- CMO is usually a physician serving as the liaison between upper management and the medical staff at an HCO. He or she has responsibility for clinical care, quality improvement and sometimes, graduate medical education.
- CIO is the executive leader of an organization's health IT department. He or she is often in charge of planning, choosing, installing and supporting an HCO's IT and network operations and processing operations.
- CMIO and CNIO provide a liaison between clinicians and IT services. This, too, has become a critical role with the implementation of EHRs. The CMIO often reports to the CIO, CMO or CEO.
- CNO is the head of the nursing department of a medical institution and is in charge of developing the programs, processes and procedures for the other nurses to follow. The CNO will be directly involved in projects involving nursing use of IT systems.

Healthcare Administrators

Healthcare administrators are responsible for planning, directing, coordinating and supervising the delivery of healthcare. They can be in charge of specific departments or manage an entire facility.

Medical Staff

The medical staff is comprised of physicians and other clinicians who practice at the hospital or hospital-based clinics. They hold a semi-autonomous position, which gives them a high degree of authority. Physicians possess the unique skills, talent and training necessary for patient treatment and care. They are directly responsible for patient safety, well-being and quality of care. Physicians may be self-employed or be employed by the HCO. Increasingly, acute care hospitals are utilizing hospitalists, who are employed by the hospital and who are responsible for managing inpatient care.

The chief of staff's office is the governing body of the physicians and works closely with nurses and other clinical staff members. Elected by the staff physicians, the office manages physician privileges and accreditation, medical policies and continuing medical education.

Nursing Staff

Nursing staff, or the nursing division, is typically headed by the CNO. Nursing is responsible for managing and staffing all nursing units. This includes ambulatory units that may comprise primary care or specialty clinics, or inpatient nursing units that provide care in the hospital setting.

Critical care nurses typically work in cardiac intensive care, surgical intensive care, medical intensive care, pediatric intensive care and neonatal intensive care units in general hospitals or in more specialized units in academic or specialized hospitals. Other specialty areas in which nurses work include the ED, labor and delivery and surgery (operating rooms and the post anesthesia care unit).

The nursing division is also responsible for nursing education and professional development. The nursing staff may include nurses with specialized training in clinical informatics. These nurses are directly involved in clinical system selection, implementation and training.

Advanced nursing professions include nurse practitioner, clinical nurse midwife, clinical nurse specialist and nurse anesthetist. Other nursing roles include licensed practical nurses and nursing aides and assistants.

Physician Practices

A physician practice is administered by a physician or physicians and an office manager. The medical staff may consist of only a few physicians or a larger group of many physicians. The practice will also most likely have registrars, nurses and a back-office administrative team. Optionally, the practice may include medical assistants or physician assistants.

The registrar and other office staff are responsible for scheduling and registration. They identify the patient, collect and record demographic and insurance data needed for billing, and sometimes collect co-pays or deductibles at the point-of-service. These personnel routinely interact with a practice management system. If the patient has not been seen before, the output of the registrar's process will be the creation of a unique medical record number for the patient. This medical record number is essential in the creation of an EHR. Medical assistants provide administrative and limited clinical duties in physician practice settings.

Non-Physician Services

Patient care may include care not provided by licensed physicians. These include optometrists, physical therapists, dentists, chiropractors, podiatrists, dietitians and psychologists.

Diagnostic and therapeutic service areas. Within an HCO, there are a variety of departments that provide clinical support. They provide specialized diagnostic and therapeutic services for patients. Diagnostic ancillary services are generally provided in-office or in support of physician services at a hospital, an ASC or a freestanding diagnostic testing facility, and they include audiology, radiology, pulmonary testing services and clinical lab services. Therapeutic ancillary services include physical therapy, occupational therapy, speech therapy, radiation therapy, nutrition therapy and weight management, which may be provided in freestanding medical facilities or hospital-based clinics. Custodial ancillary services focus on hospice, home health or nursing home care.[8]

Pharmacy. Pharmacies can be hospital based or may be freestanding retail pharmacies. Often, a hospital pharmacy also provides retail pharmacy services. When a physician prescribes a drug to a patient on an outpatient basis, the patient fills the prescription at a pharmacy. A pharmacy is a retail store where medicinal drugs are dispensed and sold. These stores may also sell general merchandise, food and health-related products.

Pharmacists, sometimes called chemists, have specialized education and training and are responsible for preparing and dispensing medications.

Many modern pharmacies have expanded their healthcare-related services beyond dispensing drugs to include the following:

- Reviewing medications for safety and efficacy
- Providing drug information
- Providing basic primary care services, such as giving flu shots and monitoring blood pressure

Diagnostic imaging. Imaging tests may include x-rays, CT scans, MRIs, mammograms and PET scans. Commonly, diagnostic images are stored in a picture archiving and communication system (PACS), where images can be accessed by radiologists and other physicians.

Within pharmacy and diagnostic imaging, medical technicians play a key role and often operate specialized medical equipment to provide patient care.

Departments Having a Focus on Patient Information

An HCO must link together various types of information about patients: demographic data, insurance details, medical histories, laboratory test results, diagnoses, treatments, prescriptions and more. Accurate data is essential for safety and quality of care, as well as for billing purposes.

In an HCO, registration and scheduling, information services (health IT) and health information management (HIM, sometimes referred to as the medical records department) are the three departments responsible for:

- Collecting patient information essential for unique identification of the patient and billing
- Ensuring the integrity and completeness of patient data
- Making all information readily accessible for patient care needs
- Securing all patient information

The security and privacy of patient information is one of the most important responsibilities of the organization. The organization must ensure that technical, administrative and physical security safeguards are in place including:

- Continuing education for staff on requirements for privacy and security
- Technical security mechanisms that limit access to the data to those have a work-related need for the information

- A disaster recovery plan
- Mitigation strategies for organization to reduce security vulnerabilities

Registration and Scheduling (Sometimes Called Patient Access)

Registration and scheduling are responsible for registering patients and scheduling appointments. A registrar obtains patient demographic data, payer information and other information needed for billing and the creation of a new record if this is a new patient. The registration process must uniquely identify a patient, and the output of registration of a new patient is a medical record number.

Health Information Management

The HIM department ensures that the record meets legal and regulatory requirements related to the creation, maintenance and use of a patient's medical record – whether paper or electronic. Generally, HIM staff are responsible for these functions: analysis and completion of the medical record, coding of diagnoses and procedures and release of information.

Information Services

Information services (often called by different names, such as health systems technology department, IT department) is responsible for the design, development, creation, use and maintenance of information systems for the HCO as well as the network and IT infrastructure.

With the implementation of EHR systems and greater linkage of data across the continuum of care, an organization's health IT department must support many clinical functions across diverse sites. This expansion has resulted in the need for both a CIO and a CMIO and the addition of clinical analysts in the IT department. These analysts often have the skills needed to reengineer clinical workflow when systems are implemented.

Other Departments

Facilities Department

Facilities departments are led by senior managers who often report to the COO or CFO. The departments are largely involved in managing the facility as a whole; this can include structures and grounds. For example, the housekeeping department is responsible for cleaning and may include the laundry. Maintenance involves day-to-day repairs and replacement but also includes complex maintenance such as electrical, backup generators and heating and cooling. Security is often included in facilities management and is responsible for security issues such as parking control, identification badges and securing patient belongings upon admission.

Facilities management in a delivery network may be a combination of the office staff and contracted cleaning and maintenance staff. As facilities grow, these functions tend to require more personnel.

Teaching and Research Departments

Academic medical centers add the need for two new functions – teaching and research. These can be substantial undertakings requiring specifically allocated divisions and personnel to accomplish these tasks. Research in healthcare might be referred to as health research, medical research or clinical research and refers to research that is done to learn more about human health and focuses on finding better ways to prevent and treat disease across the world.

Healthcare Financing and Regulation

Healthcare spending is growing faster than most other sectors of the U.S. economy and faster than the economy as a whole. This rapid increase in spending places great strains on companies and individuals. The total health expenditure is the sum of public and private health expenditures as a ratio of total population.

According to the Peterson Kaiser Health System tracker, "Over the past four decades, the difference between health spending as a share of the economy in the U.S. and comparable OECD countries has widened. In 1970 the U.S. spent

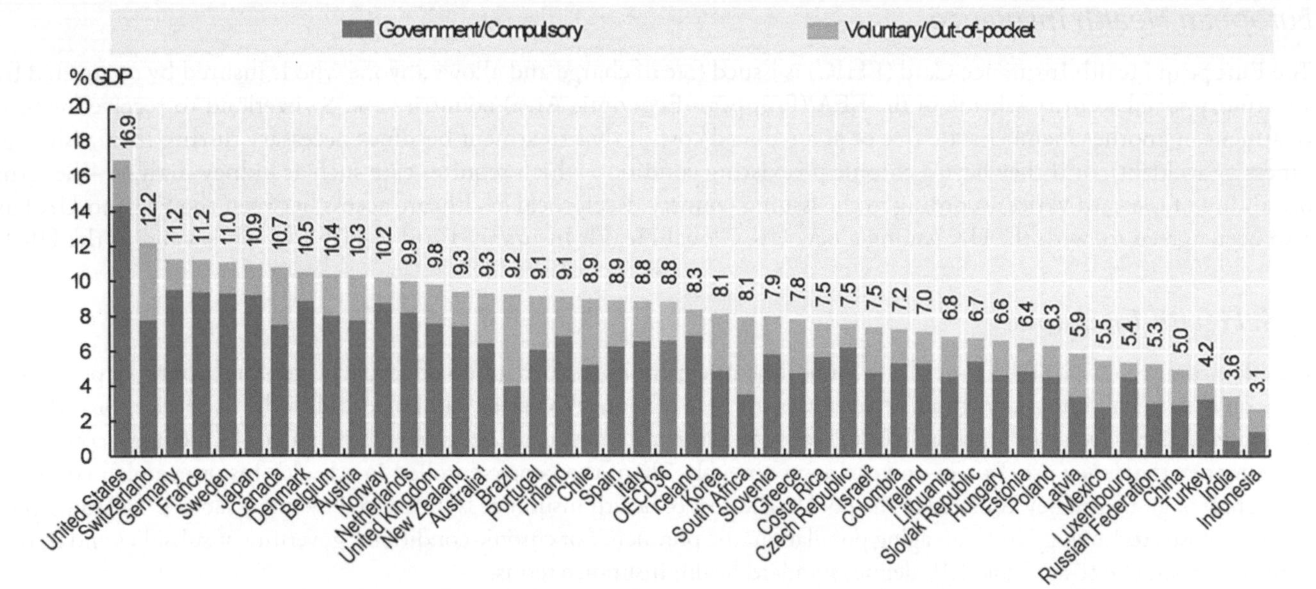

Figure 1.2 Organisation for Economic Co-operation and Development (OECD) health expenditure as a share of GDP, 2018. (From OECD, health expenditure in relation to GDP, in *Health at a Glance 2019: OECD Indicators*, OECD Publishing, Paris.)

about 6% of its GDP on health, similar to spending by several comparable countries (the average of comparably wealthy countries was 5% of GDP in 1970). The U.S. was relatively on pace with other countries until the 1980s, when its health spending grew at a significantly faster rate relative to its GDP. In 2017, the U.S. spent 17% of its GDP on health consumption, whereas the next highest comparable country (Switzerland) devoted 12% of its GDP".[9] Figure 1.2 further illustrates health expenditure as a share of GDP as reported by the OECD in 2019.

It is easy to see that healthcare is consuming our national economies at an unsustainable rate, making governmental engagement in these factors essential.

To address the growth in healthcare costs, many nations' governments are considering changes to their health programs. Among these are enhancements to the primary care delivery system to manage chronic diseases more effectively in Australia, experimentation with privatization in Canada, global budgeting and competition among sickness funds in Germany, requiring long-term care residents to pay for room and board in Japan, and consideration of pro-market reforms in the United Kingdom.[10] Similarly, the development of ACOs in the U.S. is being encouraged with a goal of producing better health outcomes at lower cost. Such trends will continue as we collectively grapple with the best ways to balance quality, access, cost and safety for the greatest proportion of our populations.

Over the years, technology has led to advances in medicine that have prolonged the life expectancy of the average person, but it has come at a price. The Congressional Budget Office (CBO) estimates that almost one half of the healthcare expenditures in the U.S. are due to the cost of technology.[11]

It has been argued that although these technologies are expensive, increased utilization of these devices and techniques can improve quality and reduce costs through their advanced diagnostic capabilities or by reducing complications and shortening the length of hospital stays.

Care and treatment of individuals with chronic diseases constitutes another large portion of the expenditures on healthcare in the U.S. Chronic diseases are ongoing, generally incurable illnesses or conditions, such as heart disease, asthma, cancer and diabetes. These diseases are often preventable and frequently manageable through early detection, improved diet, exercise and timely medical treatment.

Health Insurance Coverage

Across EU member states, healthcare systems are organized and financed in different ways but universal access to quality healthcare, at an affordable cost to both individuals and society at large, is widely regarded as a basic need; moreover, this is one of the common values and principles of EU health systems.[12]

European Health Insurance

The European Health Insurance Card (EHIC) is issued free of charge and allows anyone who is insured by or covered by a statutory social security scheme of the EEA (European Economic Area) countries and Switzerland to receive medical treatment in another member state free or at a reduced cost, if that treatment becomes necessary during their visit (e.g. illness or accident), or if they have a chronic preexisting condition which requires care such as kidney dialysis. The term of validity of the card varies according to the issuing country. Reciprocal healthcare access between the EU and UK has also been agreed to, with the UK issuing a new UK Global Health Insurance Card (GHIC) which is valid in the UK.[13]

U.S. Health Insurance

Health insurance spreads the financial risk for healthcare expenditures for a group of people by pooling money, or premiums paid, on their behalf into a large fund. A payer uses the pool of money to pay or reimburse for healthcare services provided to the individual members of the group. Health plans stay solvent in most cases because each year all of its members contribute more money than they use. In a given year, approximately 5% of the people enrolled in a health insurance plan consume about half of all the money available in the pool.[14] The cost of health insurance is influenced by many factors, including prescription costs, technology costs, an aging population, the prevalence of chronic conditions, government subsidies and health plan administrative costs. Table 1.1[15] defines standard health insurance terms.

Consumers often obtain private insurance through their employer. In 2018, the average company-provided health insurance policy totaled $6,896 a year for single coverage. On average, employers paid 82% of the premium or $5,655 a year. Employees paid the remaining 18% or $1,241 a year. In some cases, employers self-insure, in which case they finance and pay for all the healthcare expenditures of their employees. In these plans, the employer administers the plan and assumes all the risk for the healthcare expenditures of its employees. An employer may contract the claims paperwork to a third-party administrator (TPA).

The contract that an insurance company offers is either an indemnity plan or a managed care plan. Generally, the contract for insurance is between the individual or family and the insurance company or payer, and not between the insurance company and provider.

Table 1.1 Definitions of Standard Health Insurance Terminology

Term	*Definition*
Authorization for service	Commonly known as preauthorization or precertification, the process of preapproving a patient for coverage of a specific medical procedure, such as a surgery or prescription drug.
Co-insurance	The amount a patient is obliged to pay for covered medical services after satisfying any copayment or deductible required by his/her health insurance plan.
Copayment (co-pay)	A specific charge a health insurance plan may require a patient to pay for a specific medical service or supply; an example may be a co-pay for an office visit.
Deductible	A specific dollar amount that a health insurance company may require a patient to pay out-of-pocket each year before making payments for claims.
Eligibility	Conditions that must be met for an individual or group to be considered eligible for insurance coverage.
Out-of-pocket max	An annual limitation on all cost sharing that patients are responsible for under a health insurance plan. Note: This does not apply to premiums, balance-billed charges from out-of-network healthcare providers or services that are not covered by the plan.
Premium	The total amount paid to the insurance company for health insurance coverage, typically a monthly charge.
Subscriber	A person or organization that pays for health insurance premiums; it can also refer to the person whose employment makes him/her eligible for group health insurance benefits.

Indemnity plans are "traditional" plans based on a fee-for-service model. Under these plans, providers are paid according to the services they perform. For example, if a patient goes to the doctor with a broken arm, the company pays a different fee for each service provided, such as taking x-rays and applying a cast.

Managed Care Plans

Managed Care Plans seek to control medical costs by contracting with a network of providers and by requiring preauthorization for visits to specialists. The three main types of managed care plans are:

- **Health Maintenance Organizations (HMOs).** Subscribers pay a predetermined fee in return for a range of medical services from physicians who are either directly employed by the HMO or who have signed contracts with the HMO, becoming "participating providers".
- **Preferred Provider Organizations (PPOs).** Subscribers utilize providers in a contracted network but have the option to pay more if they use doctors, hospitals and other healthcare providers outside of the plan's network. The PPO negotiates contracts with physicians who form the plan's network and who agree to charge discounted rates.
- **Point of Service Plans.** Plans combine elements of HMO and PPO plans and do offer some out-of-network coverage.

Privately funded health plans are state-licensed insurance organizations, also known as commercial health insurers, or simply insurance carriers. Most of these companies are publicly owned through stockholders. Alternatively, these companies can be mutual insurance companies, which are owned by their policyholders. Managed care organizations are also state-licensed insurance organizations.

Government-Funded Insurance

Public insurance is run by the federal government and is funded by the taxpayer. In the U.S. government-run public programs include Medicare, Medicaid and the Children's Health Insurance Program (CHIP). The federal agency responsible for Medicare, Medicaid and CHIP is the Centers for Medicare & Medicaid Services (CMS). Medicaid and CHIP receive federal funding, but are administered by the states. Some people are eligible for both Medicaid and Medicare (Medi-Medi or dual eligible) or for both Medicaid and CHIP.

Medicaid. Medicaid provides care primarily to low-income individuals and families. Medicaid programs vary from state to state, each having different eligibility requirements and reimbursement structures. The rules for determining income and resources vary from state to state and group to group. However, some rules have been mandated by the federal government: States must provide payments for hospital and physician services; they may provide payments for pharmacy, dental and eye care; and no state may provide payments for abortions.

States are not required to offer Medicaid, although all 50 states now have a program. Each state formulates and administers its own Medicaid plans subject to federal regulations and guidelines. In these plans, each state outlines the nature and scope of services to be provided, then selects vendors to provide the services outlined in their plan.

Medicaid programs have different names in different states. Some examples are Badger Care Plus in Wisconsin and Medical in California. The Medicaid program is jointly funded by the federal government and states. The federal government pays for a specified percentage of program expenditures. The federal government's share of Medicaid expenditures varies by state, ranging from 50% in wealthier states to up to 75% in states with lower per capita income.[16] States that accept Medicaid funding must provide coverage to families and individuals who receive assistance under the federal programs called Temporary Assistance to Needy Families (TANF) and Supplemental Security Income (SSI).

CHIP. CHIP covers children whose families cannot afford private insurance. Children who are covered under CHIP may also be covered by Medicaid. If so, they receive a range of benefits, including doctor visits, emergency care, hospital care, prescription drugs, and vision, hearing and dental care. Children also get free preventive care, such as vaccinations. For other services, families may pay low premiums and deductibles.

Workers' compensation. Workers' compensation provides several types of benefits to an injured employee, or to his or her family after he or she is deceased. It can replace wages, acting as a form of disability insurance. In addition, it can compensate for past and future economic loss, provide medical benefits, acting as a form of health insurance and provide benefits to survivors of employees killed in work-related accidents, acting as a form of life insurance. Workers' compensation, however, is not the same as disability insurance or unemployment income.

Medicare. Medicare provides healthcare to persons 65 and older and the disabled. It is divided into a number of "parts", each paying for a different type of care. These are:

- **Medicare Part A** is hospital insurance but is not limited to acute hospital care. Part A also covers SNFs, rehabilitation centers, long-term care facilities, home healthcare, hospice programs and certain outpatient care.
- **Medicare Part B** is medical insurance for outpatient service. It covers doctors' services, laboratory and diagnostic imaging services, home health services and other medical services delivered in an ambulatory setting. Patients are required to pay a monthly premium and annual deductible.
- **Medicare Part C** refers to Medicare Advantage Plans. These HMO-type plans are offered by private companies that have been approved by Medicare. The plans provide Medicare Parts A, B and sometimes D and may offer extra coverage, such as vision, hearing and dental care. Enrollees in Medicare Advantage Plans pay a premium to the private companies for their coverage and also pay a deductible. Each Medicare Advantage Plan charges different out-of-pocket costs and has different rules for services, which can change each year.
- **Medicare Part D** was created in 2003 and provides prescription drug coverage. Enrollment is voluntary, and enrollees pay a premium to an insurance company or other private company that is approved by Medicare. Deductibles and co-pays vary by plan. In addition to the monthly premium paid to the insurance company, the subscriber also pays a monthly Medicare premium that is normally withheld from the monthly Social Security payment. After a certain point, enrollees may have to pay a greater portion of their prescription drug costs themselves for a portion of the year.

The Medical Billing Process

Medical billing involves the creation of a claim that is normally transmitted electronically from the provider to the payer. While standardized transaction sets are utilized in the submission of a claim, requirements for billing may vary by payer. Key to a claim is the codes, including the International Classification of Diseases 9th Revision or 10th Revision (ICD-9 or ICD-10) and Current Procedural Terminology (CPT) codes that identify and diagnose procedures and services for all patient encounters. In an inpatient environment, diagnosis and procedure codes are utilized in the generation of a diagnosis-related group (DRG). DRG reimbursement methodology is a form of prospective payment where a standard fee is associated with an acute episode of care. Another prospective payment methodology is the use of Ambulatory Payment Classifications (APCs).

The Medical Billing Cycle

When an individual seeks medical services, the medical billing cycle is initiated. Practice management software or hospital management software is used extensively during part or all of this cycle. The components of the billing cycle are:

- **Scheduling.** An appointment is made for medical services. This appointment could be in a physician's office, at a hospital, or in a clinic. Demographic, insurance and diagnosis and procedure information may be collected during the scheduling process.
- **Registration.** During patient registration, an account record is created. If this is a new patient, a medical record number is also assigned. Demographic information is collected, and accurate patient and responsible-party information is taken. The recording of this information, including the guarantor, is a legal record and can be used to hold the patient or responsible party accountable for the bill for medical services. In the case of a minor, the responsible party is the responsible adult, usually the parent or guardian. Insurance information, including deductibles, copayments and coinsurance, is gathered.
- **Delivery of medical services.** Medical services include all diagnostic and therapeutic services provided to a patient.
- **Charge capture.** Charge capture is the recording of charges for all medical services. Charges may be captured electronically as a by-product of other documentation or may be entered manually.
- **Coding.** Coding is the process of translating treatments, diagnoses and other medical services into established codes so they can be submitted as part of a claim. Accurate diagnosis and procedure codes have a direct impact on reimbursement. In a hospital environment, coding is usually supported by specialized coding software that supports the accurate documentation of diagnosis and procedure codes. Most practice management systems also have a function that associates diagnosis and procedure codes with an encounter or visit.

- **Claim processing.** Claims are submitted to the payer or to a contractor who processes the claim for the payer. For instance, CMS utilizes Medicare Administrative Contractors to process claims. Often, claims are submitted to a clearinghouse where they can be edited prior to submission to the payer.
- **Explanation of benefits (EOB).** The payer issues an EOB, which contains the date of service, the code used to bill a particular service to an insurance company, the fee charged by the healthcare provider, the payment made by the payer and the patient's responsibility under the terms of his or her coverage. The final entry of each line item usually shows what the patient's responsibility is.
- **Reimbursement.** The healthcare provider receives reimbursement for medical services delivered. Normally reimbursement is sent in the form of an electronic remittance.
- **Patient billing and generation of patient statements.** After the insurance company has issued an EOB, the provider will bill the patient for the remaining balance. In this step, normally a system generates patient statements.
- **Final settlement.** Final settlement occurs when the patient's balance is settled. The provider has the option to write off a portion of what is owned or to send the account to a third-party for collections.

Medical Code Sets

ICD-10, developed by WHO, is a set of medical codes for complaints, diseases, injuries, symptoms and abnormal findings. ICD-10 was implemented as the agreed upon code set in the U.S. starting on 1 October 2015 to allow more specific reporting on patient care.

Other code sets are used for various purposes. CPT[17] codes, for example, are used to document medical procedures. The ICD-10 code structure is as follows:

Characters 1 to 3: Category
Characters 4 to 6: Etiology, anatomic site, severity or other clinical detail
Character 7: Extension

Reimbursement

Reimbursement to healthcare providers is based upon a variety of payment methods.

Fee-for-service methodology. In the fee-for-service payment method, third-party payers reimburse a provider for each service, according to a fee schedule, which is a list of allowable services and procedures, and the amounts payable for each. Some medical services may not be allowable or payable; one example is cosmetic plastic surgery. The fee schedule is developed from historical claims data using the average of the usual, customary and reasonable charges that have been submitted by providers over time.

A variation on this method is the resource-based relative value scale (RBRVS), used by Medicare and other third-party payers. These payments are based on the cost of services in terms of effort, overhead and malpractice insurance.

Self-pay. With self-pay, patients pay directly for the services they receive. One self-pay scheme involves large employers who self-insure under the Employee Retirement Income Security Act of 1974 (ERISA), which will be explained later in this chapter. The employer agrees to pay for an employee's medical care and assumes all the risk for the cost of care and administers and pays for all of an employee's healthcare costs. In some cases, employees may share some of the costs with the employer. This scheme usually involves a TPA, which may be an insurance company, to assist in processing employee claims.

Managed care reimbursement. In managed care reimbursement, managed care organizations (MCOs) contract with providers to limit fees. The MCO may use a fee-for-service methodology in which payments are made according to a discounted fee schedule, or an MCO may use an episode-of-care reimbursement, such as a prospective or global payment. MCOs provide an incentive to patients to use resources effectively, by either lowering in-network costs, or raising costs for out-of-network care.

Capitation. MCOs may also employ capitation, a type of reimbursement in which there is a single "capitated" payment made for the covered member – regardless of services used. The provider or HCO receives the same amount from the third- party payer per length of time, usually a month, for the care provided at the HCO to all of its members. Regardless of the number of patients enrolled in the plan requiring care, the frequency of the visits, or the severity of an illness, the provider receives a preset amount per enrolled patient each month. The term used to describe this payment is per member per month, or PMPM.

Episode-of-care methodology. In the episode-of-care methodology, reimbursement is provided as a lump sum payment for all care provided to and received by the patient during the episode, regardless of the cost of providing the services.

Global payment methodology. The global payment methodology pays a fixed dollar payment for each episode of care a patient receives in a given time period, such as a month or a year.

Prospective payment methodology. Another type of episode-of-care methodology is the prospective payment method in which payers establish reimbursement rates in advance for packages of healthcare services for specific problems. The rates are established based on average resource use for the level of care and the services provided. Individual patients may require different levels of resources that correspond to different costs; however, the total resource use should average out over time. There are two types of prospective payment methods:

- **DRGs**, a prospective payment methodology utilized for acute care, were implemented originally by Medicare to reduce costs. In DRG-based reimbursement, the DRG code determines what the hospital will be paid for all acute care services associated with the case. DRGs are assigned by the payer utilizing software that combines diagnosis and procedure codes with a subset of patient data. An example of one of the most common DRGs is chronic obstructive pulmonary disease (COPD).
- **APCs** are the U.S. government's method of paying for facility outpatient services for Medicare. Through part of the Federal Balanced Budget Act of 1997, CMS created a new Medicare "Outpatient Prospective Payment System" (OPPS) for hospital outpatient services – analogous to the Medicare prospective payment system for hospital inpatients (DRGs). OPPS was implemented on 1 August 2000. APCs are an OPPS applicable only to hospitals. Physicians are reimbursed via other methodologies for payment in the U.S., such as CPTs.

Health Insurance Regulation

Private insurance in the U.S. is regulated by both state and federal laws. States control the legal structure of private insurers and monitor their finances to make sure they can meet their obligations to the people they insure. Health insurance companies must prove they have enough money to pay all anticipated claims for the year, along with their administrative and operating costs. In addition, they must maintain a certain amount of excess funds or reserves, in case claims exceed projected experience.

There are multiple federal laws regulating both public and private health insurance, including the following:

ERISA

ERISA sets certain minimum standards for employer-provided health plans. For any ERISA-organized health plan, states laws may not preempt federal regulations that require employers to provide an appeals process and also allow employees to sue for benefits.

Consolidated Omnibus Budget Reconciliation Act (COBRA)

COBRA is a 1986 amendment to ERISA that allows employees to continue their healthcare insurance in certain cases, including voluntarily leaving a job, involuntary job loss, the death of a spouse and divorce. Individuals usually have to pay at least some of the premium themselves, and they may even pay slightly more than what the insurance formerly cost. Companies with fewer than 20 employees are not generally required to offer COBRA benefits.

Health Insurance Portability and Accountability Act (HIPAA)

HIPAA, passed in 1996, provides protection for the privacy of an individual's health information. Under HIPAA, providers must notify patients of their privacy rights and how their information can be used upon their first visit to the healthcare entity (and upon subsequent revision) within the Notice of Privacy Practices. HIPAA also gives employees and their families access to group insurance regardless of their health status. For many employees who lose insurance coverage, it provides opportunities to join other group plans or buy individual insurance. HIPAA also mandated the use of standardized transaction sets for communication between providers and payers.

HIPAA Privacy Rule

- Requires HCOs, defined as covered entities, to notify patients of their privacy rights
- Allows patients access to their designed record set, which includes their legal medical and billing records within a defined time frame
- Requires implementation of privacy procedures for HCOs
- Provides elements of required privacy and security education and training for workforce members
- Mandates covered entities to designate someone to oversee privacy procedures and be named the privacy officer
- Includes a defined set of rules and regulations in outlined technical and administration controls for entities to maintain patient privacy and secure their protected health information including their entire medical patient record

The Women's Health and Cancer Rights Act (WHCRA)

WHCRA provides coverage of certain post-mastectomy benefits for women who undergo mastectomy, including reconstructive surgery and treatment of complications.

ACA

The Patient Protection and Affordable Care Act, enacted in 2010, improves access to health insurance for children, young adults and people who have been denied insurance due to a preexisting condition. In addition, insurance companies are no longer allowed to impose lifetime limits on most benefits, and the law is phasing out the annual limits that companies can impose. Patients in some plans get free access to certain preventive services, and there were provisions to reduce the cost of drugs for Medicare.

ARRA and the HITECH Act

The American Recovery and Reinvestment Act (ARRA), otherwise known as the "stimulus package", was signed into law by President Barack Obama on 17 February 2009. ARRA provided over $787 billion in funding, including grants to states for infrastructure and jobs and increased funding for healthcare research. Its many other provisions are designed to increase jobs and stimulate the economy.

One of the provisions of ARRA is the Health Information Technology for Economic and Clinical Health (HITECH) Act. The HITECH Act legislation provided over $19 billion in funding to guide important initiatives to improve healthcare through the use of health IT.

The goals and vision of the HITECH Act are:

- Improved individual and population health outcomes
- Increased transparency and efficiency
- Improved ability to study healthcare
- Improved care delivery

The HITECH Act seeks to improve patient care and promote patient-centered healthcare through the use of interoperable EHR systems. Interoperability – or the connection between EHRs – —enables improved provider workflow, access to comprehensive patient information and allows data transfer among EHR systems and healthcare stakeholders. Ultimately, an interoperable environment improves the delivery of healthcare by making the right data available at the right time to the right people.

A key premise is that information should follow the patient. Therefore, secure information exchange needs to occur so that the appropriate information is available to improve coordination and improve quality of care for patients. This act is also intended to enhance the capabilities of healthcare researchers.

Promoting Interoperability (Formerly Known as Meaningful Use)

The Promoting Interoperability (PI) Program was created by CMS to encourage healthcare providers to demonstrate effective, or meaningful use, of certified EHR technology.

Meaningful Use[18] is defined by a set of standards being developed by HHS, in collaboration with CMS and the Office of the National Coordinator for Health Information Technology (ONC), to govern the use of EHRs. Compliance with meaningful use criteria allows eligible providers – eligible professionals, eligible hospitals and critical access hospitals (CAHs) – to earn incentive payments.

The milestones for this project were established by the Centers for Medicare and Medicaid in 2011 and are now referred to as the PI Program Milestones. The PI program is the most recent expression of the original Meaningful Use program.

Eligible providers who use EHRs in a meaningful way earn financial incentives, which are paid by CMS. The focus of meaningful use is to promote the application of EHRs in ways that improve the outcomes of care.

Because meaningful use requires new function and data to be in place as an EHR is adopted, health IT professionals and clinicians must collaborate in helping their organization to meet meaningful use requirements. Some of the capabilities meaningful use will require EHRs to have been described as follows:

- **Structured documentation** is data entered into predefined fields in the EHR. It also includes codified data stored in a standard, coded format. The allergy list, problem list and medication list supported in an EHR are examples of codified data.
- **Electronic prescribing (also called ePrescribing)** enables physicians to create and electronically transmit prescriptions to a pharmacy.
- **Computerized provider order entry (CPOE)** is a clinical module that enables a provider to enter an order. Used primarily for medication orders, the system can also be utilized for other types of orders, including laboratory orders. Although used primarily by physicians, other providers who have authority to enter specific types of orders may also use CPOE. CPOE, when utilized for medication ordering, is tightly integrated with the Pharmacy system and employs clinical decision support (CDS) to issue alerts and reminders during the ordering process. Orders are transmitted electronically to pharmacy, laboratory, or other departments where they are then processed.
- **Clinical decision support systems (CDSS)** enhance clinician workflow by issuing alerts and reminders at the point of care (POC). **CDSS,** when embedded in an EHR, assists providers at all stages of care – diagnostic, treatment and follow-up – and is increasingly seen as a tool for preventive health and chronic disease management.

In 2014, Stage 2 Meaningful Use required providers to offer secure electronic messaging to patients, as well as enabling patients to securely view online, download and transmit their health information.

For 2020 the Medicare program requires the following:[18]

- Finalized a minimum EHR reporting period of any consecutive 90 days for new and returning participants.
- Converted the query of prescription drug monitoring program (PDMP) measures from required to optional and eligible for five bonus points.
- Removed the verify opioid treatment agreement measure beginning in CY 2020.
- Requires all eligible hospitals and CAHs utilize 2015 edition certified edition EHR technology (CEHRT).
- Requirement that EHR technology be certified to all electronic clinical quality measures (eCQMs) available to report for CY 2020 reporting period.
- Aligned the CQM submission requirements with those of the hospital inpatient quality reporting (IQR) programs for the reporting period in CY 2021.
- Finalized an eCQM reporting period of one, self-selected quarter of discharge data for four self-selected eCQMs in the IQR Program for CY 2020 and subsequent reporting years.

Accreditation, Certification and Licensure

Accreditation

Accreditation entities, regulatory bodies and professional associations serve important roles in setting standards, regulating healthcare, enforcing compliance and evaluating an HCO's performance. Two accreditation organizations with which most U.S. healthcare workers are familiar are The Joint Commission and URAC (formerly known as the Utilization Review Accreditation Commission). All healthcare workers, to varying degrees, are involved in helping facilities pursue the accreditation process.

The Joint Commission, a nongovernmental, nonprofit agency, is the nation's oldest and largest standards-setting and accrediting body in healthcare. To earn and maintain The Joint Commission's Gold Seal of Approval, an HCO must undergo an on-site survey by a Joint Commission survey team at least every three years.[19] The team evaluates criteria in a wide range of areas, such as infection control procedures, emergency preparedness, medication management, patient safety protocols and management of patient information.

URAC is one of the fastest-growing healthcare accreditation agencies with more than 25 programs. The accreditation process includes a review of policies and procedures plus an on-site visit to the organization to determine that it is operating according to its stated policies and national standards.

Certification

Certification is the documented confirmation that a person has demonstrated skills or knowledge necessary to competently complete a job or task. Certification is voluntary and usually requires the applicant to pass an examination. Certification is normally granted by a professional organization. For instance, the Healthcare Information and Management Systems Society (HIMSS) offers the CAHIMS℠, CPHIMS℠ and CPDHTS℠ certifications. Normally, certification is provided at a national level but HIMSS certification is internationally relevant.

Licensure

Licensure is the state of legally being able to practice or work in a profession as stipulated by a license, which is a document giving permission to practice. Both physicians and nurses must hold state licenses in order to practice. Licensing requirements vary by state. In California, for instance, other types of providers, such as acupuncturists, audiologists, chiropractors, physical therapists and occupational therapists, must hold licenses.

Most healthcare licenses are granted by the states. The requirements can range from completing a few hours of coursework to completing advanced degrees involving several years of coursework, education and training. For licensure, requirements vary, sometimes greatly, among states and across the range of healthcare professions.

Summary

Much of the globe has UHC, giving everyone equal access to quality healthcare. However, that does not come without its problems such as long wait times for elective procedures and healthcare costs may overwhelm government budgets. Many recipients of UHC believe this system is still better than the U.S. healthcare system.

The U.S. healthcare system is a complex network of public and private providers and payers focused on delivering a broad array of healthcare services to the American public. It is delivered in a host of locations, ranging from hospitals to virtual care clinics, and paid for by both public and private entities.

A range of both state and federal government agencies are involved in the delivery and regulation of healthcare services, and in the private sector both for-profit and nonprofit organizations are dedicated to delivering, managing and improving patient care.

Encouraged by legislative actions such as the HITECH Act, and promoted enthusiastically by advocates across the healthcare sector, health IT is playing an ever-increasing role in the evolution of U.S. healthcare, contributing to more efficient care, better outcomes, patient empowerment and team care.

References

1. A Leadership Resource for Patient and Family Engagement Strategies. Health Research & Educational Trust, Chicago: July 2013, www.hpoe.org (accessed 5 January 2014).
2. Slaybaugh, Chris. International Healthcare Systems: The US Versus the World. https://axenehp.com/international-healthcare-systems-us-versus-world/ (accessed 12 November 2021).
3. Kruse, Adang, & Groenewoud, Jeurissen, Wiley On-line Library, 2 March 2018, https://onlinelibrary.wiley.com/doi/full/10.1002/hpm.2502 (accessed 5 January 2021).
4. Federal Bureau of Prisons. http://www.bop.gov/about/agency/ (accessed Nov. 7, 2014).

5. Winslow, C.E. (1920). The untilled fields of public health. *Science.* no. 51.
6. Risk factors. http://en.wikipedia.org/wiki/Risk_factor.
7. Preventive healthcare. http://en.wikipedia.org/wiki/Preventive_healthcare.
8. Bankrate Ancillary Services, https://www.bankrate.com/glossary/a/ancillary-services/ (accessed 20 December 2020).
9. Kamal, R., Ramirez, G, & Cox, C. How Does Health Spending in the U.S. Compare to Other Countries? Peterson-KFF. Health System Tracker. https://www.healthsystemtracker.org/chart-collection/health-spending-u-s-compare-countries/ (accessed 11 February 2020).
10. Shi, L, & Singh, DA. (2012). *Delivering Health Care in America: A Systems Approach* (5th ed.). Burlington, MA: Jones & Bartlett Learning, pp. 20–27.
11. Congressional Budget Office. PDF. (accessed 4 November 2014). Technological Change and the Growth of Health Care.
12. Eurostat Statistics Explained. https://ec.europa.eu/eurostat/statistics-explained/index.php?title=Healthcare_expenditure_statistics#Healthcare_expenditure (accessed 20 December 2020).
13. European Health Insurance Card. https://en.wikipedia.org/wiki/European_Health_Insurance_Card.
14. Affordability: The Most Urgent Health Reform Issue For Ordinary Americans. https://www.healthaffairs.org/do/10.1377/forefront.20160229.053330. (accessed 8 April 2022).
15. Medical Mutual Glossary of Healthcare Terms. https://www.medmutual.com/For-Individuals-and-Families/Health-Insurance-Education/Glossary-of-Terms.aspx (accessed 4 November 2014).
16. Rudowitz, R., Orgera, K., & Hinton, E. (March 21, 2019). https://www.kff.org/medicaid/issue-brief/medicaid-financing-the-basics/view/print/ (accessed 4 November 2014).
17. Current Procedural Terminology. https://en.wikipedia.org/wiki/Current_Procedural_Terminology
18. CMS.gov; Centers for Medicare and Medicaid Services. https://www.cms.gov/Regulations-and-Guidance/Legislation/EHRIncentivePrograms/Basics.html
19. The Joint Commission; Facts about the Joint Commission. PDF. https://www.jointcommission.org/-/media/deprecated-unorganized/imported-assets/tjc/system-folders/topics-library/the_joint_commission_3_10pdf.pdf?db=web&hash=ADF3210071154EF26FD6B399DAFDCCE5 (accessed 4 November 2014).

Chapter 2

Technology Environment

Learning Objectives

At the conclusion of this chapter, the reader will be able to:

- Differentiate characteristics of applications (e.g., clinical, administrative, financial) and clinical technologies commonly used in healthcare
- Recognize basic characteristics of the information and communication technologies that support the healthcare environment (e.g., diagnostic imaging, data warehouses, data models, infrastructure, servers, web services)
- Recognize trends in healthcare technology (e.g., telemedicine, patient portals, wearable devices, population health)

Introduction

As computer technology has advanced, its use and application in healthcare has expanded to include just about every aspect of care delivery. Governments and regulatory entities around the world have enacted laws and rules to support, and in some cases require, the use of healthcare technology. In some countries, reimbursement for care for targeted populations is tied to the use of technology.

This increasing implementation of healthcare technology is helping transform both the clinical and the financial side of the sector.

In order to be able to effectively manage and make optimal use of current and future health information technology (health IT), it's important for health IT professionals to understand both the technologies themselves and the role they play within healthcare organizations and the broader sector, while also recognizing the myriad efforts underway to continue to introduce and improve upon the use of health IT.

Global Trends in Health IT

In the United States (U.S.), the passage in 2009 of the Health Information Technology for Economic and Clinical Health (HITECH) Act put health IT front and center in the minds of healthcare stakeholders, policymakers and the general public as a key tool in the effort to transform the U.S. healthcare system. HITECH focused largely on facilitating the spread of electronic health records (EHRs) among providers, but there are numerous ways in which health IT is contributing to more efficient and effective healthcare delivery.

These same factors are at play in countries around the world. Rising healthcare costs, aging populations, labor shortages and a desire to improve care are universal drivers resulting in efforts to improve the use of technology in the delivery of care worldwide.

In Australia, the My Health Record initiative was opened to all Australians so their medical records would be available via the Internet anytime and anywhere. Australians were provided a six-month window (July 2018–January 2019) to determine whether they wanted to participate in My Health Record or to opt out. This national initiative makes key

DOI: 10.4324/9780429443862-3

medical data available to providers, whether it's a new general practitioner in a new state or an emergency room visit after an accident.[1]

In 2003, Singapore's health minister announced the One Singaporean, One EMR initiative and in 2015, the government of Singapore underscored their commitment to healthcare IT in the Intelligent Nation (i2015) initiative.[2]

China and India, with large populations to manage, are focusing efforts on managing administrative workflows of healthcare more than the integration of clinical systems and workflows.

In Brazil, the Ministry of Health has defined standards for interoperability of health IT systems and the city of Sao Paulo adopted an open-source EHR that serves more than 14 million patients.

In Europe, there has been increasing emphasis on making health data available across borders. To address the exchange of health data across EU borders, the eHealth Digital Service Infrastructure (eHDSI) was created. It was initially set up to provide patient summary and prescription data. The program was structured to exist from 2015 to 2019. A permanent governance structure will be needed to maintain this initiative into 2020 and beyond.[3]

A 2011 survey of 300 acute hospitals in 30 European countries found that more than 80% had a computer system connected to the Internet, more than 70% had an EHR, just over 30% shared medical data with other healthcare organizations in their area, and less than 5% exchange data outside their country. The most commonly shared data across borders were radiologic reports.[4] In the years since this report, more organizations have implemented EHR systems and interoperability is increasing both within countries and across borders as technology and interfaces have become more standardized.

Many African countries, including Kenya, Mozambique, Nigeria, Algeria and Ghana (to name just five), are deploying open-source EMR systems. Open-source EMR systems are also deployed in India, Nepal, Afghanistan, Ukraine, Greece and the Philippines, to name a few. In many areas, the cost of deployment and the reliability of infrastructure continue to pose challenges to widespread deployment and interoperability, but these implementations provide a starting point for the proliferation of EMR systems in the future.[5]

Clearly, as healthcare technology evolves, it is being deployed in increasing numbers of organizations worldwide. This trend will continue as all countries strive to find cost-effective ways to provide healthcare to their populations.

Health Information Technology and Health Information Systems

The development and use of different types of health IT have grown significantly over the past two decades. According to the U.S. federal government, health IT is "a broad concept that encompasses an array of technologies to store, share and analyze health information".[6] Another way of viewing health IT is to consider it an umbrella concept that describes the computerized devices and systems that are used to collect, manage and make multifaceted use of health data by patients, providers, payers and policymakers.

Health information systems (HIS) then, are automated, connected systems consisting of computer hardware and software that receive, process and output data as they support the functions of healthcare-related organizations.

HIS can be centralized where a single vendor provides most of the applications or modules, or it can be best of breed. In a best of breed environment, organizations utilize different vendors for different modules or applications which are part of the larger HIS environment. Within a HIS are a variety of applications including those that provide clinical capability like the EHR and computerized provider order entry (CPOE) that support clinician workflow, financial modules like billing and collections, administrative applications like human resources and payroll, and departmental systems including laboratory, radiology, pharmacy and medical records.

Worldwide, there are numerous software vendors providing EHR software. Many focused on smaller practices are comprehensive providing both medical record management as well as back-office functions such as supply chain management, human resources (HR), payroll, billing and financials. Many of these systems are focused on medical clinic operations or small hospitals. Other larger vendors focus primarily on providing a wide array of clinical functions (which include coding, charging, billing, collection) but exclude other more business-focused functions such as HR or Payroll. These systems are often used by larger healthcare providers who deploy best-of-breed solutions to address business functions not offered by their EHR system.

Cost Concerns as a Driver of Health IT Use

For healthcare organizations, decreasing revenues and increasing costs have been a persistent concern over the past 50 years. In response, healthcare organizations and policymakers have been working on several fronts to find ways to reduce costs while also working to improve care. Some of the approaches focus on the methods providers use to deliver care, while others focus on altering how providers are compensated with an eye toward giving them an incentive to improve efficiency and achieve savings by targeting areas such as chronic disease management. Increasingly, regardless of the specific strategy, health IT is being looked to as a critical part of controlling costs across the healthcare sector as it facilitates quicker, more seamless and more efficient access to both clinical and financial data, thus helping reduce the overall cost of care delivery.

Quality-of-Care Concerns as a Driver of Health IT Use

One of the key areas of focus in healthcare since the 1990s is quality of care. This concern was heightened by Institute of Medicine (IOM) reports, such as *To Err Is Human*,[7] that pointed out the significant number of medical errors that were routinely occurring in the U.S. healthcare system. The IOM called for major improvements in the quality of care and emphasized the use of IT in reducing medical errors. In the early 1990s, hospitals began to use a variety of methods for overall quality improvement. These efforts in quality improvement activities, including outcomes analysis and the use of evidence-based medicine (EBM) supported by clinical guidelines, critical pathways and protocols, were enhanced by the increased use of health IT.

Outcomes analysis involves analyzing the impact of medical treatment on patient health outcomes. Clinical guidelines are care guidelines for healthcare providers that are typically developed by expert consensus and/or are based on evidence from research studies. Guidelines recommend actions to be taken to diagnose or treat a given condition and are a cornerstone of preventive health and chronic disease management. Through health IT, this information can be made available to physicians at the point-of-care (POC), in both inpatient and outpatient settings.

Protocols (in a healthcare setting) are standards of care, often expressed as standard order sets that guide care surrounding particular clinical conditions. POC systems also support online access to reference materials that support clinical decision-making. The use of EBM that incorporates standardized order sets, critical pathways and protocols, along with system-generated alerts and reminders, support an organization's efforts to deliver high-quality care while minimizing adverse events.

Nursing's use of pathways (standardized, structured nursing care plans) has been shown to reduce patient falls, infection and other avoidable complications. The use of EBM, implementation of critical pathways, clinical guidelines and protocols did not originally involve computers, but these activities are now increasingly computerized and have been incorporated into both physician and nursing workflow. For instance, nursing may be prompted by the system to perform a fall-risk assessment for an elderly patient; or during an office visit, the system may generate a reminder that a pediatric patient is due for a specific vaccination; or the system may generate a reminder that a diabetic patient is overdue for a retinal examination; or a physician in the emergency department (ED) may utilize a standard set of orders, adopted by the medical staff, for a patient with a stroke.

Health IT Application Foundations

Health IT applications, which range from EHR software to imaging systems to lab, pharmacy and supply chain systems, all run on hardware and software platforms. All systems, regardless of whether they are installed locally or remotely in the cloud, run on servers, which are computers that have processor speeds and memory that far exceed that used in most personal computers. These servers run operating systems (OSs) that differ from personal computers as well. Server OSs may be installed on a single computer, often referred to as a physical server, or on a group of computers, often referred to as virtual servers. Servers run application software, connect to network resources in order to "serve data" and often connect to external storage as well, as shown in Figure 2.1.

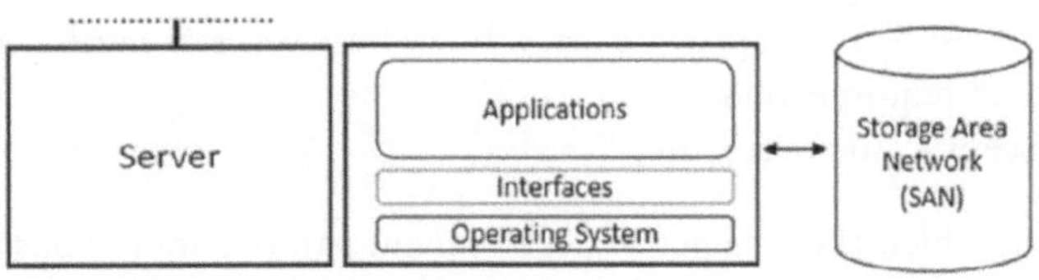

Figure 2.1 Components of computer information systems.

Computer Software

In essence, software is a set of instructions telling a computer how to behave. The instructions are called programs, and they are written in languages understood by computers. The job of software is to control and maintain the operations of a computer. All software – everything from OSs to word processing programs to enterprise EHR applications – is written in some sort of programming language.

Like natural languages, computer languages have syntax, a set of specific commands and statements with rules as to how these statements can be used and combined. Programming includes specific keywords that are used, along with certain punctuation for combining and defining the statements.

There are many types of software, including application software, system software, including the OS, and software used specifically for development, such as software for web development or software testing tools.

Role of the OS

An OS is a required component of every computer. It controls all the functions of the computer and acts as an intermediary between the hardware and software. It also provides a way for the user to interact with the computer.

All computers have an OS, and there are several types, including OSs for personal computers, servers, handheld devices and embedded computers. All of them provide some level of the same core functionality but differ in complexity and size. OSs may contain programming errors or security vulnerabilities and must be updated ("patched") on a regular basis. Providers of OSs will issue patches to fix bugs, address security vulnerabilities or to provide enhanced capabilities throughout the support life cycle of the OS. When an OS is no longer supported by the vendor, it must be upgraded to a newer version. Because OSs and applications work in tandem, they often must be upgraded in a coordinated manner.

Utility Programs

Utility programs contain instructions to perform specific tasks to manage a computer, its devices or its programs. They may come with the installation of the OS or may need to be installed later. The OS and the utility programs work together to make computer hardware usable. Utility programs perform system tasks that include backing up files, diagnosing system problems, searching for a file and compressing files.

Software Development

The process of creating software is complex and time consuming. Ultimately, the end product is application software that achieves intended outcomes, but actual programming is only one of the steps in a broader systems development life cycle (SDLC).

The first set of activities in the SDLC involves analysis and planning. Developers determine and document specific requirements for the software and create initial design specifications. The specifications are high-level descriptions of each piece of the application software. As the software is being written, it will be tested thoroughly to make sure that it functions correctly, is easy to use and meets requirements. The stages of software development are:

- **Planning/exploratory phase.** Focuses on research, analysis and exploration, which help determine the need for new software along with any existing software.
- **Requirements gathering.** Determines who the intended users are and what the software must do to achieve intended outcomes.
- **Design of software.** Requires creating specifications that outline all components of the software.
- **Coding phase.** Includes the actual programming, also referred to as writing code.
- **Testing.** Occurs during various stages of development. The code is tested thoroughly, using a test plan and various testing methodologies. The test plan will provide traceability between test results and requirements; e.g., there will be test cases for documented requirements.
- **Deployment/maintenance.** Occurs over time.

There are many different ways in which these stages of development can occur. Various software development methodologies (also known as frameworks) can be used in the SDLC. Each describes how the different stages of development will occur and how prototypes are used during these stages. A development team will follow one particular methodology, which will guide how the team progresses through the development stages.

For instance, in a Waterfall Methodology, the stages of analysis, design and testing occur sequentially. As each stage is completed, the next begins. In Rapid Cycle development methodology, analysis and design often involve using a prototype for validation, with iterative analysis and design cycles.

Programming Languages

There are many different programming languages available. The choice of programming language is dependent on several factors, including what the program is intended to do and what environment it will run in. Current programming languages include those listed here, but this is just a small sampling of popular programs today:

- JavaScript is a scripting language and is often used in web-based programs.
- Python is a general-purpose coding language used for writing system scripts, mobile apps, desktop apps and processing big data.
- Java is a freely available portable object-oriented language.
- Rust is an open-source system programming language similar to C++ but with better memory management features in some use cases.
- Ruby on Rails (or Ruby) was originally designed to develop games, but is often used for web development.
- C++, an object-oriented version of C.
- C#, a portable object-oriented language developed by Microsoft.
- VB.Net, an object-oriented version of Visual Basic developed by Microsoft.
- MUMPS, a general-purpose programming language that supports a novel, native hierarchical database facility.

The Evolution of Electronic Health Record Applications

In the early days of EHR systems, most were single applications or a collection of single applications loosely stitched together to run a healthcare organization. One of the modules that has been used for decades and was often one of the first deployed in healthcare organizations is CPOE. As EHR software vendors and the markets matured, additional capabilities were added. Today's EHR systems are comprehensive, end-to-end systems with robust reporting, data warehouse and analytics capabilities that continue to rapidly evolve.

EHR Functions

EHR functionality can be as simple as a web-based interface used for entering, storing and retrieving data or as complex as an integrated system that facilitates communication among multiple healthcare systems or even assists clinicians in making medical decisions.

The IOM[8] outlined the following as capabilities that all EHR systems should address (see Figure 2.2):

- A longitudinal collection of electronic health information for and about persons, where health information is defined as information pertaining to the health of an individual or the healthcare provided to an individual;
- Immediate electronic access to person and population-level information by authorized, and only authorized, users;

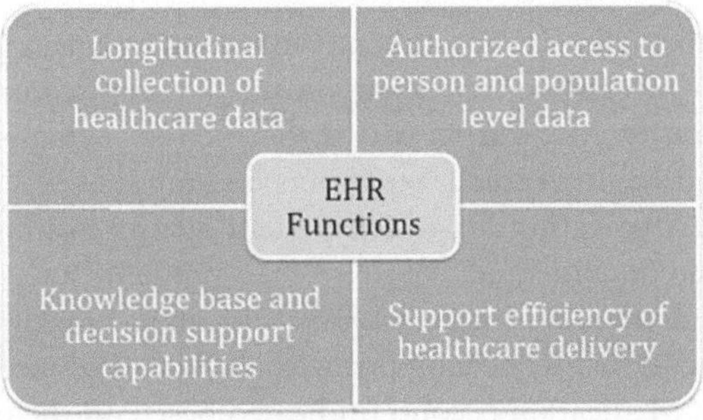

Figure 2.2 Capabilities all EHR systems should address, as outlined by the IOM.

Source: CC-BY by CAST.

- Provision of knowledge and decision support that enhance the quality, safety and efficiency of patient care; and
- Support of efficient processes for healthcare delivery.

In the U.S., the federal Office of the National Coordinator for Health Information Technology (ONC) has expanded the definition and that standard is evolving. In addition, ONC has developed a certification program that aims to ensure that EHR programs meet the standards and criteria adopted by the Secretary of the U.S. Department of Health and Human Services (HHS).[9]

To meet the capabilities defined by ONC, EHR systems must have both basic and advanced features, including data storage, secure accessibility, information retrieval, access to current clinical data and communication mechanisms to improve efficiency. To this end, EHR systems should contain the following key functions: demographic data; medication, allergy and problem lists; CPOE; clinical decision support systems (CDSS); ePrescribing; health information exchange (HIE); and privacy and security capabilities. While these features are defined by the U.S. ONC, these features are part of EHR systems used worldwide. Regulation and requirements for features vary, of course, but all EHR systems used internationally provide these functions.

EHR Feature: Computerized Provider Order Entry (CPOE)

CPOE helps medical practitioners create and manage orders for medications and medical services. Traditionally, orders were written on paper, given verbally (in person or by telephone) and often faxed. A CPOE module, normally integrated within a system that supports clinical workflow, provides electronic order entry that can greatly reduce errors associated with transcribed orders and illegible handwriting. Additionally, the use of CDS at the point of order can reduce error associated with medications. CPOE requires electronic communication between sender and receiver and interfaces with existing information systems, primarily pharmacy, laboratory and radiology.

CPOE has been implemented to automate and manage patient care more effectively and efficiently and, as a consequence, to improve patient safety and outcomes. Physicians, nurses, physician assistants (PAs), nurse practitioners (NPs) and ancillary staff such as pharmacists, therapists, dieticians and laboratory and radiology personnel all use CPOE. The kind of orders that a healthcare professional can write is determined by his or her professional role. Nurses may write certain orders concerning a patient's plan of care. Medication orders can be entered by those providers licensed to prescribe (e.g., PAs and NPs).

How CPOE Works

In a CPOE system, an order is entered, evaluated for potential error by a CDS module at the point of entry, and then transmitted electronically to a hospital or retail pharmacy. If it is a medication order, the pharmacist will also evaluate the order. For an order to be executed, it must be digitally signed by the clinician.

Common Medication Errors That CPOE/CDS Can Prevent

Regardless of inpatient or outpatient setting, CPOE can prevent serious medication error by incorporating these types of safety checks at the point of order.

- **Therapeutic duplication.** Medication that has a therapeutic overlap with another new or active order; it may be same drug, within the same drug class or involve components of combination products.
- **Single and cumulative dose limits.** Medication with a specified dose that exceeds recommended dose ranges or that will result in a cumulative dose that exceeds recommended ranges.
- **Allergies and cross allergies.** Medication for which patient allergy has been documented, or allergy to other drugs in same category has been documented.
- **Contraindicated route of administration.** Medication order with an incorrectly specified route of administration (such as oral, intramuscular or intravenous) that is not appropriate for the identified medication.
- **Drug–diagnosis Interactions.** Medication is contraindicated based on the patient diagnosis or the need for dosing that is diagnosis-specific.

- **Contraindications/dose limits based on age and weight.** Medication is contraindicated for this patient based on age and weight that must be considered in appropriate dosing.
- **Contraindications/dose limits based on laboratory studies.** Medication is contraindicated for this patient based on laboratory studies.
- **Contraindications/dose limits based on radiology studies.** Medication is contraindicated for this patient based on a recorded interaction with contrast.

When the electronic order is received by the ancillary system (most often laboratory, pharmacy or diagnostic imaging), the order will have a system status. All orders are processed electronically, whether entered using CPOE or entered manually, and an order communications module will display the status of orders. These statuses are useful for ancillary departments in managing workflow and for clinicians in understanding the stages of an order.

- **Processing.** The order has been received and is being processed.
- **Pending.** The order is not yet complete or finalized.
- **Waiting.** Waiting for an event to occur such as approval of a medication ordered that is not in the hospital formulary.
- **Complete.** The order has been processed.
- **Discontinued.** An active order is canceled; for example, the physician discontinues an intravenous (IV) line because the patient no longer requires it.
- **Voided.** The clinician cancels the order before signing.

Where Is CPOE Used?

CPOE is used in a wide variety of clinical settings and healthcare venues, including hospitals, clinics and physician offices. Examples of its application in the hospital ED, in surgery and in inpatient hospital care are discussed here.

Emergency Department. A good way to understand the advantages of CPOE is to consider an ED physician who is examining a patient with a chief complaint of upper abdominal pain. The CPOE module, in tandem with a CDSS, provides standard order sets built for the most common chief complaints. The physician selects the upper abdominal pain order set. This order set suggests specific laboratory studies, medications and/or tests that are appropriate for this chief complaint. To further enhance the capabilities of the system, the physician can then customize the order sets to suit the way he or she treats patients with certain chief complaints.

If the physician orders blood work, the order is immediately transmitted to the laboratory that manages the workflow of the phlebotomist or nurse who will draw the blood. If there is an injury or trauma that requires an x-ray, the CPOE system transmits an order to the radiology system that then manages the workflow needed to perform the test including scheduling of the room, technician and equipment needed. An advantage to CPOE, in this case, is that if there is a recorded patient allergy to dye, the CDS module incorporated into CPOE will issue an alert about a potential adverse reaction.

Surgery. CPOE is invaluable in surgery. If, for instance, the antibiotic required prior to surgery has not been administered, the system can alert the surgical team of the omission. In addition, standard drug-allergy checking is performed along with other standard medication safety checks including drug-drug interactions. CPOE/CDS systems can also evaluate a medication order against laboratory values to ensure the drug or dosage is appropriate. For instance, the system can check the dose against a laboratory value that indicates poor renal function. In this case, the system might issue an alert that the dosage should be reduced. Beyond basic medication checking, CPOE takes advantage of standard order sets, based on EBM. A standard surgical order set might include prophylactic antibiotics and other medications needed after surgery.

Inpatient care areas. CPOE/CDS systems are utilized in a variety of ways during inpatient care. For example, when patients are admitted to the hospital, they often see the following series of physicians:

- An *admitting physician* who writes the order to admit a patient to the hospital
- An *attending physician* who manages the patient's care while he or she is in the hospital (an attending physician is often a hospitalist)
- One or more *consulting physicians* who may advise the attending physician

With this array of physicians assigned to a patient, orders can often be duplicated. For example, multiple doctors could see the patient at different times and then order the same blood test. A CPOE/CDS system would display a duplicate order alert to advise the physician that a laboratory or medication has already been ordered. The doctor could then cancel the order before it is completed or could modify the order if desired.

Or, for a surgical patient, the physician might receive an alert that indicated a prophylactic antibacterial medication had not been correctly discontinued within 24 hours of completed surgery. For nursing, the system might display a standard nursing care plan for a diagnosis or might display recommended assessments used to identify patients at risk for depression.

Expert Systems/CDSS

Expert systems use rules and direct input from the user to support decision-making. They are composed of three parts: a knowledge base, an inference engine and an interface. The knowledge base is the set of rules the expert system knows. The inference engine takes these rules and produces reasoning based on them. There are many applications of expert systems in healthcare. These systems support diagnostic and therapeutic decision-making.

Various Interventions of CDSS. CDSS offer interventions such as alerts and reminders or makes EBM available in the form of standard order sets, linkage to reference databases and education or workflow orchestration. For instance, if a nurse performs a risk assessment for fall-injury, the system might immediately present the standard care plan for a patient with these risk factors. Or perhaps, if vital sign entry indicated the possibility of a nosocomial infection, the system would generate either an alert or task for the Infection Control practitioner.

The six main types of CDS interventions are:

1. **Documentation forms/templates.** Standard and customized forms, including those for patient self-assessment, clinician encounters and specific health problems, streamline the often-tedious documentation process.
2. **Relevant data presentation.** Data flowsheets and patient summary sheets, for example, organize pertinent patient information (laboratory results, medications, problem lists, etc.) in easy-to-view formats to make ordering, administration and documentation tasks more accurate and efficient. For example, in an endocrinology clinic that treats diabetic patients, the system may display a laboratory flowsheet that highlights and shows trends in laboratory values that are most important in diabetic patients.
3. **Order/prescription creation facilitators.** Standardized, evidence-based order sets provide quick access to clinical best practices, protocols and external knowledge.
4. **Protocol/Pathway support.** This intervention utilizes EBM to help clinicians manage treatments for specific health conditions.
5. **Reference information and guidance.** A knowledge base of drugs, laboratory tests and diseases is at the clinician's fingertips, greatly reducing the need to log out of the system to look up this information.
6. **Alerts and reminders.** This intervention consists of built-in reminders or warnings, such as drug allergy or dangerous drug-drug interaction alerts and performance indicators to avert potential omission/commission errors and hazards.[10] Alerts and reminders are also a key component in chronic disease management where they can be used to identify patients needing vaccination or patients needing follow-up care, essential for diseases like diabetes, asthma or congestive heart failure.

The purpose of CDS interventions is to put relevant knowledge at the fingertips of clinicians to ensure they can make well-informed decisions. Interventions also help streamline tasks and add quality checks to the many processes in which healthcare professionals engage every day. The numerous benefits of CDS interventions, from the promotion of standards adherence to optimized decision-making, ultimately lead to improved quality of care.

EHR Feature: ePrescribing

As defined by the ONC, electronic prescribing, known as ePrescribing or eRx, "With electronic prescribing, or "e-Prescribing", healthcare providers can enter prescription information into a computer device – like a tablet, laptop, or desktop computer – and securely transmit the prescription to pharmacies using a special software program and connectivity to a transmission network. When a pharmacy receives a request, it can begin filling the medication right away".[11]

CPOE is usually associated with hospital medication ordering, and ePrescribing usually refers to outpatient prescribing. The capability for ePrescribing is integrated within an EHR and includes CDS for basic medication checking. In the U.S., ePrescribing is required functionality in all certified ambulatory EHR systems. The function is integrated with patient information such as a patient's age, weight and allergies.

EHR Data Warehouse

A data warehouse is a centralized repository for data, which can come from multiple areas of a single application or from multiple applications. The most basic data warehouse is often referred to as a data mart, as smaller datasets allow for fast, simple analytics to be performed. Data marts are not robust enough to provide enterprise-wide predictive analytics such as those needed for population health management. In these cases, much larger datasets are required as input so that data can be correlated across vast volumes of inputs. The data warehouse is the structure used for these enterprise-level initiatives. Analytics follow the maturity (or complexity) model of descriptive (what happened), predictive (what is likely to happen) and prescriptive (here's what you should do). While most healthcare organizations are using descriptive analytics, some are using predictive analytics. Still fewer are using prescriptive analytics, but as data warehouse platforms evolve and healthcare organization's capabilities increase, the use of prescriptive analytics is mere years away from being a catalyst for rapid change in healthcare delivery.[12] For more on this topic, also see Big Data/Business Intelligence (BI) and Analytics section later in this chapter.

Other Health IT Applications

Patient Monitoring Systems

Patient monitoring systems monitor physiological data. They capture raw data, process it into human-readable form and then communicate and display it. They also write the data to a storage device. In some cases, patient monitoring systems may interface data directly to an EHR where it can also be displayed. A physician who did not have direct access to these monitoring systems would then be able to view critical patient information via access to the EHR. This device integration reduces the amount of time needed by nurses to chart data, such as vital signs and makes data available to any provider with access to the EHR.

Monitoring can be performed locally or remotely. A patient monitoring device in a critical care unit that tracks and records vital signs would sound an alarm should a life-threatening event be detected. Patient monitoring systems may include data interpretation and the use of information exchange protocols. Data can be output as charts, graphs, tables and flow sheets.

Patient monitoring systems are used in many settings, both inpatient and outpatient and are critical tools in intensive care units, critical care units, operating suites, post-operative recovery areas (Post Anesthesia Care Units or PACUs), ambulatory surgery centers and many other sites.

Medical Imaging Systems

Biomedical imaging, sometimes referred to as diagnostic imaging, is the science and branch of medicine concerned with the development and use of imaging devices and techniques. Imaging is the visual display of structural or functional patterns of organs or tissues for diagnostic evaluation. In addition to visualizing the parts of the body, biomedical imaging techniques are used to measure physiological and metabolic responses to physical and chemical stimuli.

Historically, physicians have been limited in their role as diagnosticians by the inability to "see inside a patient" without resorting to exploratory surgery. Exploratory surgery is a serious and sometimes necessary step that can entail considerable risk. Traditionally, it was often a final alternative that physicians had to take in order to make a diagnosis. Because of advances in medical imaging systems, exploratory surgery is performed much less frequently.

Common tests supported by medical imaging devices include:

- **X-ray** is a diagnostic procedure using electromagnetic waves to create a one-dimensional image of the body. X-rays are widely used in EDs due to the speed of the procedure and result, which can help make initial diagnoses quickly.

- **Computed tomography (CT) scan** is a diagnostic procedure that uses special x-ray equipment (the scanner) to obtain cross-sectional pictures of the body.
- **Positron emission tomography (PET) scan** is a nuclear medicine imaging technique that produces a three-dimensional image of functional processes in the body.
- **Ultrasonography (US)** uses sound waves to produce an image. Echoes are received as input from a device called a sonographic probe and then are translated into pixels for creation of an image.
- **Magnetic resonance imaging (MRI) device** works by surrounding the human body with a magnetic field and then flooding it with a radiofrequency pulse that produces an image of the body's interior structure.
- **Electrocardiography (EKG) machine** provides an interpretation of the electrical activity of a heart over time, captured and externally recorded by skin electrodes. Skin electrodes are the input devices.

Diagnostic imaging tests are normally managed by a Radiology or Diagnostic Imaging Department that utilizes a Radiology Information System (RIS) to process orders for these diagnostic imaging tests. RIS supports scheduling, result reporting and imaging tracking and stores, organizes and distributes patient radiological data, including a report of the interpretation by a radiologist. Radiologist reports are often interfaced to the EHR and are considered "results" that are displayed in an EHR. Many EHR systems provide a RIS module so that these functions are native to the EHR and orders, results, diagnoses, charging and billing are all captured within one system.

Diagnostic images are typically stored in a picture archiving and communication system (PACS) that is designed to store digital images and that enables physicians to view these images remotely.

OR Integration and Surgical Video Systems

Today, an increasing number of surgeries are performed using minimally invasive techniques. Minimally invasive surgery (MIS) inflicts less trauma on the body and allows for faster recovery times with less patient discomfort compared with traditional invasive surgery. With improved imaging capabilities through laparoscopes (or other endoscopes), only small incisions need to be made in the body, but the surgeon can visualize the surgical site through these powerful scopes that provide light, magnification and surgical instruments. Surgical video systems (SVS) allow images from the scopes to be displayed on large monitors in the OR alongside other images such as x-ray, CT or MRI images and other relevant data. OR integration system would allow the nurse or physician to have centralized control of audio visual signals, including inputs and outputs. Common components in these systems include a video camera or camera head, light source, video processor and video displays. Currently, the highest resolution systems available are 4K, but 8K is on the near horizon. This level of resolution provides sharp images that can be enhanced to assist the surgeon in visualizing the surgical area. Enhancements include zoom, color (to identify blood vessels, for example) and more.

Clinical Laboratory Systems

Clinical laboratory systems manage the collection, testing, analysis and reporting of patient specimens. The information is used to diagnose and treat patients and to monitor the effectiveness of treatment. Laboratory information systems (LIS) manage the collection and processing of samples for testing and analysis. Common tests include (this is a short list):

- **Blood chemistry testing** (cholesterol, glucose, white blood cell counts, etc.)
- **Blood gas analysis** (oxygen saturation, for example)
- **Therapeutic drug monitoring** (identify if a drug dose is too low, too high or having the desired effect)
- **Toxicology testing** (tests for the presence of toxic substances including illicit drugs, overdoses of therapeutic drugs, poison, etc.)
- **Urinalysis** (tests that assess the presence of various substance in urine that may assist in diagnosis and treatment decisions)
- **Pathology/histology** (tests for the presence or absence of cell types or characteristics such as cancer cells in a tissue sample)
- **Microbiology** (tests for infectious elements such as bacteria or viruses to assist in diagnosis and treatment)

Labs receive specimens from patients in a variety of settings from physician offices to lab locations to hospitals. The process begins with specimen collection. Specimens are transported to the appropriate laboratory systems for processing.

Results and reports must be accurate, consistent and easily available to the referring provider. These testing processes are often handled by laboratory automation systems (LAS), which include both electronic and manual devices to automate the laboratory testing processes. In addition, labs must perform related administrative functions such as regulatory compliance, billing and sending results. These functions are typically managed by an LIS system.

In some hospitals, there are also POC testing devices that enable the collection, testing and resulting of samples at the bedside. Patients presenting at an ED with chest pain can be tested for the presence of certain cardiac enzymes to assist in the diagnosis and rapid treatment of the patient. These rapid turnaround times (compared to sending samples to the central Lab) can positively impact patient outcomes.

Data from POC testing is sent to the LIS, which is often part of the EHR software suite or is interfaced so data flows bi-directionally between systems. The EHR may send data regarding the patients for whom lab orders have been submitted; the LIS may send results and reports back to the patient record in the EHR.

Revenue Cycle Management

Revenue Cycle from a Healthcare Provider's Perspective

Revenue cycle is a complex process and healthcare providers must perform multiple tasks to ensure they are reimbursed for their services. The provider's responsibilities in the revenue cycle involve front office functions such as patient registration, collection of demographic and insurance information, charge capture and back-office functions such as coding and claims submission. Figure 2.3 illustrates the cycle in a typical outpatient setting.

Registration and Front-Office Functions

During scheduling and registration at a hospital, doctor's office or other healthcare setting, patient information needed for billing is gathered by the healthcare provider, including:

- Patient demographics such as name, address, phone number, gender, sex, race, date of birth, ethnicity, preferred language
- Insurance information and guarantor information
- Copayments and deductibles

Figure 2.3 Revenue cycle in a typical outpatient setting.

Source: CC-BY by CAST/Gary Lockhart.

Care Delivery, Capture of Charges and Documentation

Care that is delivered must be accurately documented in the patient's EHR. As care is delivered, charges may be automatically generated by the system as a by-product of documentation, or charges for services may be manually entered in the system. When the account is billed, the provider transmits this information to the payer including specific services, dates and times along with other information needed for billing. Documentation of clinical care must be sufficient to justify specific charges as well as the diagnosis and procedure codes assigned for the visit or inpatient stay.

Medical Coding

Before a claim can be submitted to a payer, it must be coded using code sets that include the International Classification of Diseases (ICD), 10th Revision, Clinical Modification (ICD-10-CM) and a set of codes used for diagnoses and procedures, and CPT4, a code set utilized for procedures.

Inpatient coders review physician documentation, including transcribed documents, in order to assign the appropriate code. In an outpatient environment, the physician or other office personnel can utilize the practice management system to assign a code, based on the diagnosis, for the visit. These systems, most of which incorporate EHR functionality, also provide templates for documentation of the outpatient encounter note.

Admission-Discharge-Transfer

The admission-discharge-transfer (ADT) system is a software system that tracks a patient from admission through discharge. The ADT system displays census information (e.g., lists of patients in a particular setting). When patients are admitted, discharged or transferred to another location within the facility, the system notifies other systems – such as Pharmacy, Radiology or Laboratory – of the patient's current location.

Practice Management Systems

Practice management systems (PMSs) are used to automate a physician office. Practice management software provides a combination of financial and administrative functions. Many PMSs fully interface or are integrated with clinical EHR software. Common practice management software functions include:

- Registration
- Scheduling
- Billing and receivables management
- Electronic collection and reporting of patient demographics
- Management of clinical data and interface and integration with EHRs

Health Information Exchange (HIE)

HIE involves the sharing of electronic health information across organizational boundaries, often within a city, a state or a region. It may involve any site where care is provided. For example, if a patient is transferred from a hospital to a rehabilitation clinic, a HIE would make it possible for that patient's records to be electronically shared between the hospital's EHR system and the clinic's EHR system.

An HIE is not only useful for a patient transferring between healthcare organizations within a particular area but also can give people within a region immediate access to their health records. Like HIEs, regional health information organizations (RHIOs) support exchange of healthcare information in a region, often across state boundaries.

The U.S. federal government has put a priority on being able to share patient data across the entire nation. Ultimately, the aim is to have information exchanged over a nationwide health information network so that all authorized providers have access to patient information where and when it is needed. These goals have been articulated by governmental entities in countries around the world. The goals are the same. To share patient data across geographic and physical boundaries, across nations, states and organizations to enable safe, effective and timely patient care. Key to that goal of data sharing is the ongoing development and adoption of standards needed to harmonize disparate information systems and facilitate the secure transfer of data.

Health IT Infrastructure

Information technology (IT) infrastructure is the foundation of all computer systems, including healthcare IT. The foundations are servers, storage and databases that manage the computing and storing of data from applications, such as the EHR or LIS, for example. In order for data to flow between systems, a network infrastructure is required. Both wired and wireless networks provide needed connectivity for systems and devices.

Servers, Storage and Databases

Servers form the foundation of healthcare IT systems. Servers typically run the Microsoft Windows Server OS or any one of a number of Unix-based OSs including Unix and Linux. Servers can run on individual computers (stand-alone servers or physical servers), or many servers can be run on a computer using virtualization software. In this case, another layer of software is used to manage many server OSs running on a single hardware platform. This configuration allows many servers to be run and managed via a virtualization software application. Virtualized servers can be easily spun up, configured, patched, moved and decommissioned. One of the benefits of virtualization is that the server instance is disassociated with specific hardware, allowing more flexibility in managing the servers.

Storage is a form of computer memory. Computers have some amount of memory, or storage, in the computer itself to enable the computer to store code that allows the computer to load the OS. The OS and applications are typically stored on hard disk drives. Disk drives come in a number of different formats. The older Serial AT Attachment (Serial ATA) drives have platters on a spindle that spin the disks while heads write or read the data on those platters. Newer drives are solid-state drives and use computer memory chips to store data. The technology is similar to that used in USB or thumb drives. These types of storage devices have the benefit of being far faster than Serial ATA drives because data can be retrieved instantly rather than waiting for the platter to spin to a location where the head can access the specific piece of information requested. Solid-state drives historically have been more expensive than spinning drives, but prices for solid-state drives have continued to come down over the past decade.

Databases are software applications that store data in a very structured manner. Pieces of data are stored in defined fields. As a result, a single data element can be associated with multiple other data elements, creating new relationships between data elements. Most databases contain many different fields and tables. In healthcare, databases store EHR data, lab, pharmacy, supply chain and financial data, to name just a few.

Networks

When you have two or more computers connected to each other, you have a network. The purpose of a network is to enable the sharing of files and information between multiple systems. The Internet is working as a global network of networks. Computer networks can be connected through cables, such as Ethernet cables (Category 5 or 6, often referred to as CAT5 or CAT6) or phone lines, or wirelessly, using wireless networking cards that send and receive data through the air. A network includes the collection of hardware, such as printers, modems, servers and terminals/personal computers that enable users to store and retrieve information, share devices and exchange information.[13]

To visualize a network, examine Figure 2.4. Servers run applications and provide access to those applications via network connections. Those servers may be in a local data center, or they may be hosted in the cloud and accessed via Internet connections. Servers may connect with network connected storage systems (network attached storage, NAS or storage area network, SAN) to store, retrieve and send stored data. This is depicted at the bottom of Figure 2.4.

End user devices, depicted at the top of Figure 2.4, include scanners, printers and computers that connect to a network using a wired and/or wireless connection. The network to which those devices are connected may be connected to the Internet. An Internet connection requires the use of an Internet service provider (ISP), which is a company that connects users to the worldwide Internet network.

Wired connections require that devices have a network interface card (NIC) installed. It can be either wireless or wired. The wired NIC must provide a port to plug in the network cable. The network cable plugs into an outlet that is connected to a network switch, from which network connectivity is provided.

PCs, laptops and tablets can be connected via wired connection or wireless connection, as shown in Figure 2.4. Wired connections are more reliable as they are more resistant to interference, but they are more expensive to install

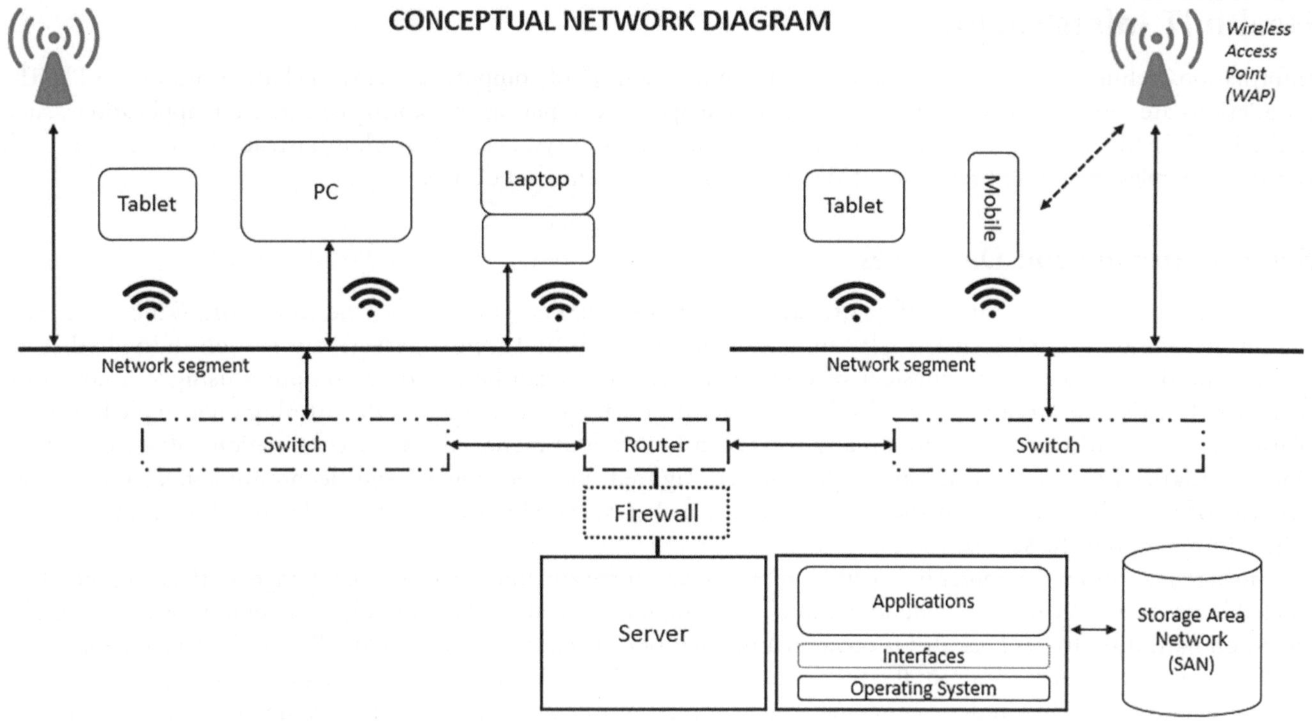

Figure 2.4 Diagram of a network.

and limit the location of the device. Wireless provides more flexibility, including the ability to roam or move about, but wireless signals can be subject to interference. Determining the best type of connectivity involves understanding how and where the device is to be used and what will best meet the end user's needs.

To make wireless connections, devices must have a wireless NIC and a wireless access point (WAP) to send and receive wireless signals and connect them to the network infrastructure.

Network Speeds

Networks measure speed with the terms *bandwidth* and *throughput:*

- **Bandwidth.** Bandwidth is the highest number of bits that can be sent at any one time. The bandwidth of a home network might be 100 megabytes (100 MB) per second using typical network cabling. Typical business networks often run at 1 gigabyte (1 GB) or 10 gigabytes (10 GB) speeds.
- **Throughput.** Throughput is the rate of successful message delivery over a communication channel. Errors and network congestion can reduce throughput, regardless of bandwidth specifications.

Routers

Routers manage the movement of network traffic using Internet protocol (IP) addressing. If a computer needs to communicate with a server in another country, the routers have to find the IP address of the other server. A networking device that forwards data packets between computer networks, a router is connected to two or more data lines from different networks. When a data packet comes in one of the lines, the router reads the address information in the packet to determine its ultimate destination. Then, using information in its routing table or routing policy, it directs the packet to the next network on its journey. Routers perform the "traffic directing" functions on the Internet. A data packet is typically forwarded from one router to another through the networks that constitute the internetwork until it reaches its destination node.

IP Address

Also known as an *IP number* or simply an *IP*, this is a code made up of numbers separated by three dots that identifies a particular computer on the Internet. For example, an IP address might be 10.147.122.5. Each segment can have a maximum of three digits, and there are four required segments. Every computer, whether it be a Web server, a database server or a home computer, requires a unique IP address to connect to the Internet. IP addresses – a type of identification label – can be purchased or leased and used by the holder of that IP address for the duration of the purchase or lease. Public IP addresses are generally purchased by ISPs from regional organizations that are responsible for managing public IP addresses. Then, companies or households lease public IP addresses from the ISPs.

Domain Names

A domain name is a unique name, corresponding to one or more numeric IP addresses, used to identify a particular computer, web page or set of web pages on the Internet. Every domain name has a suffix that indicates which top-level domain (TLD) it belongs to. There are only a limited number of such domains, but in recent years there has been a significant expansion to accommodate the growing use of domains worldwide. For example:

- gov: Government agencies
- edu: Educational institutions
- org: Organizations (nonprofit)
- mil: Military
- com: Commercial business
- net: Originally indented for network organizations, now open for public use
- tv: Television
- info: Alternative to. com
- life: Alternative to. com
- us: Country codes can be used in each country (.ar – Argentina, .ca – Canada, .ch – Switzerland, .fi – Finland, .in – India, etc.). Some, but not all, countries have residence requirements.

Networks and the Internet support the use of domain names. People and organizations can purchase a domain name from the Internet Corporation for Assigned Names and Numbers (ICANN). Because all computers communicate through IP addressing, a domain name has no meaning unless that name can be resolved, or translated, into a specific IP address. Domain names may be private if not connected to the public Internet, may use any name desired if it resolves to a valid IP address.

Trends Affecting Health IT

Technology constantly evolves and the application of technology in the delivery of healthcare also has been rapidly changing. Some of these technologies are making their way into mainstream use, others are still only at the leading edge, but all have the potential to positively disrupt healthcare delivery in the future. This partial list is presented in alphabetical order.

Artificial Intelligence

Artificial intelligence (AI) is the automated performance of tasks normally performed by a human. A related concept is machine learning in which algorithms are programmed to modify outputs or results based on changing inputs. An algorithm that can identify tuberculosis in an x-ray is a good example because the inputs vary (different x-rays from different people) but the algorithm is able to "adjust" so that it can identify tuberculosis in lung images. There are numerous use cases for AI in healthcare and uses are expanding annually.

Big Data/Business Intelligence (BI) and Analytics

The massive amounts of data (big data) generated in healthcare are increasingly being used in aggregated forms to develop actionable data for healthcare organizations. In addition to financial and quality requirements tied to value-based payment models, BI and analytics help organizations organize, process, analyze and develop data-based plans.

In healthcare, this capability can be used in just about any area of the organization – from population health to supply chain to OR scheduling and beyond.

BI activity in organizations typically follows a maturity model from descriptive (what happened) to predictive (what's likely to happen) to prescriptive (what should we do). As healthcare organizations mature along these levels, the ability to more effectively manage care and quality outcomes can increase exponentially. The danger, of course, is lack of required competencies in managing big data, BI and analytics. There is a distinct difference between those on the BI team who develop data universes and produce reports and those clinical leaders who need to be well versed in asking the right questions, understanding the underlying data elements and interpreting the results.

Blockchain

Blockchain is the foundation of digital currencies, also referred to as cryptocurrencies (though not all digital currencies are cryptocurrencies), like Bitcoin, Ethereum and Tether to name three. Blockchain is the digital ledger mechanism that enables financial (and other) transactions without an intermediary such as a bank. The potential for blockchain in healthcare seems substantial, but the development of commercialized solutions is still slowly evolving. Understandably, this is an area where large companies are investing resources. Though a few large healthcare organizations have begun to work with blockchain technologies, most healthcare organizations are waiting to see how this technology will evolve over time.

Cloud Computing

Cloud computing is probably the oldest technology platform in this list. Cloud computing includes any computing function that is delivered via the Internet. Private cloud functions are delivered via private connections across the Internet. The large providers of cloud computing are Amazon, Microsoft and Google, though there are millions of cloud computing providers worldwide. The benefits to healthcare organizations include lower capital costs, flexible and on-demand capacity, scalability, data backup and recovery. The potential downside to cloud computing in healthcare, as evidenced by headlines related to HIPAA breaches, includes risk of misconfiguration and lack of specialized expertise to manage proprietary or hybrid cloud environments. In addition, healthcare organizations have to be able to address decentralization of data, management and administration, third-party access and the potential inability to repatriate data. Finally, though capital costs are reduced, operational costs increase and can often spiral out of control if the team is unfamiliar with managing cloud resources.

Information Security or Cybersecurity

Information security or cybersecurity is not a technology, per se, but it is a significant trend in healthcare IT and requires health IT leaders to have a level of awareness and understanding about this growing risk. Attackers have increasingly targeted healthcare organizations for a variety of reasons. Healthcare data, unlike credit card account numbers, cannot be changed. When your bank sends you a new credit card after declaring "there has been some unusual activity, so we are giving you a new credit card account number", it's easy enough to change the number. Your health data is not changeable. You were born on a certain day in a certain year. You have certain diagnoses or medical conditions. These cannot be simply modified if your health record is compromised. Attackers have stolen health data to conduct insurance fraud (receive healthcare on someone else's insurance), to gain entry into a country by presenting a false "clean bill of health" (someone else's medical record), or to blackmail an individual or organization, for example. More recently, ransomware attacks have been perpetuated in order to force organizations to pay large sums of ransom (usually via cryptocurrency so as to be untraceable) to unlock files. Ransomware encrypts files and requires a unique key, which is a long sequence of random numbers, to unlock the files. When files are locked, the organization cannot use that data. This often means that EHR systems are unusable, and organizations have to resort to paper processes. The goal of the attacker is to make fast money. Unfortunately, not all attackers will provide keys that work or provide keys at all after ransom is paid. Ransomware is a large and growing threat to healthcare IT, and health IT leaders must have a basic understanding of health IT risk and mitigation strategies in order to help guide the organization as it deploys an increasingly complex set of computer technologies for patient care.

Internet of Things (IoT)

The Internet of Things (IoT) describes connectivity and a variety of data in everyday objects such as wristwatches, refrigerators, thermostats and scales, to name a few. In healthcare, the growing number of connected devices creates both opportunity and risk for patient care. Opportunities such as being able to automatically upload a diabetic's blood sugar levels for immediate analysis and feedback are exciting in terms of improving patient's lives outside of traditional healthcare settings. On the other hand, data from these types of devices is not always clinically accurate, it may not be stored or transmitted in a secure manner, and not all data is immediately usable in a clinical manner. Flooding the EHR with unstructured consumer data can pose challenges to healthcare providers. However, other uses such as tracking supplies, transmitting par levels, locating beds or wheelchairs or collecting data points from medication refrigerators, negative pressure rooms or other environmental controls can leverage the power of IoT in healthcare. The uses are numerous and growing. Security of these devices is of concern to healthcare information security teams, so involving the information security team prior to implementing and deploying solutions is important.

Interoperability

Interoperability is a critical element of health IT systems. In early days of health IT, systems were stand-alone systems and did not have the ability to share data easily (or at all). The early solution for data sharing was the exporting and importing of static data files on a periodic basis in order to sync data across disparate systems. With newer software platforms, systems can now more easily share data using defined interface standards including HL7, FHIR and open APIs. The benefits to interoperability are faster access to patient data across various systems, reduction in duplication of tests, orders, procedures, etc., and the ability to analyze and optimize workflows to deliver more efficient care to patients. As a health IT leader, it's important to assess a new system's ability to share critical data in an easy, efficient manner (vs. file import/export) as well as to assess whether the software vendor is actively trying to block data sharing. If so, the vendor may be in violation of governmental mandates (which differ across countries and regions) and may simply be a vendor to exclude from consideration as you work toward developing your health IT strategies of the future.

Mobile Health (mHealth)

Possibly one of the greatest influences on modern healthcare is the expanded use of mHealth. Mobile devices such as smartphones and iPads satisfy provider requirements for accessing real-time information in a variety of settings. For instance, mobile devices free providers from being tethered to a desktop computer. There are a variety of mHealth applications, targeted to both providers and patients:

- Review of results data to providers and/or patients
- ePrescribing
- Access to physician reference databases, including those for medications
- Patient access to his or her PHR
- Patient educational materials available via a handheld device
- Hospital "wayfinding" that enables patients to use their own mobile device to navigate through a large hospital
- Home health tracking where patients monitor aspects of their care

mHealth Adoption

Researchers have noted some patterns emerging in the adoption of mobile devices. One study verified what most people would suspect, that "younger doctors, medical students and physician residents are more likely to use mobile devices".[14]

Challenges with Mobile Devices

Mobile computing in healthcare brings a few challenges for healthcare systems and network administrators, namely:

- **Security.** Mobile devices are wireless, so healthcare network administrators must provide encryption and security measures that protect patient information and ensure adherence to HIPAA standards.
- **Regulations.** From a regulatory perspective, the issue of mobile devices used in healthcare is an evolving topic. While an EHR system must meet the certification requirements in many countries, there are few regulations concerning the subset of EMR functionality that might be available on a mobile device.

The pace of change in the mHealth sector is bound to continue to present challenges to developers and regulators alike. There is, however, the potential of mHealth technologies to present providers and patients alike with a steady stream of new opportunities for greater efficiency and convenience in the delivery of care.

Multifactor Authentication (MFA)

Multifactor authentication (MFA) uses two or more methods of validating identity before providing electronic access to secured systems. Most financial systems now require the use of two-factor authentication (2FA) by requiring a username and password followed by entering a one-time unique code provided to the end user via another method such as text message, phone call, security application or security fob, for example. 2FA and MFA are often used interchangeably. This improves security by requiring multiple methods of validation. If a username and password are compromised, the second factor should (in theory) stop an intruder. Though there are ways to circumvent 2FA/MFA, the use of these technologies is increasing in healthcare to reduce the possibility of user credential abuse.

Natural Language Processing (NLP)

Many healthcare systems have implemented speech recognition to assist providers in entering data into EHR systems. However, much of the data still resides in unstructured formats, such as notes fields (vs. structured fields such as forms, fields, check boxes, lists, etc.). Unstructured data is vast and growing in most EHRs. That data may be of significant clinical use, but processing it is challenging. Natural language processing (NLP) is a form of AI that is focused on processing language. In healthcare, this can be used to process unstructured data to provide insights and information for providers. Challenges remain in using NLP for clinical data including common problems when entering data such as using shorthand, abbreviations, misspelling words or assuming context. However, there is a lot of potential for using NLP to process the massive amounts of unstructured data in EHRs with the goal of improving patient care.

Patient-Generated Health Data (PGHD)

Related to the IoT is patient generated health data (PGHD), which can be generated from Internet-connected devices. Mobile applications, wearables (watches, sensors, etc.), medical devices and user input (surveys, logs, diaries, etc.) are all sources of PGHD. One of the key differences between PGHD and traditional health data is that with PGHD, the patient creates and enters data and ultimately controls the distribution and use of the data. As expectations about healthcare in many countries shifts from episodic to holistic, the use of PGHD may be useful in developing care and wellness plans.

Personalized Medicine

Developments in basic science research, clinical research and bioinformatics obviously have a significant impact on healthcare. One of the most important research developments in the last few decades was the sequencing of the entire human genome through the Human Genome Project. The ultimate purpose was to "provide a greater understanding of the genetic underpinnings of disease".[15] This research can yield a multitude of healthcare benefits for individuals. For example, if a person has a genetic marker for a disease such as Alzheimer's, he or she could be treated early to potentially delay onset or progression. Drug companies could determine which drugs work and which do not work for patients with a particular genetic makeup.

The concept of customized treatment based on information about an individual's genetic makeup is called personalized medicine. As stated by the Personalized Medicine Coalition: "Personalized medicine is a multifaceted approach to patient care that not only improves our ability to diagnose and treat disease but offers the potential to detect disease at an earlier stage, when it is easier to treat effectively".[16]

Telemedicine

Telemedicine can also provide access to healthcare services to those who are "isolated by poverty, geography, and disability".[16]

Telehealth, which promotes "virtual" patient visits or "virtual" consultation with specialists, can enable small rural hospitals to provide high-quality care at lower costs. Also, rural patients receiving care via telehealth can avoid driving long distances to access specialty care.

Using telehealth services is more feasible for rural healthcare facilities than staffing their facilities with specialist providers. Telehealth allows specialists to visit rural patients virtually.[17] Specialties that have incorporated telemedicine in rural areas include:

- Teleradiology
- Telepsychiatry
- Teleopthalmology
- Teledermatology
- Teledentistry

New uses for telemedicine continue to expand the boundaries of the use of technology to treat patients who might otherwise not be able to seek care. Telemedicine has been successfully used with elderly patients who are less able to travel or who may be depressed and fail to seek care. Telemedicine is now used for a wide array of remote services including cardiac monitoring, asthma, Irritable Bowel Disorder (IBD), depression and behavioral health, to name just a few.

Telemedicine can reduce barriers to quality healthcare created by geographic location. Patients benefit in many ways. Those with chronic ailments are more likely to receive the type of regular care that can help them manage their conditions. Individuals who need specialized care but lack specialists in their region can receive the care they need. It is particularly beneficial in rural areas where access to regular and specialized healthcare remains a challenge. Providing greater access to care when needed creates better outcomes for patients and lower overall costs.

Use of telemedicine is dependent upon the communication infrastructure being present. Fast, reliable Internet access or cellular data service is not globally available nor is reliable electricity in some areas. Therefore, the reach of telemedicine is limited by the reliability of the needed infrastructure to provide these services.

Three-Dimensional (3D) Printing

While three-dimensional (3D) printing is not a particularly new technology, the cost of 3D printers is now low enough to be affordable for many organizations. 3D printing is accomplished by adding successive layers of a material as dictated by the software program controlling the printed output. 3D printing in healthcare includes uses in surgical planning, developing prosthetics and implants and forensics. There are growing number of bio programs involving 3D printing from polymers or donor cells or other biomaterials to print functioning organs, blood vessels and more. Forensic teams are using 3D printing to replicate skulls of unidentified victims for forensic artists to use in hopes of identifying missing persons. This is a rapidly evolving field that has significant potential in the healthcare space.

Virtual Reality (VR)/Augmented Reality (AR)

Virtual reality (VR) completely replaces one's field of vision with computer-generated images. Augmented reality (AR), on the other hand, augments natural vision with computer-generated images. Both are used to some extend in healthcare, though use is still relatively low. Uses currently include education, training and pain management. As the costs come down, use cases will likely increase.

X-as-a-Service (XaaS)

One of the earliest forms of [*something*]–as-a-Service was Software-as-a-Service (SaaS), which was when cloud-based computing began to surface as a viable alternative to installed software on a computer or in a local data center. From there, other cloud-based services have emerged including (but certainly not limited to) Infrastructure-as-a-Service, Platform-as-a-Service, Security-as-a-Service, Container-as-a-Service (container as in a computer runtime environment), Disaster Recovery-as-a-Service, Network-as-a-Service, Unified Communications-as-a-Service and even (unfortunately) Ransomware-as-a-Service. Essentially, these are managed services provided by a vendor with the proposed value proposition that these services can be provided faster, better and at a lower cost by an external expert than by the IT team internally. Depending on the nature of the organization and its IT functions, these services may be viable options for some health IT providers.

Summary

To a considerable extent, medicine has always been an exercise in gathering, storing and sharing patient information. But with the increasing pace of IT development and implementation across the healthcare sector, that practice can now take place faster, among more people and across greater distances than ever before. For health IT professionals, it is important to understand the core functions of IT and to stay abreast of the range of ways IT is being used to facilitate the efficient delivery of healthcare. That means understanding the "mechanics" of computer technology, the structure and role of networks and the range of financial and clinical applications that are increasingly in use. By expanding networks and facilitating the exchange of information, policymakers and providers alike hope the day will soon come when patient data can be retrieved, shared and acted upon wherever and whenever it is needed.

References

1. Australian Government, Australian Digital Health Agency, My Health Record. https://www.myhealthrecord.gov.au/ (accessed 10 December 2020).
2. Kankhar, S. Asian Hospital and Healthcare Management. https://www.asianhhm.com/information-technology/healthcareit-asiapacific (accessed 10 December 2020)
3. HIMSS Europe. (17 March 2017). https://www.himss.eu/himss-blog/data-portability-and-sharing-personal-health-data-across-national-borders (accessed 10 December 2020).
4. U.S. Department of Commerce, U.S. Commercial Service, Getman, Susana and Sabina Kroigaard. (April 2013). "Health IT/eHealth in Europe". http://files.export.gov/x_4040002.pdf (accessed 20 November 2020).
5. Ibid.
6. HealthIT.gov. Basics of Health IT: Learn the Basics of Health Information Technology. www.healthit.gov/patients-families/basics-health-it (accessed 20 November 2020).
7. Institute of Medicine (US) Committee on Quality of Health Care in America. (1999). *To Err Is Human: Building a Safer Health System*. https://pubmed.ncbi.nlm.nih.gov/25077248/.
8. Institute of Medicine. (2001). *Crossing the Quality Chasm: A New Health System for the 21st Century*. Washington, DC: The National Academies Press. Retrieved 29 June 2006.
9. The U.S. Office of the National Coordinator for Health Information Technology (ONC). https://www.healthit.gov/playbook/certified-health-it/.
10. Health IT Workforce Curriculum, Version 3.0. (2012). Component 6: Health Management Information Systems. Unit 5a: Clinical Decision Support Systems. This material, Comp6_Unit5a, was developed by Duke University, funded by the Department of Health and Human Services, Office of the National Coordinator for Health Information Technology under Award Number IU240C000024. https://www.healthit.gov/topic/health-it-resources/health-it-curriculum-resources-educators.
11. Electronic prescribing. Office of the National Coordinator for Health Information Technology. Ver 1, 2. (November 2020). https://www.healthit.gov/test-method/electronic-prescribing.
12. Bresnick, J. (25 January 2016). Defining the Basics of the Healthcare Big Data Warehouse, *HIT Infrastructure*. https://hitinfrastructure.com/news/defining-the-basics-of-the-healthcare-big-data-warehouse.
13. Healthcare Information and Management Systems Society (HIMSS). (2013). *Healthcare Information and Management Systems Society. HIMSS Dictionary of Health Information Technology Terms, Acronyms and Organizations*. Chicago, IL: HIMSS.
14. Garritty, C., & El Emam, K. (2006). Who's using PDAs? Estimates of PDA use by health care providers: A systematic review of surveys. *Journal of Medical Internet Research*, 8, 2.
15. Girard, P. (2007). Military and VA telemedicine systems for patients with traumatic brain injury. *Journal of Rehabilitation Research & Development*, 44(7), 1017–1026.
16. Personalized Medicine Coalition. (2014). *PMC Personalized Medicine Coalition* (4th ed.). http://www.personalizedmedicine-coalition.org/Userfiles/PMC-Corporate/file/pmc_age_of_pmc_factsheet.pdf (accessed 20 November 2020).
17. Caramenico, A. JAMA Study: Isolated, Rural Hospitals Have Poorer Quality. https://www.fiercehealthcare.com/healthcare/patients-at-small-isolated-rural-hospitals-us-more-likely-to-receive-lower-quality-care.

CLINICAL INFORMATICS II

Chapter 3

Clinical Informatics

Learning Objectives

At the conclusion of this chapter, the reader will be able to:

- Identify basic clinical vocabulary/terms frequently represented in healthcare informatics (e.g., dosage frequency, dosage routes, body systems)
- Identify basic healthcare IT vocabulary/terms frequently represented in healthcare informatics (e.g., LAN, SMS, VPN)
- Identify basic clinical metrics frequently represented in informatics (e.g., average daily census, turnaround time, adherence, barcode medication administration)
- Identify and support opportunities to optimize clinical effectiveness and efficiencies
- Understand various data visualization techniques (e.g., tables, graphs, charts)
- Maintain clinical content and decision-support tools

Introduction

Many professional associations define the profession of clinical informatics. Healthcare Information and Management Systems Society (HIMSS) defines clinical informatics as activities that promote the understanding, integration and application of information technology (IT) in healthcare settings.[1] The American Medical Informatics Association (AMIA) differentiates clinical informatics by explicitly noting that the information used in healthcare is actually *by clinicians*.[2] Whereas, the American Nursing Informatics Association (ANIA) defines nursing informatics as explicitly addressing improvements for "the health of populations, communities, families and individuals by optimizing information management and communication".[3] Likewise, Canada has a comparable association to ANIA, the Canadian Nursing Informatics Association (CNIA), with a stated purpose of engaging internationally to partner on initiatives related to informatics and health IT.[4] CNIA endorses the International Medical Informatics Association (IMIA) definition for nursing informatics as follows: "Nursing Informatics science and practice integrates nursing, its information and knowledge and their management with information and communication technologies to promote the health of people, families and communities worldwide".[5]

Globally, clinical informatics has been increasingly impactful to the healthcare world. Diana Nole, the Chief Executive Officer (CEO) of Wolters Kluwer, Health, states that in 2018 there was more than USD $8 billion in digital health deals made.[6] Clinical decision support (CDS) continues to be a powerful tool guiding today's clinicians. Drug usage and cost are analyzed with new methods and use of data including artificial intelligence (AI) and machine learning. With the increased focus on social determinants of health and patient-driven care, AI development and usage will continue to escalate in use with new demands for clinical informatics specialists.[6] Clinical informaticists will be needed in various roles including translators between data scientists, computer scientists and actually serving in the data scientist

DOI: 10.4324/9780429443862-5

role within interprofessional teams. As a professional that speaks clinical, informatics and healthcare, the role is a critical component of the interprofessional team with use of big data and advanced analytics.

Basic Clinical Vocabulary and Terms

Understanding the basics of healthcare is vitally important for health IT workers and clinicians alike. To be able to speak the same language, and understand each other, common ground must be found. In this section, we will review frequently used clinical terminology found in the healthcare environment. At the root of clinical language is the use of prefixes, or letters, words or numbers placed before a medical term. Any tables listed are merely a sampling of existing terminology; they are not meant to be a complete catalog (Tables 3.1 and 3.2). It is notable that the prefixes in Table 3.1 are Latin root words and relevant globally when communicating medical terminology. Additionally, there is an overlap with the European Medical Agency and their list of common vocabulary and terms along with the Canadian Glossary of Health Care Terms.[7]

National Standards for Health Information Technology

This section will examine important data standards that support certification of electronic health records (EHRs) and the ability to capture and report data with consistency. These standards have evolved over time in the United States (U.S.) and are critical to building the digital highway to capture and transmit healthcare data effectively across institutions, regions and states, nationally and even internationally. Data standards are developed and maintained by a number of global organizations. This section will describe these standards and the organizations that develop, govern and maintain these standards. The importance of these standards to the infrastructure of digital healthcare data and the role of the clinical informatics professional will also be discussed.

Table 3.3 includes some of the more essential standards to national strategies to leverage EHRs and the interoperability of EHRs within and across organizations. Examples of these standards reflected in Table 3.3 include the messaging standards upon which the standard is based and notes of examples of these types of standards and what the standard is used for in healthcare.

Table 3.1 Frequently Used Clinical Terminology Prefixes

Brachi/o	*Arm*	*Lapar/o*	*Abdomen, loin or flank*
Cardi/o	*Heart*	My/o	*Muscle*
Cyt/o	*Cell*	Neur/o	*Nerve*
Derm/a, derm/o, dermat/o	*Skin*	Ocul/o	*Eye*
Encephal/o	*Brain*	Ophthalm/o	*Eyes*
Gastr/o	*Stomach*	Or/o	*Mouth*
Hemat/o	*Blood*	Ot/o	*Ear*
Intestin/o	*Intestine*	Pulmon/o	*Lungs*

Source: Adapted from American Institute of Medical Sciences & Education (AIMS). *All Essential Medical Terms in One Place*. Retrieved from https://www.merriam-webster.com/dictionary/prefix (accessed 16 July 2019).

Basic Information Technology Vocabulary and Terms

Table 3.2 Frequently Used Clinical Abbreviations

Abbreviation	*Definition*	*Abbreviation*	*Definition*
AM	Morning	L	Liter
AC	Before meals	LMP	Last menstrual period
AD	Right ear	MCG	microgram
Ad lib	Freely	mEq/L	Milliequivalent per liter
Amp	Ampule	mL	Milliliter
Ante	Before	Mm	Millimeter
AS	Left ear	N/V	Nausea and vomiting
ASA	Aspirin	NKDA	No known drug allergies
AU	Both ears	NPO	Nothing by mouth
BID	Twice a day	OD	Right eye
BMI	Body mass index	OS	Left eye
BP	Blood pressure	OU	Both eyes
BS	Blood sugar	Oz	Ounce
CC	Chief complaint	PRN	As needed
Cap	Capsule	PM	Evening
CM	Centimeter	PMH	Past medical history
CXR	Chest x-ray	Q	Every
DC	Discontinue	Q2h	Every two hours
Disp	Dispense	Q6h	Every six hours
ER/EC/ED	Emergency Room	Qam	Every morning
G	Gram	Qpm	Every night
Gr	Grain	QID	Four times a day
HR	Hour	QOD	Every other day
H/O	History of	Rx	Prescription
HR	Heart rate	SL	Sublingual
HS	At bedtime	SQ	Subcutaneous
HX	History	STAT	Immediately
ID	Intradermal	Supp	Suppository
IM	Intramuscular	T	Temperature
IN	Intranasal	TID	Three times a day
INJ	Injection	w/o	Without
IV	Intravenous	WNL	Within normal limits

Source: Adapted from Drugs.com. Prescription Abbreviations. (n.d.). Retrieved from https://www.drugs.com/article/prescription-abbreviations.html.

Table 3.3 Technology Standards for Healthcare

Technology Standards for Healthcare	
Messaging Standards	*Used for*
HL7	Clinical data
X12N	Financial data, HIPAA-mandated transactions, transport of data
DICOM	Images
NCPDP	Standards for pharmacy business functions, HIPAA-mandated transactions
IEEE	Bedside instruments, medical information bus
Terminology Standards	
LOINC	Lab interoperability/data exchange
Drugs	NLM/FDA/VA collaboration on RxNorm, NDF-RT
Billing	CPT, ICD-10-CM
Clinical	UMLS, SNOMED and others

Source: National Health Information Infrastructure. (n.d.). Standards and standards organization. Retrieved from http://www.aspe.hhs.gov/sp/nhii/standards.html.

CPT, Current Procedural Terminology; DICOM, Digital Imaging and Communication in Medicine; FDA, US. Food and Drug Administration; HIPAA, Health Insurance Portability and Accountability Act; HL7, Health Level Seven; ICD-9-CM, *International Classification of Diseases*, 9th edition, Clinical Modification; ICD-10-CM, *International Classification of Diseases*, 10th edition, Clinical Modification; IEEE, Institute of Electrical and Electronics Engineers; LOINC, Logical Observation Identifiers Names and Codes; NCPDP, National Council for Prescription Drug Programs; NDF-RT, National Drug File-Reference Terminology; NLM, National Library of Medicine; SNOMED, Systematized Nomenclature of Medicine; UMLS, Unified Medical Language System; VA, Veterans Administration.

Computers in Healthcare

Computers in healthcare are not a new phenomenon and have been around for decades in the form of legacy systems that manage billing, laboratory information, pharmacy information and supplies. However, the massive update and enormous expansion of EHR adoption and implementation in the U.S. is a result of a Federal Act passed in 2009 under the American Recovery and Reinvestment Act. This bill is known as The Health Information Technology for Economic and Clinical Health Act (HITECH Act). The HITECH Act was created to motivate the implementation of EHRs and supporting technology in the U.S. This Act as it was intended to do created an economic stimulus effect and created new jobs to help support this massive infrastructure within the U.S.. Many of these roles were roles supporting expansion of EHRs and clinicians' use of these systems. Through a collaboration with the U.S. and the European Union (EU), there are extensive efforts to examine competencies needed for the digital age of healthcare. This collaboration is referred to as HITComp.org. Phase I of this work to identify competencies related to roles and levels of competency began in May 2015. For a complete list of the competencies, levels and roles, see HITComp.org.[8]

Communication of information is the essence of the role of computers in healthcare and the primary function of any EHR or machine intelligence. Clinical informatics professionals need to understand the basic underpinnings of computers and how they work to manage healthcare information. Therefore, this section will discuss the basics of computer technology including hardware, software and networking; describe hardware specifications and criteria that should be taken into account when making purchases. Additionally, this section will discuss the ergonomics requirements needed when implementing health IT for clinicians.

The basics of computer technology encompass fundamental building blocks. These building blocks to be described and defined include "bits", "bytes", "hardware," and "software" and conclude with connectivity considerations. Table 3.4 are key internal components of a computer that the clinical informatics professional should understand and often fills a role to manage these components for clinical teams alongside their IT colleagues.

Table 3.4 Internal Components of the Computer

Component	*Definition*	*Function*
Motherboard	The backbone of the computer	Connects all of the parts of the computer together
Central processing unit (CPU)	Often thought of as "the brains" of the computer	Responsible for interpreting and executing most of the commands from the computer's hardware and software
Random-access memory (RAM)	The working memory of the computer	Allows a computer to work with more information at the same time in active memory processing
Power supply	A converter that supplies the power to the machine	Used to convert the power provided from the outlet into usable power for the many parts inside the computer case
Video card	Graphics adapter or expansion card	Allows the computer to send graphical information to a video display device such as a monitor, TV or projector
Hard disc drive (HDD)	Data storage device and an electromechanical magnetic disc drive	The HDD is the main, and usually largest, data storage hardware device in a computer where the operating system, software and most files are stored
Solid-state drive (SSD)	Data storage device; no moving (mechanical) components	Storage device that is typically more resistant to physical shock, runs silently and has lower access time and less latency, but more expensive than HDD
Optical drive (e.g., Blu-ray/DVD/CD drive)	Optical storage devices	Optical drives retrieve and/or store data on optical discs like CDs, DVDs and Blu-ray discs (BDs)

Hardware Specifications

The considerations noted here take into account hardware specifications – specifications that typically include parameters such as processing speeds, memory requirements (RAM and HDD requirements), necessary interface equipment and operating system requirements for running the clinical software. Table 3.5 presents a sample of what a technical specification for a clinical information system setup might look like for a clinical environment application server.

Table 3.5 Sample Recommended Specifications for a Clinical Information Server

Processor	2 × Six Core Xeon E5-2620 or higher
Memory	8 GB RAM
Network interface card	1 Gbit
Primary hard drive(s)	2 × 300 GB SAS in RAID 1
Repository hard drives	6 × 300 GB SAS or more in RAID 5
Operating system	Microsoft Windows 2008 R2 (64-bit) Standard Edition SP1
Database software	Microsoft SQL (structured query language)

Software Considerations

Software can be categorized as (a) system software that is used to start and run the computer, (b) application software that generally has a purpose or function specific to its use (e.g., accounting/financial applications) or (c) programming tools that are used to compile programs and link or translate computer program source code and libraries that belong to either the system software or the application. Table 3.6 features the types of system software used across industries. Systems software is related to what the software does within the computer system to support the use of the computer. For example, the device-driver software operates and manages all devices attached to the computer. The application software is typically categorized by intended use, such as business software that is used for managing admissions, discharge and transactions for patients in hospitals and healthcare systems.

Connectivity Considerations

Communications and interoperability in health IT is fundamental to understand for clinical informatics professionals. Connections from various mechanisms that seamlessly transmit data from one system to another have become common features in our lives. One may consider the simple function of our cell or mobile phone technology that we are so dependent on in this day and age to understand important considerations for clinical information management. Short messaging services (SMS) are experiencing rapid growth because of our ability to establish virtual private networks (VPNs) within our homes and work environments. Many individuals automate all kinds of home-based technologies by cell or mobile phone connectivity. We can turn on and off our security system, view who is at our front door from video streaming on our mobile devices and even turn on and off our utilities, water sprinklers and robotic vacuum cleaners – all thought mobile devices in our homes.

Healthcare has also seen an explosion of mobile technologies in our hospitals and clinics that can send mobile alerts for patients to return to follow-up or view their lab or diagnostic results through their patient portals. Bar code administration and secure messaging via mobile devices are also routinely done, but a major consideration for healthcare as we use this type of interoperability and communications relates to the ability to secure the message and maintain privacy of patient information that is transmitted. In healthcare we have federal mandates in the form of

Table 3.6 Types of Internal Components of Computer Software

Type	*Description*
Operating system	The software that is responsible for the direct control and management of the hardware and running application software
Open-source software	Free source code access licensed for use by an open community of developers and end users; proprietary software is owned and distributed for commercial use
Boot loader or bootstrap	The small program that loads and executes the command to "boot up" the computer; the program is stored in the RAM
Device drivers	A program that operates the various devices on the computer, such as printers and peripherals; the driver provides software interface to the hardware device
Firm ware	Controls the devices typically seen in items such as mobile phones and digital cameras
Graphical user interface (GUI)	A graphics display with user-friendly point-and-click capability that allows the end user to interact with the computer through the mouse and touchpad
Middleware	Software that resides as an interface between the operating system and the applications that allows developers to control input/output devices, also referred to as "software glue"
Utility software	Software that helps analyze, configure, optimize or maintain the computer

the Health Insurance Portability and Accountability Act (HIPAA) and other regulation at federal and state levels requiring protection of confidential information that may result in exposure of personal health information (PHI) or identity theft. The EU has similar compliance using the General Data Protection Regulations (GDPR). These regulations came into effect in 2018. These EU compliance requirements are similar to the U.S. HIPAA requirements for secure sockets layer (SSL) protection for patient data, data security protocols and established methods of disposing of patient data.[9]

In addition to mobile technologies, computers in healthcare often reside on local area networks (LAN). LANs can take on a number of configurations, some with simple, cost-effective setups and some more complex but generate a more secure network for organizations. Cloud computing is another area we see rapidly expanding in healthcare. Cloud computing is also known as "software as service".[10] With EHRs the software is housed on a massive server and is networked in cloud services provided by the vendor, where the server is secured and often has redundancy (another server) with data mirrored in a different part of the country, also secured. Many healthcare organizations are moving to this type of service because large companies can better secure and monitor issues such as cybersecurity threats.

Ergonomics

When considering ergonomics, the science of human factors underpins important considerations for clinical informatics. In the U.S. the term ergonomics describes the physical use of computer equipment. In Europe this term is synonymous with human factors.[11]

The positioning of the computer hardware within a clinic or hospital with easy, safe and efficient use are important considerations. When you think in terms of proper posture and position of the equipment with height of the equipment and whether the end user will use the equipment in a seated or standing position these considerations are relevant for ergonomically positioned use.

Optimizing Clinical Effectiveness of Health Information Technology

With the rapid expansion of EHRs in healthcare under the HITECH Act, many providers are indicating that the ability to capture clinical data may be improved but these new systems are creating burdens of documentation,[12] interoperability challenges and unintended consequences often leading to health IT safety considerations and undue clinicians stress.[13–15] Given these challenges, using quality improvement techniques to optimize technology is an important skill set for clinical informatics professionals. One area that is important to consider are applying methods of workflow redesign to some of these common challenges.

The Agency for Healthcare Quality and Research (AHRQ) defines workflow as "Workflow is defined as a series of steps, frequently performed by different staff members and often dependent on related workflows, that accomplishes a particular task. Workflows represent how work actually gets done, not the protocols that have been established to do the work".[16] For example, when considering a patient safety issue that has occurred due to health IT, it is important to consider details of the event. Techniques that can be used to detect details include a root cause analysis or a Failure Modes and Effects Analysis (FMEA). For further information on these techniques visit the Institute for Healthcare Improvement website (IHI.org). These techniques help to determine how a workflow might be redesigned to address the unintended consequence (patient safety issue).

In addition, the "as is" or current state workflow is mapped using flipcharts and sticky tabs with clinicians and other stakeholders involved in the process. This visual depiction of the workflow can then be translated into a software that helps to map roles, responsibilities and when actions and decisions are made within the workflow. Common software used is Microsoft Visio and LucidChart. This mapping is followed by redesign of the workflow to address what happened that created the patient safety issue and to mitigate the error from happening in the future. This map is referred to as the "to be" map or future state map of the workflow. This redesign uses a similar technique to map the workflow out with stakeholders using flip charts and sticky tabs, followed by a formalized diagram in the software.[17] In addition to mapping workflows, the team should consider how to measure whether your redesign has made a difference. Measures that are process, outcome and balancing measures are important considerations. We will consider these types of measures as we examine common clinical metrics in healthcare that are typically categorized in these three categories.

Common Clinical Metrics Used in Healthcare

Common measures in healthcare can be organized into three categories, process, outcome and balancing measures. Examples of common outcome measures include mortality rates, 30-day readmission rates for hospitals, surgical site infections. Often, outcome measures need to be risk-adjusted to account for comorbidities and other factors that might influence the metric. Statistical procedures are used to "control" and "adjust for" these factors to get an apples-to-apples comparison of hospitals and providers. This method adjusts for the "my patients are sicker" factor that can influence ability to compare providers fairly and equitably.

Process measures are reflective of a clinical guideline and key interventions that impact a clinical outcome. For example, door to balloon time for a heart attack also called myocardial infarction (MI) patient is a common process measure to improve mortality rates for MI patients. The mortality outcome is impacted by how quickly we can get the patient into the cardiac catheterization (cath) laboratory (lab), determine where the coronary blockage might be in a very timely manner and insert a balloon to inflate the area of blockage and place a stent in the area to keep it open. The expression, "time is muscle", refers to a timely response in order to save cardiac muscle that is damaged as the coronary artery remains blocked. So, the metric of measuring total time from emergency department triage, to getting the patient on the cath lab table to intervene to save cardiac muscle and prevent mortality (outcome) due to the acute MI, is a critical measure of success.

Balancing measures are metrics that address potential unintended consequences as we address quality improvement interventions to improve process or outcomes. Take for example our focus on the opioid epidemic and metrics to measure outcomes such as opioid-related mortality, and an intervention that might be prescribing rates of opioids by providers. An unintended consequence of addressing this major public health crisis in the U.S. might be a reluctance to prescribe pain medications for patients. So, a balancing measure to address this unintended consequence might be satisfaction of the patient and family related to pain management.

The National Quality Forum (NQF) is an organization tasked through a federal contract to oversee quality measures development in the U.S. The U.S. is at a critical juncture in transforming healthcare through how we pay for healthcare. With these changes NQF outlines three interdependent levels of measurement, including individual performance measures, measure sets and measurement systems. This approach establishes a next generation approach to measuring quality in healthcare. For an expansive view of common metrics in healthcare and this new approach to measurement strategy, we recommend that the reader visits the NQF website to look at the hundreds of outcomes, processes and balancing measures to measure quality and safety in healthcare.[18]

Outside of the U.S., there are several organizations and societies related to healthcare quality and standards. The International Society for Quality in Health Care (ISQua) is a not-for-profit community that works to maintain healthcare quality and safety through, "education, knowledge sharing, external evaluation, supporting health systems worldwide and connecting like-minded people …."[19] They support over 70 countries on six continents. Three organizations with international implications for quality improvement and measurement in healthcare include the International Organization for Standardization (ISO), the ISO 9001 standard. ISO was founded in 1947 with a purpose of establishing an international quality standard. The European Foundation for Quality Management (EFQM) Excellence Model is another approach focused on European quality for hospitals founded in 1988 with the approval of the European commission. This model is originally based on eight concepts of quality and later expanded to a public model including nine criteria. The nine criteria include five enablers (leadership, people, policy and strategy, partnership and resources and processes) and four "results" (people results, customer results, society results and key performance results).[20]

Common Data Visualization Methods

Common data visualization techniques include graphs, charts and tables. There are best practices in developing and presenting data that clinical informatics professionals should understand. According to Tufte, graphical display of data can convey complex ideas with clarity, precision and efficiency when the best practices are followed.[21] These best practices should include:

- Clear display of the data
- Induce the viewer to think about substance rather than methods

- Avoid distortion
- Present numbers in small space
- Make a large data set coherent
- Encourage the eye to compare different pieces of data
- Review the data at multiple levels
- Serve a clear purpose to describe, explore, tabulate or enhance a report
- Be closely integrated with verbal or descriptive information in a report.[21]

Some common visual displays of data are noted in Figure 3.1. These graphs include line charts often used to reflect a metrics variability over time, in Figure 3.1A. The line chart reflects mortality risk-adjusted rates by quarter from 2010 through 2017. Line graphs can also show multiple series of data points overtime, such as multiple hospital mortality rates compared to overtime depicted by different colored lines. Bar charts are used to reflect frequency, counts or percentages as reflected by a total frequency of gender (males and females) in Figure 3.1B. Bar charts can also be used to reflect multiple variables as in Figure 3.1C, whereas, histograms can reflect distributions of data for discrete (categories) or continuous data. The bars represent numerical data by showing the number of data points that fall within a specified range of values often called "bins".[22]

Pie charts have a bad reputation and can be messy and hard to read; however, pie charts can be effective at comparing differences and to illustrate the percentage breakdown of a small number of data points. The figure reflects two pie charts comparing distributions of males compared to female income differences.

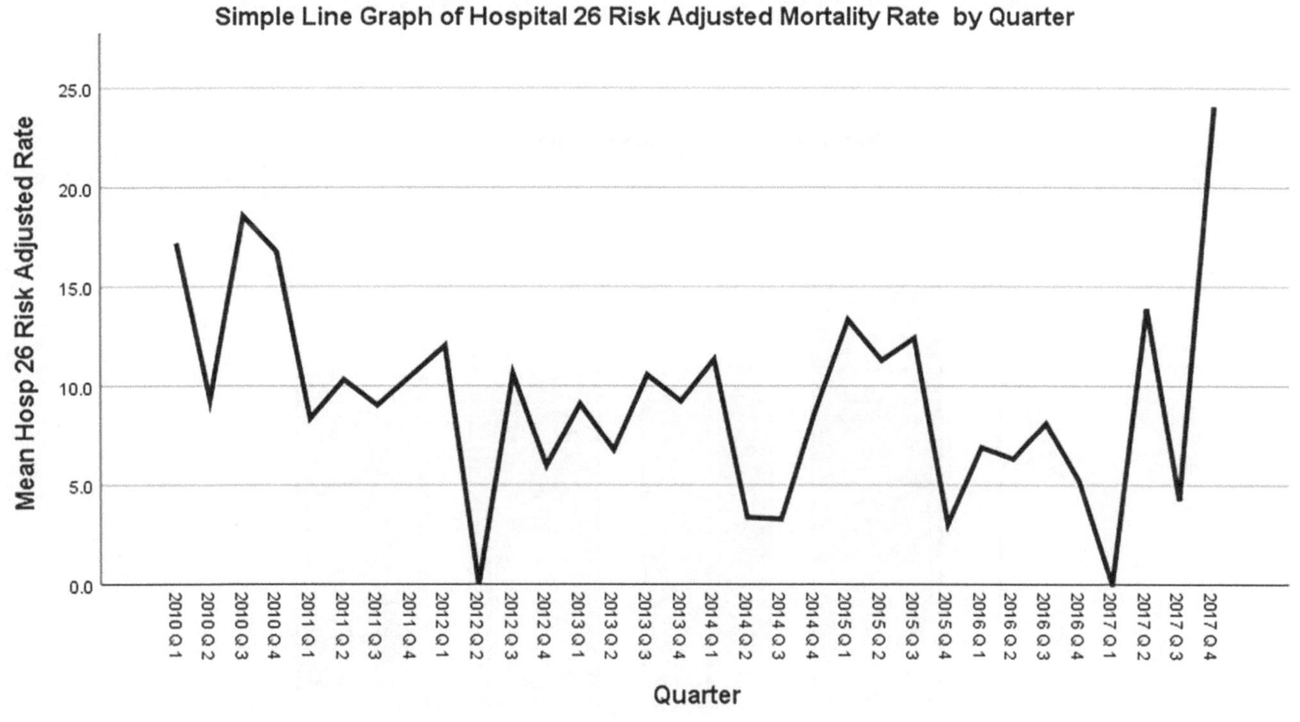

Figure 3.1 Common visual displays of data *(Continued)*

gender

		Frequency	Percent	Valid Percent	Cumulative Percent
Valid	male	255	36.4	36.6	36.6
	female	441	62.9	63.4	100.0
	Total	696	99.3	100.0	
Missing	System	5	.7		
Total		701	100.0		

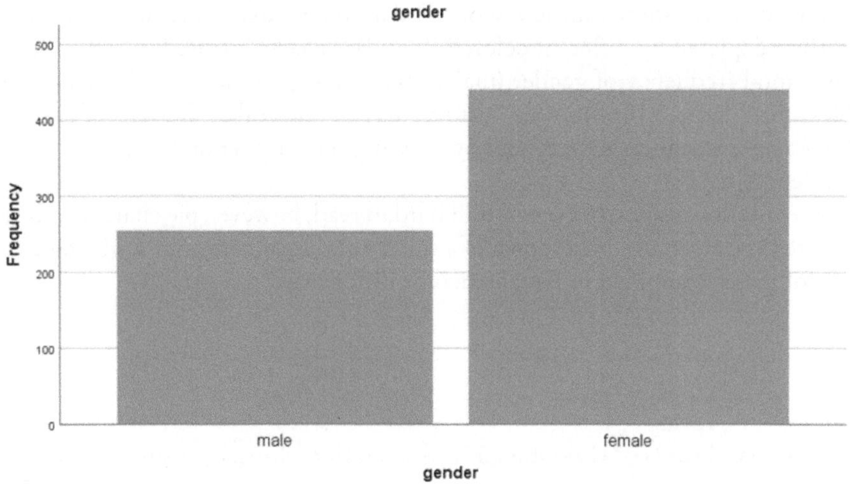

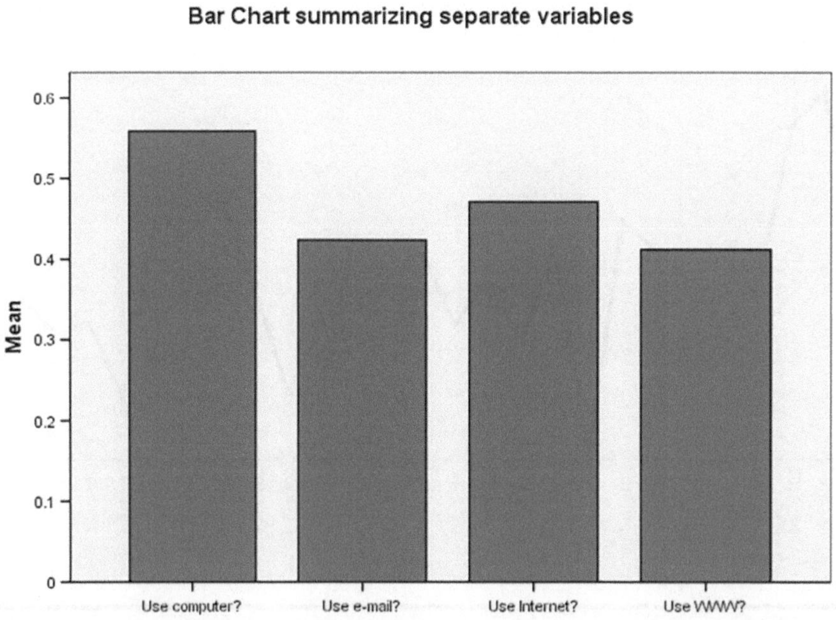

Figure 3.1 *(Continued)*

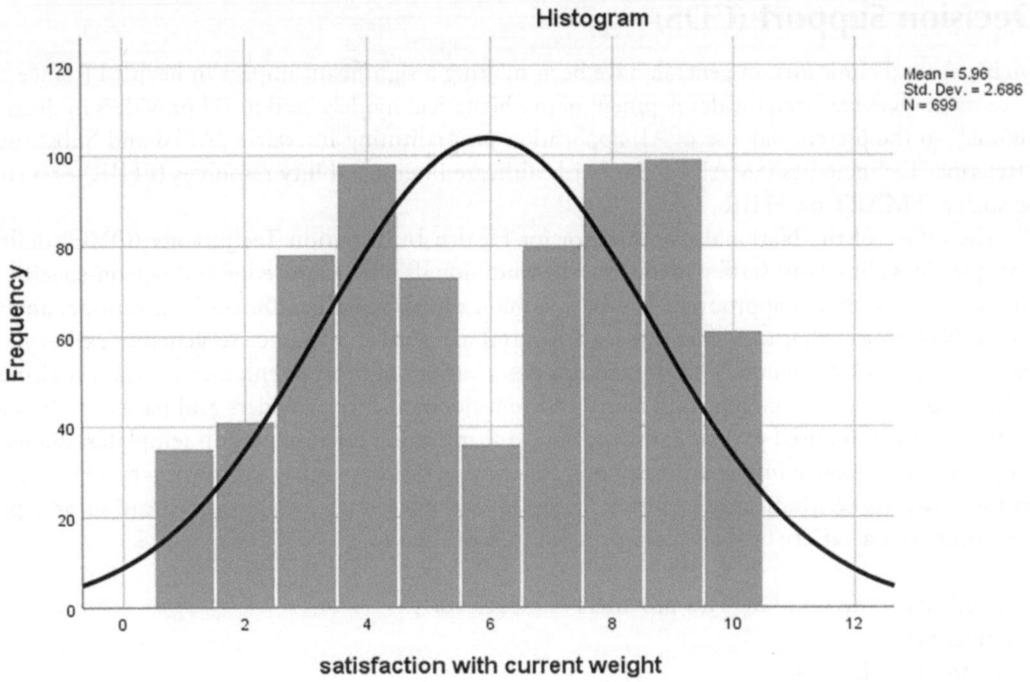

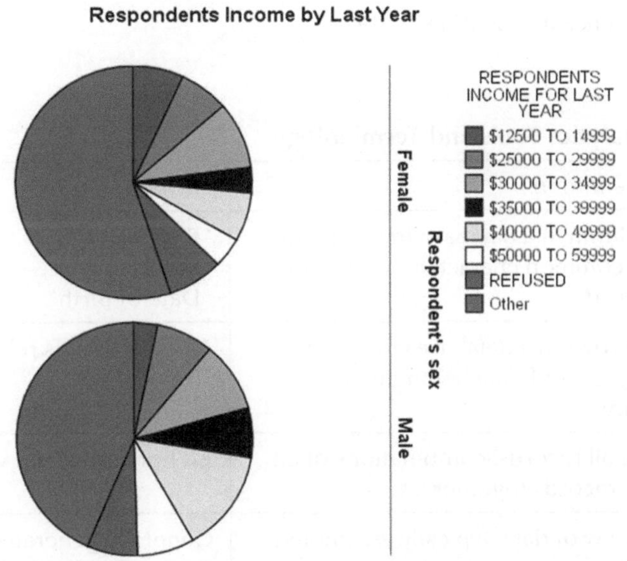

Figure 3.1 ***(Continued)***

Clinical Decision Support (CDS)

Clinical informaticists and clinicians, in general, have been making a significant impact in health IT since the late 1950s (Table 3.7). Since then, there has been the development of mathematical models used to aid providers in diagnosing various medical conditions[23] to the present-day use of AI, application programming interfaces (APIs) and Substitutable Medical Applications, Reusable Technologies (SMART), the fast healthcare interoperability resources (FHIR) or a combination of several of these such as SMART on FHIR.

In the U.S., the Office of the National Coordinator for Health Information Technology (ONC) defines CDS as a component that "provides clinicians, staff, patients or other individuals with knowledge and person-specific information, intelligently filtered or presented at appropriate times, to enhance health and healthcare.[24] In Europe, an example is the EU-funded PredictND project that uses machine learning and artificial intelligence to generate earlier neurodegenerative disease diagnoses, such as dementia.[25] CDS encompasses a variety of tools to enhance decision-making in the clinical workflow. These tools include computerized alerts and reminders to care providers and patients; clinical guidelines; condition-specific order sets; focused patient data reports and summaries; documentation templates; diagnostic support, and contextually relevant reference information, among other tools" (n.d., para. 1). According to a fact sheet distributed by the Centers for Medicare & Medicaid Services (CMS), CDS is not simply an alert, notification or explicit care suggestion. CDS encompasses a variety of tools including, but not limited to:

- Computerized alerts and reminders for providers and patients
- Clinical guidelines
- Condition-specific order sets
- Focused patient data reports and summaries
- Documentation templates
- Diagnostic support
- Contextually relevant reference information.

Table 3.7 Common Data Analytics Tools and Terminology

Tool	*Purpose/Definition*	*Example*
Fields	Vertical column in a database that contains data with common characteristics for the entire record	"First Name" "Last Name" "Date of Birth"
Records	Horizontal rows in a database containing different pieces of data belonging to a given entity	All of the fields related to the row of "Billy"
Tables	Consists of all records; combinations of all fields and records together	All horizontal and vertical rows together
Reports	Alternate view of data; typically assembled from a query	Generally generated on paper, can also be electronic for distribution of data
Query	Process of selecting desired records; pulling the data	Pulling data related to all female patients older than 50 with a history of colon polyps
Graphs and charts	Tool for examining and presenting data	Scatter plot, pie charts, bar charts, flowcharts
Control charts	Tool for looking at a process over time	Common and special-cause variation, upper and lower control limits
Predictive modeling	Instead of retrospective data analytics, the data is used to predict future outcomes	Pulling last five years of financial data to predict next years' budget needs

Source: Englebardt, S., & Nelson, R. (2002). *Health Care Informatics: An Interdisciplinary Approach.* St Louis, MO: Mosby, Inc.

Osheroff et al. recommend combining all of these types of CDS to strategically use CDS within an organization following a framework that includes five rights of CDS.[26] The five rights address the who, what, where, when and how of a CDS program and emphasize the importance of clear goals and objectives that identify all five components. These strategies are outlined and applied to a number of important clinical priorities on a HRSA website developed by Osheroff, we recommend the reader review strategies outlined on the website for further application of these CDS best practices to clinical conditions.[26]

Summary

In summary, this chapter has covered important foundational information for clinical informatics professionals to understand and begin to master. Information covered has included the basics of clinical vocabulary and important terms frequently represented in healthcare informatics. We have also examined basic definitions for IT vocabulary and terms frequently represented in healthcare informatics. Also covered has been important types of metrics, including process, outcome and balancing measures with clinical examples of how these measures tie together. Methods to optimize technology to improve care delivery such as workflow redesign methods were examined, as well as important data visualizations and some basic types of graphics often used in healthcare were also covered. Finally, CDS strategies and best practices were defined and described.

References

1. HIMSS. (2019). Clinical Informatics. Retrieved from https://www.himss.org/library/clinical-informatics.
2. AMIA. (2019). Clinical Informatics. Retrieved from https://www.amia.org/applications-informatics/clinical-informatics.
3. ANIA. (2019). American Nursing Informatics Association. Retrieved from https://www.ania.org/about-us.
4. CNIA. (2020). About CNIA. Retrieved from https://cnia.ca/about (accessed 15 December 2020).
5. International Medical Informatics Association. (2009). IMIA-NI definition of nursing informatics updated. Retrieved from https://imianews.wordpress.com/2009/08/24/imia-ni-definition-ofnursing-informatics-updated/.
6. Nole, D. (2018). 5 Healthcare trends to watch in 2019. *Becker's Hospital Review.* https://www.beckershospitalreview.com/healthcare-information-technology/5-healthcare-trends-to-watch-in-2019.html.
7. Ontario, HQCanada. (2020). A Glossary of Health Care Teams: For Patient and Caregiver Partners. Retrieved https://hqontario.ca/Portals/0/documents/pe/glossary-resource-en.pdf (accessed 15 December 2020).
8. HITComp.org. (N.D.). HITComp.org: About Us. Retrieved from http://hitcomp.org/about/ (accessed 15 December 2020).
9. Venkatesiah, K. (2017). GDPR Vs. HIPAA – Noting the differences. https://www.healthitoutcomes.com/doc/gdpr-vs-hipaa-noting-the-differences-0001.
10. McBride, S., & Tietze, M. (2018). *Nursing Informatics for the Advanced Practice Nurse: Patient Safety, Quality, Outcomes, and Interprofessionalism* (2nd ed.). New York: Springer Publishing Company.
11. McGonigle, D., & Mastrian, K. G. (2012). *Nursing Informatics and the Foundation of Knowledge* (2nd ed.). Burlington, MA: Jones & Bartlett Learning.
12. Bodenheimer, T., & Sinsky, C. (2014). From triple to quadruple aim: Care of the patient requires care of the provider. *Annals of Family Medicine*, 12(6), 573–576. https://doi.org/10.1370/afm.1713.
13. Staggers, N., Elias, B., Makar, E., & Alexander, G. L. (2018). The imperative of solving nurses usability problems with health information technology. *The Journal of Nursing Administration*, 48(4), 191–196.
14. Bloomrosen, M., Starren, J., Lorenzi, N. M., Ash, J. S., Patel, V. L., & Shortliffe, E. H. (2011). Anticipating and addressing the unintended consequences of health IT and policy: A report from the AMIA 2009 health policy meeting. *Journal of the American Medical Informatics Association*, 18(1), 82–90. https://doi.org/10.1136/jamia.2010.007567.
15. McBride, S., Tietze, M., Hanley, M., & Thomas, L. (2017). Statewide study to assess nurses' experience with meaningful-use based electronic health records. *Computers, Informatics, Nursing*, 35(1), 18–28. https://doi.org/10.1097/CIN.0000000000000290.
16. AHRQ. (2019). Module 5: Mapping and Redesigning Workflow. Retrieved from https://www.ahrq.gov/ncepcr/tools/pf-handbook/mod5.html.
17. McBride, S., & Tietze, M. (2018). *Nursing Informatics for the Advanced Practice Nurse: Patient Safety, Quality, Outcomes, and Interprofessionalism* (2nd ed., pp. 209–228). New York, NY: Springer Publishing Company.
18. National Quality Forum. http://www.qualityforum.org/Home.aspx.
19. International Society for Quality in Health Care. (n.d.). *Welcome to the International Society for Quality in Health Care (ISQua).* https://isqua.org.

20. Yousefinezhadi, T., Mohamadi, E., Safari Palangi, H., & Akbari Sari, A. (2015). The effect of ISO 9001 and the EFQM model on improving Hospital performance: A systematic review. *Iran Red Crescent Medical Journal,* 17(12), e23010–e23010. https://doi.org/10.5812/ircmj.23010.
21. Tufte, E. (2013). *The Visual Display of Quantitative Information* (2nd ed.). Cheshire, CT: Graphics Press.
22. Plichta, S., & Kelvin, E. (2013). *Munro's Statistical Methods for Health Care Research* (6th ed.). Philadelphia: Wolters Kluwer/Lippincott Williams & Wilkins.
23. Ledley, R. S., & Lusted, L. B. (1959). Reasoning foundations of medical diagnosis. *Science,* 130(3366) (accessed 8 November 2020).
24. Office of the National Coordinator for Health Information Technology. (2014). Clinical decision support rule. Retrieved from https://www.healthit.gov/topic/safety/clinical-decision-support (accessed 8 November 2020).
25. European Commission. (2018). *PredictND: Clinical decision support systems for dementia.* https://ec.europa.eu/digital-single-market/en/news/predictnd-clinical-decision-support-system-dementia (accessed 8 November 2020)
26. Osheroff, J. A., Teich, J. M., Levick, D., Saldana, L., Velasco, F. T., Sittig, D. F., & Jenders, R. A. (2012). *Improving Outcomes with CDS: An Implementer's Guide* (2nd ed.). Chicago, IL: Healthcare Information and Management Systems Society.

HEALTHCARE INFORMATION AND SYSTEMS MANAGEMENT

III

Chapter 4

Analysis

Learning Objectives

At the conclusion of this chapter, the reader will be able to:

- Identify and differentiate fundamental concepts of systems development (e.g., systems development lifecycle or SDLC, rapid application development, extreme programming)
- Identify and differentiate fundamental IT project management methodologies (e.g., Agile, waterfall) and components (e.g., needs analysis, gap analysis, defining and prioritizing requirements)
- Identify and differentiate fundamental concepts of process improvement (e.g., DMAIC, PDCA)
- Describe business and clinical processes utilizing standard visualization tools such as Gantt charts, fishbone, swimlane
- Conduct basic data analysis and interpretation
- Understand the basic elements of common business documents such as RFPs, RFIs, proposals, SLAs, NDAs, etc.)

Introduction

Implementation of new health information technology (health IT) can be a challenging experience for members of the healthcare workforce, but proper planning can make the adjustment easier for users and the information technology (IT) support staff. A detailed and comprehensive understanding of how a new technology will achieve desired outcomes of high-quality patient care or organizational efficiency is essential for IT professionals who participate in a clinical implementation. Participation in analysis and design activities includes an analysis of clinical process and workflow.

Process analysis is the method by which a health IT professional examines a process and identifies opportunities for improvement. It is important for health IT professionals to understand the fundamentals of health workflow process analysis and redesign. Process analysis enables the organization to develop workflow that takes advantage of new application capabilities. This analysis also validates workflow requirements and provides a base for change management activities, like the training of end users in a new capability.

The complexities involved in implementing a health information system (HIS) makes thorough systems analysis, planning and design of workflow necessary to ensure success. A solid understanding of what is required of a system, as well as what the system can do in a clinical or other setting, is the foundation for the system's design. The design process is part of planning for a system implementation. The goal of process analysis in the context of an HIS is to ensure that the organization has the best system for its needs and that the system meets requirements and enables the organization to achieve expected outcomes.

DOI: 10.4324/9780429443862-7

Analysis

The Role of the Analyst

The role of the health IT analyst involved in process design is to assist in designing workflow that takes full advantage of the features of a health IT system. The successful healthcare process analyst must have a basic understanding of data systems and clinical workflows. Further, the analyst must be able to identify areas where the current process is inefficient. Finally, it is crucial that the analyst be able to communicate these concepts to members of the implementation team, including both IT and the end user community.

Process Analysis

There are many ways to analyze processes. Often the methods concentrate on one or more aspects of a process. One process analysis methodology for implementing an electronic health record (EHR) focuses on identifying processes used at a clinic and translating information about the processes into a list of functions, supported by the EHR, that are needed at that clinic. The purpose of this type of process analysis is to ensure that the clinic has made the best match possible between an EHR and its needs and to optimally leverage health IT to improve patient care.

To get an idea of what this work entails, it might be good to begin with some basic definitions. The Norwegian Ministry of Health and Care Services defines process as "set of interrelated or interacting healthcare activities which transforms inputs into outputs".[1] The word *procedure* is related to process. The Solutions for Quality Environmental and Shipping Safety (SQSS) Certification Body defines a procedure as, "The steps in a process and how these steps are to be performed for the process to fulfill a customer's requirements".[2]

Processes have a number of important characteristics:

- They happen in a sequence or order.
- They have steps, inputs and outputs.
- They happen over and over again.

For example, appointment scheduling is a common process in healthcare facilities that has steps in a defined sequence: inputs (information about the appointment being scheduled), outputs (the appointment) and activity that occurs repeatedly during the day.

Aspects of a process analysis include looking at the various steps and the relationships between them, such as:

- What steps can be done at the same time, as opposed to sequentially?
- Who or what performs each step?
- Where are steps performed?

Because the goal of a healthcare process analysis is to ultimately improve the process, it is important to look for things like gaps, lack of conformity with best practice, undue delays, redundancy, rework and lack of efficiency.

Healthcare is not the only industry that engages in process analysis; health IT professionals can draw from many different methods of analyzing processes. These methods have originated from other fields, including business, quality improvement, industrial engineering, cognitive science, computer science and informatics.

Process analysis usually involves using a process diagram that allows the analyst to look for clues to inefficiency, redundancy and/or opportunity for error. An analysis at this level might also collect some data about how the process operates; for example, time from patient check-in to time seen by the provider might be collected. To understand opportunities for improvement, analysis might also include interviews of practice providers and staff to understand their perceptions.

Process Analysis: Determining Requirements

Process analysis can also be utilized in identifying requirements needed to select a new system like an EHR. For this activity, a less detailed approach could be used that involves identifying the clinic's core functions and how an EHR might contribute to accomplishing each of them.

This is an example of the approach an analyst might use:

1. **Takes a process inventory and creates process diagrams.** These should provide a context diagram showing clinic functions and a flowchart for each process.
2. **Lists the process variations applicable to the clinic.** Also include exceptions that often occur for each process. For example, for a patient visit, a common exception would be that a patient cancels or does not show up.
3. **Report findings.** The findings from a process analysis would include major observations, a list of EHR functionality necessary to support clinic functions and opportunities for improvement (technology assisted and otherwise).

After the processes are listed, the analyst works with leadership at the healthcare facility to identify those that are of high priority for analysis and improvement. All of the processes can't always be assessed. Some can't feasibly be improved upon with the available resources, and for others, the gain would be too small to make the effort worthwhile. Still others can be improved, but by means other than the use of health IT.

After the processes for analysis have been identified, the analyst, working with staff from the clinic, creates diagrams of the processes. These graphical representations of the processes will be used later for process analysis and redesign as part of the implementation. It is best to start with a simple process inventory and diagram because sometimes those are all that is needed. Moreover, they often point to areas where different types of objective information may be necessary.

A health IT analyst can improve processes by

- Increasing efficiency
- Decreasing delays, errors and cost
- Increasing quality and safety
- Improving the work environment
- Improving the ability to care for patients
- Creating a better overall patient experience

Physician practices have a set of core functions. Some functions are performed by most practices, such as scheduling and registration, documentation, prescription writing, billing and referrals. Other functions vary according to the type of practice; for example, a small practice may draw blood but may not perform any laboratory tests, while large practices may have equipment to perform common blood and urine-based lab tests. Services, like laboratory tests, other diagnostic tests and procedures vary by practice size and by specialty.

The Value of Process Mapping

The ability to identify the components of a process is a critical skill for conducting process analysis and improvement. As is often the case with many job functions, documentation is also important to achieve a successful outcome. For process analysis and improvement, documentation includes process mapping (e.g., creating process maps).

Process Mapping Components. How does process mapping provide essential and effective documentation? According to C.D. Wickens and J.G. Hollands, authors of *Engineering Psychology and Human Performance*, "With some graphical representations, humans perceive more information and perceive the information faster than through verbal and written communication channels".[3] Graphical representations typically take the form of one or more symbols, which can often convey some information more efficiently than words. Symbols, then, make it easy to quickly share information with many audiences.

Likewise, symbols are used to efficiently represent process components and flows. Just as signs use symbols as graphical representations of locations, "a process map is a visual representation of a process that shows boundaries (e.g., where the process begins and ends), steps or tasks in the process and sequence or order of the steps".[4]

Tasks are the actions performed in a process, and they can be classified as physical, informational or mental, as shown in Table 4.1.

Table 4.1 Actions Performed in a Process

Type of Task	*Description*	*Example*
Physical	Actions that *humans* or *machines* perform	Moving supplies from a loading dock into a stockroom
Informational	Actions that *humans* or *machines* perform	Manipulating values or calculations
Mental	Actions that the *human mind* performs	Reading and reasoning

Informational tasks are also called *computational tasks.* Remember that when tasks must be completed in a certain order, they are broken down into *steps.* Tasks can be very complex, requiring numerous steps or so simple that they cannot logically be broken down into separate steps.

Process maps are also called *process diagrams* and are similar to the map of a subway system in that they graphically represent an entire process (or system) on one or only a few pages. Process maps use standard symbols to succinctly convey information. Just as there is a flow in a subway line, there is a flow in a process.

An important skill in performing process analysis is the ability to discern different aspects and levels of complexity within a process. Process maps can be created in ways that graphically depict the various dimensions of complex processes, including multiple roles and the data flow within or congruent with the workflow. In most processes, data flow and workflow typically overlap and affect each other. Process maps also can represent the physical and mental tasks and steps performed in a workflow, such as clicking an icon to open a Web browser (physical) or locating the correct icon to click in the first place (mental).

Understanding Process Maps

Because process maps are frequently used to convey information, health IT professionals must understand them and in some cases be able to create one. Process maps are tools utilized for a variety of purposes. The type of analysis being done will determine which type of process map will be utilized and the information needed.

The "What" of Process Maps

If a process map is the "holder of the knowledge" of a particular process, what types of knowledge can process maps represent? Process maps can represent three types of tasks: physical, informational and mental. Humans can perform all types of tasks, but machines cannot perform mental tasks. Informational tasks present a challenge in health IT because humans and computers are often interdependent in performing information-processing tasks.

Moreover, data flow and workflow typically overlap and affect each other in any process. This overlap can make it complicated for an analyst to diagram a process. Remember that process maps can be created to represent any particular aspect of a complex process, such as physical steps, data flow, information content, assigned workflow roles and relationships and even thought and decision processes. As previously noted, because a workflow is a process, it includes all of the following:

- Activities
- Location
- Roles
- Choices and decisions
- Information needs

Process maps, then, can represent each of these process aspects as well, and these aspects can be distinguished from each other, as outlined in Table 4.2.

Table 4.2 Descriptions of Seven Key Process Aspects

Process Aspect	*Description*
Context	How a system or process interacts within the larger environment. Context diagrams show main components and the ways in which the system interacts with things outside of the system, such as inputs and outputs
Process steps	The physical or mental tasks or activities required to complete a process, usually from the perspective of the patient or healthcare professional
Data/information flow	The path through which data and information travel in a process from the perspective of the data/information; involves informational tasks or activities
Data/information Content	The specific pieces of data/information required for process or informational steps or decisions
Data/information Transformation	The manipulations performed on data/information, such as calculating age from a patient's date of birth and today's date; involves informational tasks or activities
Step sequence, control and status	The order in which data or things move through a process and the logic that controls that flow
Roles involved	Who or what performs the process steps

Depending on the complexity of the process, it may be necessary to create and use different process maps that represent each process aspect individually.

Mapping Key Information

The goal of process mapping is to understand the current process as a means of improving it before and after the implementation of a process redesign. A graphical representation helps in the following ways:

- Reveals where the sequence of tasks is crucial
- Identifies bottlenecks or interruptions
- Identifies opportunities (often the same as bottlenecks)
- Creates solutions to relieve bottlenecks
- Reanalyzes the new process
- Makes efficiency improvements[5]

Clinical process maps represent how all of the tasks that support a particular healthcare process are accomplished. Some tasks, like the generation of a monthly report needed by a clinic manager, don't happen each day. Consider a clinical process map in the context of a family physician office. According to Ahmadi et al., family physician office workflow can broadly be broken down into two categories:

1. The flow of patients entering the office and having their needs met within the office environment.
2. The flow of patient information within the office environment, whether the patient is physically present or not. This information includes clinical, social and billing information.[6]

Applying the concept to information flow, the "goal when implementing a health IT solution in the office is to transition from a 'batch-and-queue' system to a system that exhibits continuous flow".[7] In other words, the goal is to avoid a system in which information stops and waits for a human to manually move it along. This is precisely the problem with paper charts and files. Information recorded on paper tends to accumulate until it is entered into an electronic system in batches, whereas information entered electronically at the point of care (POC) is recorded directly into the

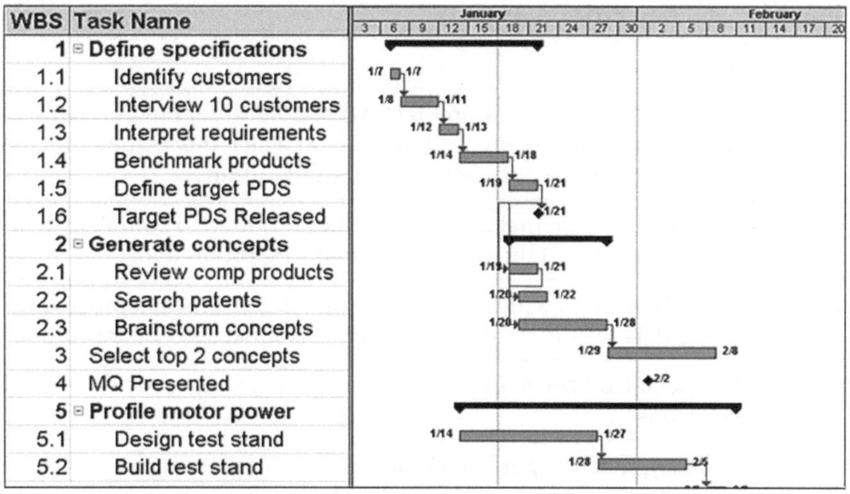

Figure 4.1 Example GANTT chart. (Minnesota.gov 2016.)

system in real time. Good process maps allow such findings of a process analysis to be much more accessible to the analyst and audience alike (Figure 4.1).

Process Map Visualization

- GANTT CHART
  - Bar chart
  - Illustrates a project schedule

- SWIM LANE
  - Visual diagram of a process from start to finish, dividing the steps into categories and identifying which departments or individuals are responsible for each step.
  - Swim lanes are represented by columns to visually separate activities of responsible departments/individuals (Figure 4.2).

Common Clinical Processes

The clinical processes that can be analyzed are far too numerous to list here. Indeed, processes vary widely depending on the type of healthcare provider. Consider, for example, the number of processes involved in a patient's single interaction with one healthcare provider, which encompasses every possible subprocess that might occur between the patient and provider within a larger process from start to finish. Included are such subprocesses as scheduling an appointment, checking in/out, receiving various forms of care and processing insurance/payment. All these subprocesses are typically performed within the larger process of a routine office visit. In addition, it is important to consider the various ways that these processes and subprocesses can be executed because they may require separate process maps. For example, patient demographics-related processes are affected by variables such as whether the patient is a child or an adult, is insured or uninsured, or is a new or existing patient. These are just a few examples; the specific process being analyzed determines the degree of possible variations.

Process Variations and Exceptions. Process variations are processes that vary from the typical or normal workflow. For instance, in an inpatient setting, there are times when a physician does not have access to an EHR with computerized provider order entry (CPOE) capability and must phone in an order. A variation, therefore, in CPOE process analysis is the handling of a phone order. When creating a process diagram, analysts should include the variation or variations used by the clinic.

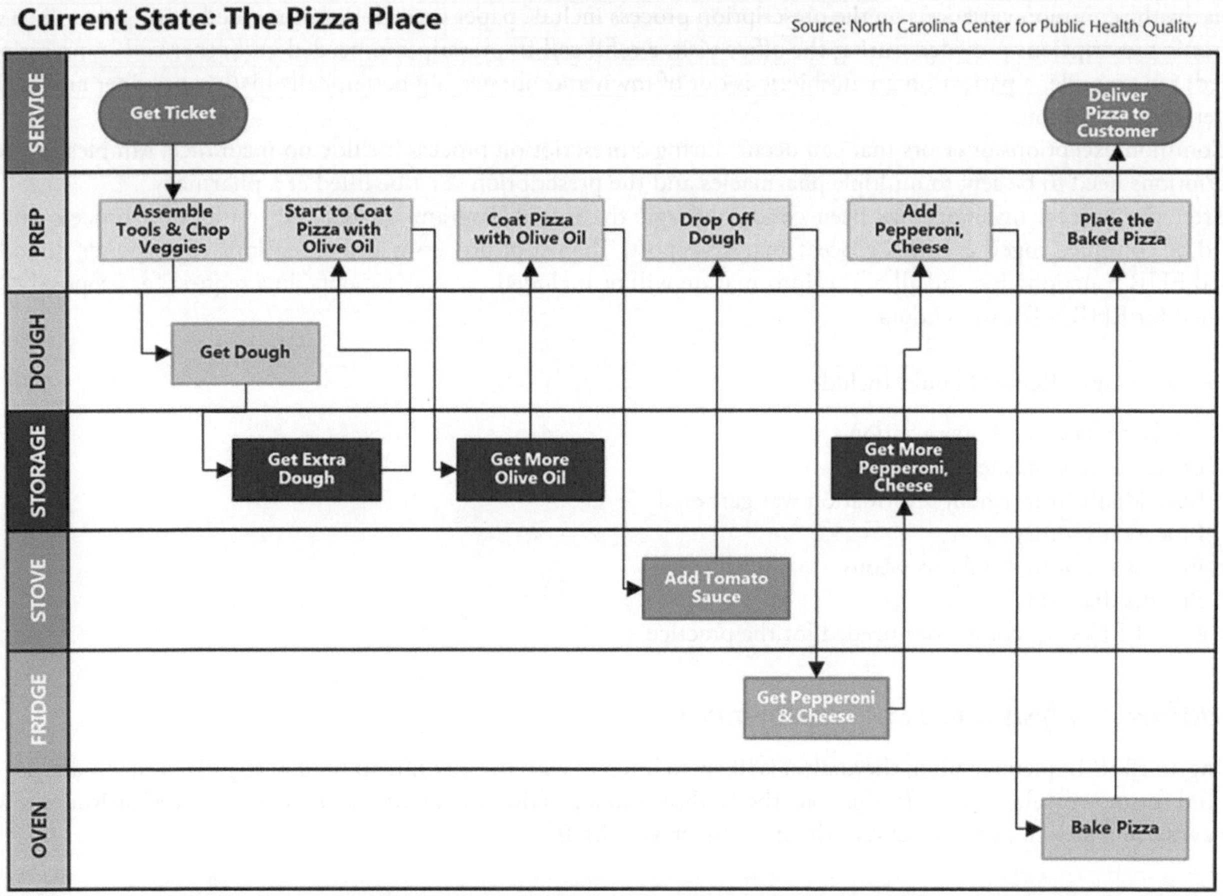

Figure 4.2 Example swim lane. (Minnesota.gov, Swim Lane Map 2020. https://www.health.state.mn.us/communities/practice/resources/phqitoolbox/swimlanemap.html.)

The occurrence of multiple variations is a signal to the analyst that (1) the EHR must support multiple options, and (2) the EHR will likely need to show different screens or otherwise facilitate the process variants. Variation, expressed as process choices – sometimes called branches, indicate important functionality needed in an EHR.

Process exceptions are deviations from the optimal process. Exceptions have the potential to prevent accomplishing an objective or outcome of the process. For instance, if a laboratory report did not arrive in time for a patient visit, the physician would not be able to complete his or her diagnostic workflow. If a patient arrived at a specialist's office without the required preauthorization, the account could not be billed. Most analysts will not have the time and resources to create process diagrams that include all exceptions. Exceptions, however, are important to note and, depending on frequency, must either be addressed within the system implementation or by a manual process.

There are many variations for patient office visits. A few of them are referral needed, procedure needed and diagnostic test needed. Likewise, there are many possible exceptions that may occur during an office visit. Some of them include emergent reason to stop the visit, a non-covered service needing a separate visit and the need to be seen by a different provider.

Process Variations for Patient Check-in Include

- New patient intake and registration
- Existing patient intake and registration
- Walk-in intake and registration

Exceptions for the Patient Check-in Include

- No insurance/non-covered service
- Patient arrives but does not speak English

Similarly, the common variations on the prescription process include paper prescriptions provided during the office visit, electronic prescriptions provided during the office visit, a refill call-in prescription needed and other call-in prescription needed; for example, a patient on an antibiotic is out of town and not getting better, calls his/her provider and asks for a different prescription.

Common exceptions or errors that can occur during a prescription process include no insurance, samples provided, prescriptions need to be sent to multiple pharmacies and the prescription can't be filled at a pharmacy.

After the process inventory has been conducted and the initial diagrams made, the results of a process analysis should be compiled together into a process analysis report. The list of processes and exceptions corresponds directly to needed EHR functionality, and all of this information will be included, as requirements, in a request for proposal (RFP) intended for EHR software vendors.

A Process Analysis Report Should Include

- Analyst's name and organization
- Dates of time on site
- Individuals from whom information was gathered
- Process inventory
- Process variations and exceptions
- Process diagrams
- List of EHR functionalities needed for the practice

Workflow Analysis and EHR Deployment

During an EHR implementation, the analyst is likely to interact with most, if not all, staff at any given site to discuss current and future workflow states. In this role, the analyst is in a position to potentially affect employees' attitudes toward the new system as well as the success of the implementation itself.

Understanding the Processes

Process improvement is defined as a systematic approach to focus, measure and redesign a critical process of any organization in order to decrease waste and achieve breakout improvement for that process. Continuous process improvement builds upon earlier work on process improvement.

Everything everyone does in an organization is part of a process. To improve the organization, you must focus on the processes (Figure 4.3). Process improvement is a fundamental step in business management. There are many different accepted ways to improve process:

- DMAIC (Deh-may-ick) A data-driven approach to process improvement
  - DEFINE the opportunity for improvement
  - MEASURE the performance of the existing process
  - ANALYZE the process to find any deficiencies
  - IMPROVE the process by addressing the root causes uncovered
  - CONTROL the improved process and future processes' performance to correct deviations before they result in defects and to prevent reverting back to the "old way"

  Diagrams are sometimes used to help professionals complete the DMAIC process (by helping identify potential causes of a defect)

- Ishikawa (aka Fishbone, Cause and Effect) diagram
  - PDCA/PDSA

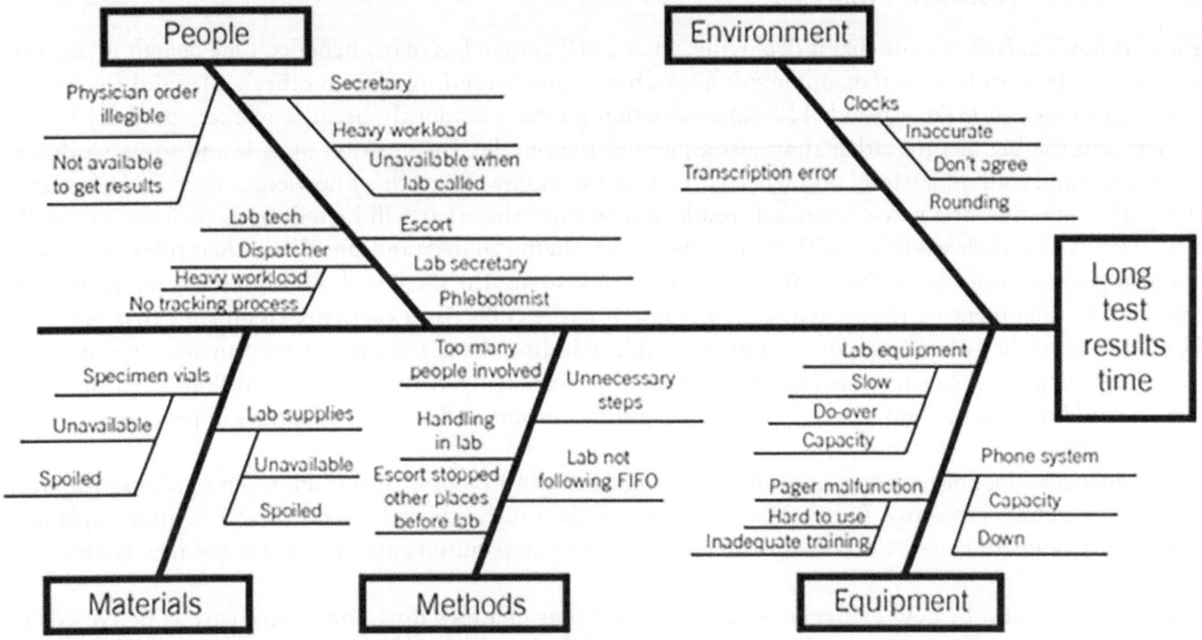

Figure 4.3 Example cause and effect diagram. (Institute for Healthcare Improvement. 2020. Example Cause and Effect Diagram. http://www.ihi.org/education/IHIOpenSchool/resources/Pages/AudioandVideo/Whiteboard16.aspx.)

The PDCA/PDSA process improvement approach is both cyclical and iterative. This approach utilizes four stages for controlled process improvement:

- PLAN
  - Identify and analyze the problem or opportunity
  - Develop hypotheses about the cause of the problem
  - Decide which to test
- DO
  - Test potential solution on a small scale
  - Measure results
- CHECK/STUDY
  - Study results
  - Measure effectiveness
  - Decide whether hypothesis is supported by data or not
- ACT
  - If the pilot solution was successful, implement it
  - If not successful, return to the beginning of the cycle

In most process improvement projects, teams will test several different changes, with each change going through more than one PDSA cycle.

The Benefits of Workflow Analysis

Doing a workflow analysis of a site that is deploying a new EHR system has many benefits. One benefit of documenting both as-is and to-be workflows is that employees have a better understanding of each other's roles and responsibilities.[8] That understanding can make a health IT implementation go more smoothly because workers perform better when they understand the big picture rather than just a piece of the puzzle. The creation of as-is and to-be workflows also helps employees and staff understand problems with current workflow. With this knowledge, they are better able to see how the implementation of a new system will result in new capability that will benefit both patients and staff. Once staff understands how their workflow will change, they have a better understanding of how their roles may also change and can also get the most out of their training on the new system. The analyst should interview as many employees as possible while documenting the current state because it is the collective experience of all staff that best informs a workflow analysis of the current state of any process. Understanding the current processes provides a point of reference from which the employees can approach the new system. Future-state workflows may reveal skills gaps among current staff, which could require new job descriptions and retraining current staff to reflect changes in processes and roles due to EHR deployment.

Lack of adequate documentation can result in a bungled health IT implementation, often requiring the workflows to be created to address problems. But it is far more time consuming and costly to do this work after implementation than before it. Completing as-is workflows early on can reveal the requirements needed for the new system to deploy successfully.[9]

With new therapies, or new evidence-based medicine that changes how and where care is delivered, or with new regulation, healthcare processes change. Process workflows, then, will need to be adjusted to support these new requirements. Similarly, process workflows are often modified to ensure higher levels of quality and safety. Process workflows are an important part of a site's continuous improvement, ensuring the maximal benefits of an EHR.

Systems Development Life Cycle

The work of implementing a new system can be clearly defined and broken down into distinct phases. Once identified, these work phases may be used as a planning foundation for designing, building, testing and delivery of high-quality information systems that meet/exceed customer expectations.

Using the systems development life cycle (SDLC) for planning a system implementation allows the designers and project managers to progress through clearly defined phases within scheduled time frames and cost estimates. Systems are complex and may interface with many different systems that could be supplied or manufactured by different software vendors. To manage this complexity, multiple SDLC models have been created:

- **Waterfall**
  The Waterfall model is one of the oldest SDLC models still in active use today. The model originated in the manufacturing and construction industries, with the signature characteristic being that the output of each stage becomes input for the next stage.

  - **Stages**
    - Project conception
    - Initiation
    - Systems analysis/requirements definition
    - Systems design
    - Implementation
    - Integrative testing
    - Acceptance/installation/deployment
    - Maintenance

  - **Challenges**
    Since manufacturing/construction are highly structured physical environments, change was prohibitively expensive. This model therefore translates to a not easily adjustable environment for software developers.

- **Iterative**
  - The iterative model involves the breaking down of large applications into smaller blocks of code.
  - Code is designed, developed and tested in repeated cycles
  - With each iteration, additional features are designed, developed and tested until fully functional software application is ready to deploy.
  - Typically used in conjunction with INCREMENTAL development.

- **Incremental** (aka Successive Version Model)
  - Software development where longer software development cycles are split into smaller segments that build upon each other.
  - Starts with a simple working system, implementing only a few base features/functions is delivered to the customer. Then successive versions are implemented/delivered to the customer until the desired system is reached (see Figure 4.4).

- **Spiral**
  - Combines the idea of ITERATIVE development with the systematic controlled WATERFALL model with a high emphasis on risk analysis.
  - Allows incremental releases with incremental refinement through each iteration around the spiral.
  - Four phases, repeated:
    - Identification
    - Design
    - Construct/build
    - Evaluation and risk analysis
  - Costly to use – doesn't work well for small projects

- **Agile**
  - Twenty-eight percent more successful than traditional project models
  - Value-driven approach
  - Common adage: 80% of all users commonly only use 20% of software application functionality
  - Agile embraces this by focusing on creating a minimum viable product (MVP) which delivers the minimum set of features that will deliver perceived value to users
  - Continuously incrementing user feedback into each future iteration as more information about the product becomes available and as more minimum features are required by users

- **Synchronize and Stabilize**
  - Schedules and parallel teams created
  - Teams work in parallel on individual modules, frequently synchronizing their code with other teams and debugging (stabilizing) regularly throughout the development process
  - Feature-oriented approach
  - Required set of features is completely functional; at each milestone
  - Vision statement and feature list based on customer input

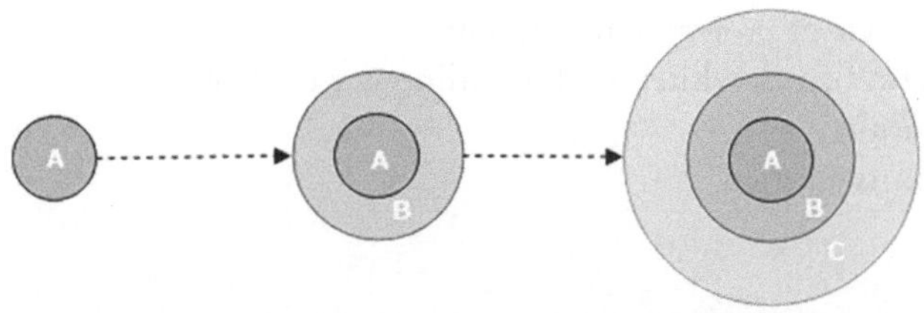

Figure 4.4 The incremental model (GeeksforGeeks 2019. https://www.geeksforgeeks.org/software-engineering-incremental-process-model/.)

- **Build and Fix** (aka Ad Hoc model)
  - Developed without any specs or design steps
  - Initial product is built and repeatedly modified until it satisfies the user
  - Lack of design requirements and repeated modifications may result in loss of acceptability of software
  - Strongly discouraged from using this development approach
  - Not well defined
- **Rapid Application Development/Rapid Application Build (RAD/RAB)**
  - Components are developed in parallel as if they were mini projects
  - Developments are time boxed, delivered and assembled into a working prototype
  - Phases:
    1. Determine requirements
    2. Build prototypes
    3. Get user feedback
    4. Repeat steps 2 and 3 until done or client requirements are met
    5. Test by engineers, users
    6. Implement
  - Users test each prototype at each stage to ensure that expectations are met
  - Development of software driven by user requirements
    - Example: Graphic User Interface or GUI
- **Scrum**
  - AGILE project management methodology
  - Allows for quick development and testing, especially within a small team
  - Complex projects are prioritized into individual tasks
  - Delegated to team members best suited to solve each task
  - Product owner: team member – represents the end user's best interests
    - Has authority over what goes into final product
  - Backlog
    - List of tasks and requirements the final product needs
    - Must be prioritized
    - Sprint
      - Predetermined timeframe within which a set of backlog tasks are completed
      - Daily stand-ups or scrums
        - Sprint reviews aka retrospectives
        - Reviews work and discusses ways to improve the next sprint
- **Kanban**
  - Japanese for "Billboard"
  - Visual method of organizing work and addressing inefficiencies in systems
  - The kanban process is based on queueing work from a backlog only as the work is needed
  - Just in time methodology
  - Kanban board
    - Central to this style of project management
    - May be a bulletin board, whiteboard or online shared tool
    - Basic configuration
      - Three columns entitled
        - To do
        - Doing
        - Done
      - Color-coded sticky notes represent different work products
      - Work card is placed in the appropriate progress column

- **Extreme Programming**
  - Type of AGILE software development
  - Increased quality of life for development team
  - Intended to improve software quality and responsiveness to changing customer requirements
  - Frequent releases
  - Short development cycles
    - Higher productivity
    - More checkpoints for customer requirements
    - Set of values for team
      - Help team work faster
      - Collaborate more frequently

    - Increased simplicity
      - Do what is needed
      - Do what is asked for – no more
      - Maximize value created for investment made to date
      - Small simple steps to goal
      - Mitigate failures as they happen

    - Streamlined communication
      - Everyone is part of the team
      - Daily face to face meetings
      - Work together on everything
      - Create the best solution that we can, together

    - Consistent constructive feedback
      - Take every iteration of software seriously by delivering working code
      - Frequent demos with customer
        - Careful attention to feedback
        - Making any changes needed
        - Adapts the process to fit the project

- Respect
  - Every team member is valued
  - Everyone contributes value even if it's enthusiasm
    - Developers respect the expertise of customers and vice versa
    - Management respects the right to accept responsibility and receive authority over work

- Coverage
  - Truthful about progress and estimates
  - No one works alone, so no fear
  - Adapt to change wherever it happens

Conducting Basic Data Analysis and Interpretation

Data analysis is defined by the Institute of Public Policy and Administration at the University of Central Asia's Graduate School of Development as the process of converting quantitative and qualitative data into information that has meaning and value for the client in light of the research questions and goals.[10] In a learning health system, processes are in place to put internal data, experience and new clinical guidelines together to provide:

- More efficient care
- Safer care
- More evidence-based care

- Lower costs
- More patient satisfaction
- Better outcomes for the patient

How does this happen? Data is analyzed, meaningful patterns are discovered. As a result, the organization incorporates actions that produce value. This process is defined as analytics. There are four types of analytics commonly used in the Data Sciences.

- **Descriptive** – usually manually performed, uses data to ask:
    - What has happened?
    - What is happening?
- **Diagnostic** – uses drill down techniques, data discovery, data mining and correlations to ask: Why did it happen?
- **Predictive** –with an increasing emphasis on ease of use, uses data, statistical models and forecasts to ask: What could happen?
- **Prescriptive** – uses data and simulation to ask:
    - What should we do?
    - What can we do to make "x" happen?[11]

RFI/RFP

The various process of systems planning and systems analysis including determining the strategic objectives, definition usability requirements, completing the various aspects that contribute to the functional needs assessment and determining the buy vs. build strategy all contribute acquisition strategy. In the earlier phases, the information gathered regarding viable products and vendor selection begins with the request for information (RFI) and request for proposal (RFP).

- Does the vendor share the same vision for the product as the organization?
- Does the product meet the key functionality needed to achieve the organizations strategic objectives?
- Does the product/vendor utilize the appropriate technology?
- Does the vendor qualify in regard to the organizations acquisition policies?
- Can the vendor support the organizations implementation strategy?
- What is the vendor's track record for operations and maintenance support?
- What is the vendor's viability in the market?

Request for Information

An RFI is a standard business process whose purpose is to collect written information about the capabilities of potential suppliers.[12] The RFI process generally consists of a formal and structured set of questions in the following areas:

- Company background (size, years in business, number of employees, product lines)
- Product information (product name, product history, technical platform, overview of product capabilities)
- Market information (major competitors and identification of key differentiators)
- Installed base and clients (number of products the company has sold, how they are currently implementing, number fully installed)
- Special criteria (anything that the vendor has identified as unique or established as critical)

It is important to employ a standardized information gathering process so that side by side comparisons of potential suppliers are possible.

Request for Proposal

An RFP is a standard business document created by an agency or company interested in procurement of a commodity, service or valuable asset. The RFP solicits a proposal, often made through a bidding process, from a potential supplier. RFPs have some fairly typical components including:

- Organizational profile (basic demographics of the organization requesting the RFP)
- Vendor information (demographics of the potential supplier)
- Functional specifications (description of required functional capabilities of the commodity, service or valuable asset)
- Operational requirements of the commodity, service or valuable asset
- Technical requirements of the commodity, service or valuable asset
- Application support (implementation schedule, testing, training and documentation to be provided, support and maintenance agreements, upgrade availability and cost)
- Licensing and contractual details for the commodity, service or valuable asset
- Evaluation criteria to be used for the commodity, service or valuable asset

Support agreements may include help desk services, which may be defined by a service level agreement (SLA). This agreement usually specifies the different levels and timeliness of support that the organization should expect from the potential supplier and the cost of these services.

The RFP is submitted early in the procurement cycle, either at the preliminary study or procurement stage.

Non-Disclosure Agreement

A non-disclosure agreement, or "NDA", creates a confidential relationship between a person or business that has confidential or trade secret information and a person that has access to that information. The NDA agreement protects these business secrets by limiting the way they can be used or disclosed. NDAs may be unilateral, in which one company seeks protection of trade secrets, bilateral where both parties are bound by secrecy, or multilateral where three or more parties are protected.[13]

Summary

Although the focus of health IT in the past has been EHR implementation, meaningfully using those EHRs by capturing data, sharing between both organizations and applications, future efforts will center around the analysis and integration of data to create new knowledge, which then may be used to make our health system more efficient, safer, more effective and more satisfying for workers and patients. EHR data capture, patient genomic information, public health data sharing, clinical trial data and other sources will combine to help create a learning health system.

References

1. A System of Concepts for the Continuity of Care. https://contsys.org/concept/healthcare_process.
2. Solutions for Quality Environment and Shipping Safety. (7 October 2014). http://www.sqss.gr/new/583-policies-and-procedures.
3. Wickens, C. D., & Hollands, J. G. (1999). *Engineering Psychology and Human Performance* (3rd ed.). Upper Saddle River, NJ: Prentice Hall.
4. Health IT Workforce Curriculum, Version 3.0. (2012). Component 10, Fundamentals of Health Workflow Process Analysis & Redesign. Unit 2a, Process Mapping Theory and Rationale. This material, Comp10_Unit2a, was developed by Duke University, funded by the Department of Health and Human Services, Office of the National Coordinator for Health Information Technology under Award Number IU24OC000024. https://www.healthit.gov/topic/health-it-resources/health-it-curriculum-resources-educators.
5. Kushinka, S. A. (2011). Workflow Analysis: EHR Deployment Techniques. California Healthcare Foundation. https://www.chcf.org/wp-content/uploads/2017/12/PDF-WorkflowAnalysisEHRDeploymentTechniques.pdf.

6. Modeling of Outpatient Prescribing Process in Iran: A Gateway toward Electronic Prescribing System. https://www.ncbi.nlm.nih.gov/pmc/articles/PMC4157049/.
7. Ibid.
8. Kushinka, S. A. (2011). Workflow Analysis: EHR Deployment Techniques. https://www.chcf.org/publication/electronic-health-record-deployment-techniques/.
9. Ibid. PDF (accessed 4 November 2014).
10. Baimyrzaev, Mahabat. (2018). Beginners Guide to Applied Research Process: What Is It and Why and How To Do It? Occasional Paper No 4, University of Central Asia. https://www.ucentralasia.org/media/ackcdaec/uca-ippa-op4-beginners-guide-for-applied-research-process-eng.pdf.
11. Gartner Glossary. (23 September 2020). https://www.gartner.com/en/information-technology/glossary/prescriptive-analytics.
12. PROFESSIONAL DEVELOPMENT, Request for Information (RFI). (April 2013). https://trainingindustry.com/wiki/professional-development/request-information-rfi/#:~:text=A%20Request%20for%20Information%20(RFI,will%20better%20inform%20buying%20decisions.
13. Haskins, Jane. (18 August 2020). Understanding Non-disclosure Agreements. https://www.legalzoom.com/articles/understanding-non-disclosure-agreements.

Chapter 5

Design

Learning Objectives

At the conclusion of this chapter, the reader will be able to:

- Identify functional requirements of software, hardware and network solutions
- Develop the documentation of compliance with applicable industry, regulatory and organizational standards
- Identify basic business continuity planning concepts (e.g., RPO, RTO, BCA, scheduled and unscheduled downtime procedures)
- Collect and compile information to assist in evaluation of existing and emerging technologies
- Understand basic data management concepts (e.g., data types, metadata, data dictionary, field formats)

Introduction

After process analysis is complete, design begins. Design refers to both a process of producing artifacts and a discipline devoted to the study of that process. No matter what type of design – be it architectural, automotive or software, they all engender a creative process in which something is produced to satisfy a population of users. They all must balance trade-offs and, sometimes, conflicting requirements.

Design concepts are communicated via representations such as diagrams and prototype sketches. Interaction design is a broad-based approach that places a premium on the role of the user in design. The focus is on enhanced usability and on the user experience. The approach is committed to an iterative methodology with ongoing validation and refinement. The key question in interaction design is how to optimize the users' interactions with a system so as to support and extend users' activities in effective, useful and usable ways.

Design choices are consequential in the arena of healthcare.[1] Despite the overwhelming challenges involved in implementing clinical information systems, there is evidence to suggest that fixing a problem in the development phase may cost 10 times more than it does in the design phases.[2] No one truly disputes that sound design can make a significant difference.

A conceptual model refers to an abstract outline of what people can do with a product and the concepts needed to understand how to interact with it. It provides a structure outlining the concepts that form the product – not the user interface. These concepts include the task domain objects, their attributes and the operations that can be performed. For example, the task domain may be personal health. The objects are the data that inform users about their health, and these particular findings or personal data have attributes. The conceptual model also defines mappings between concepts and user experience.

DOI: 10.4324/9780429443862-8

Usability

Usability engineering is a field or an approach oriented toward accentuating the user experience in the design process. Detailed usability engineering design, installation, feedback and enhancement reflect the iterative approach to refining the interface and the system to better meet users' needs.[3]

One of the central themes of interaction design and usability engineering is the importance of a user-centered approach. The approach focuses on users and tasks very early in the design and conceptualization process. The approach is also predicated on empirical measurement of users both prior to having used the system and while using the system. The measures and observations of performance feed into an iterative design process.

In a user-centered approach, it is important that the system is designed to support humans in facilitating performance on a particular task, for example determining a patient's prior health status through the retrieval of electronic documents in a clinical information system. The system needs to be shaped by an understanding of the capabilities, as well as the limitations, of the user.

The user-centered approach emphasizes that users are involved from the inception through cycles of iterative development. Furthermore, all design decisions are influenced by user considerations.[4]

User-Centered Design

User-centered design (UCD) is at the heart of system design and requires the designer to study people in their working environments. This, in turn, deepens the designer's understanding of how people deal with specific problems and tasks as they interact within the work context. For designers who utilize UCD methodology, the emphasis is on ongoing field testing, observing, listening and then redesigning.

Clinical users face many challenges when using health information technology (health IT) effectively, including work overload, constant mobility, stress and frequent interruption.

The Users

For an optimal user experience, a designer must understand his or her user base – the people who will be using the system. The designer should be aware that doctors, nurses, pharmacists and other members of a clinical team are highly mobile and are operating in highly disruptive and stressful conditions. Their environments result in cognitive overload that has the potential to increase the probability of error.

Users are further challenged by restrictions of physical space and freedom of movement. Crowded rooms, impeding furniture, visitors, equipment, constant alerts from monitors, all make maneuvering very much a challenge in healthcare. These factors make nonintrusive portable or mobile technology important for clinicians.

Interruptions in workflow that are encouraged by fixed computing devices located in areas not convenient to users – such as computers being only available at the nurses' station – contribute to efficiency losses, workarounds and higher error rates. The "I'll chart later" phenomenon results in latency of important data being available to guide care. Even portable devices such as workstations on wheels (WOWs) are not a panacea. Cumbersome WOWs are frequently left in hallways or nursing stations so that they can be plugged in for a recharge. They are too heavy and clumsy to push and take into a patient room or are too time consuming to disinfect between patient rooms.

In some provider organizations, the rate of turnover may be high – of both patients and staff – particularly in teaching institutions where residents may have rotations in various specialty areas. This turnover poses a challenge in keeping people trained and competent as new versions of software are released. User interfaces, therefore, must be intuitive and designed for ease of use.[5]

Usability in health IT systems. According to the International Organization for Standardization (ISO), the world's largest developer of voluntary international standards across various fields, usability is

> "the effectiveness, efficiency and satisfaction with which users can achieve specified goals in a particular environment".[6] In the context of EHRs, usability is often directly correlated with clinical productivity, error rate, user fatigue and user satisfaction, all of which are critical factors for provider adoption.

The six principles of usability are learnability, efficiency, memorability, errors, satisfaction and utility.[7]

- **Learnability** defines how easy is it for users to accomplish basic tasks the first time they encounter a health IT design.
- **Efficiency** is related to the quickness (after learning the basic use of the system) with which users can perform the tasks.
- **Memorability** is the ease experienced by a user returning to a system or a product after a period of not using it. It is the measurement of how long it takes to reestablish proficiency.
- **Error** is the measurement of everything related to errors made on the system: How often are they made, when are they made and why are they made? How severe are the errors? Are they life-threatening errors, or just a nuisance? How easily a user can recover from the errors is another dimension of usability quality.
- **Satisfaction** is a measure of how pleasant the design, the product or the system is to use.
- **Utility** refers to the design's functionality. Does it do what the users need it to do? It matters little that something is easy to do if it's not what needs to be done. It is also no good if the system can hypothetically do what is intended, but users can't do it because the interface is too difficult for them.

When users are forced to use a system with poor usability, user satisfaction declines and frustration increases. Safety-critical environments, such as healthcare, the cockpit of an airplane or a nuclear reactor control room, require systems that avoid dissatisfaction and frustration in users.

Usability Trends

The intent of health IT is to increase ease of use in systems, improve safety and efficiency and reduce error. As health IT use increases, purchasers will likely place a higher value on usability and select those systems that are highly useful and that meet end user usability requirements.[8]

As the patient acuity in hospitals continues to rise, there is a pressing need for usable systems that support efficient workflow in an often hectic environment. Shorter lengths of stay and complex patient presentations require very focused attention.

Aging populations (not only patients but the providers who are using the systems) require special attention to the design of systems that are usable by those with age- associated vision problems or less fine motor control. This variation points to the need for UCD that accommodates users of various ages. One size does not fit all. Adaptation is necessary.

The job of health IT professionals is to ensure that usability requirements are included as system selection criteria. Ensuring adequate access to usable workstations or devices is also imperative. When computers are in short supply, there may be competition for computers in busy clinical work areas, especially after morning rounds or at shift changes. Lack of computers leads to workarounds, missed or forgotten documentation and enhances the chance of a medical error.[9]

Usability must be considered when users have to interact with multiple systems. It is often necessary for users to have to log into several disparate systems that contain just parts of a patient's record. This additional logon requirement increases the cognitive load of users, forcing them to remember numerous passwords and to go on an information-seeking trek to find bits and pieces of data scattered across separate systems. This overly complex workflow ultimately increases the chance of error.

The Design Process

Requirements analysis is a set of activities that are undertaken prior to – or early in – the design process. Requirements are statements of what the system must do. Sometimes these are technical requirements that users are unaware of and represent a list of needs the development team will use as a roadmap. Requirements also define objectives for design and later testing.

Design requirements have multiple uses. Requirements provide clarity in communication between the user(s) and development team. They identify mismatches between user needs and designers' understanding. Such mismatches are a source of potential usability problems and end user frustration.

Requirements engineering, done thoroughly, can save significant amounts of time, effort and cost downstream. Lack of adequate requirements definition often leads to more costly changes later in the development cycle.

Requirements Progression

As author Dux Raymond Sy describes, requirements gathering is a progression that leads to the final technical requirements:

> Business requirements describe and justify the high-level business functionality that is needed.[10]

Business requirements include input such as business goals, strategies, monetary considerations, budget constraints, regulatory and legal concerns and high-level functional perspectives:

> User requirements identify what is needed from the user's perspective. These can be things that the system or product must do.[11]

User requirements include input such as current and future workflows, policies, procedures, document and data trails, environmental concerns and day-to-day operational perspectives:

> System requirements define desired characteristics of the system and properties that the system or product must have.[12]

System requirements include hardware, software, network, database and other technical considerations as well as vendor evaluations.

Documenting Requirements

Part of the process of requirements engineering is to develop documentation for requirements.

Requirements are conventionally categorized into the two groups: functional requirements and nonfunctional requirements. These in turn can also be broken down into more precise bins that can be more informative.

Functional requirements describe the capabilities of the system and specify what the user should be able to do with the system. For example, the order entry screen of a computer-based order entry system will allow the user to view the first and last name of the patient and will then display the name of the patient. That is a very basic functional requirement.

Nonfunctional requirements include everything else, such as usability requirements that align with user characteristics security, compatibility with existing system architecture and so forth.

Some requirements are specific to a particular project and will be more applicable in particular settings than others. For example, the environmental factors such as noise would be especially important if users must be attuned for certain signals that designate warnings or the completion of a process.

Methods for Eliciting Requirements

There are several methods for eliciting a user's needs, and each has advantages and disadvantages. Some of these include use of questionnaires, online surveys, interviews, focus groups and naturalistic observation.

Questionnaires are relatively common. They are particularly useful for addressing very specific kinds of questions. One advantage with them is that they can reach many people.

Online surveys are becoming increasingly popular, and there are tools available for doing this. Interviews allow a designer to explore issues in greater detail. An interview involves a degree of personal contact, which is an advantage. Interviews, however, may be time consuming and involve scheduling appointments with people who may have very little free time.

Focus groups allow a designer to solicit multiple views and build consensus. Focus groups are well suited for soliciting people's attitudes and thoughts about a particular process, but they are less useful in eliciting serious evaluations about the efficacy or usability of a product. One of the disadvantages with this method is that not all voices are heard. There may be stakeholders who were not given the opportunity to express their views.

Naturalistic observation is something particularly useful in a requirements-gathering process. This method involves observing people at work in order to understand workflow and communication processes. Naturalistic observation is also a very powerful tool for learning about the activities in a work place prior to implementation.

Failing to study a workplace will greatly diminish the likelihood of accurate requirements.

Partnership. Defining requirements necessitates a partnership with users in order to develop requirements, understand their concerns about technology and embrace their ideas for improvement.

Interpretation. Observations of the workplace are interpreted into system needs. Requirements should be based on the actual tasks people perform and the processes used within the workplace.

Focus. Maintaining a clear focus on one's goals is essential in gathering requirements. Focus keeps a designer from getting lost in enormous volumes of data.

Organizing Ideas and Data

There are a number of ways for an analyst to organize and simplify his/her data. Two good methods include: affinity diagrams, which sort and display ideas from multiple sources; and process flow, which depicts the overall flow of activities and the relationship between parts of a system and the individuals using it.

Affinity diagrams display a grouping of ideas and data. The categories can be relatively fine-grained or coarse-grained depending on an analyst's goals. The steps for making affinity diagrams are rather simple:

1. Write down individual ideas on a note card or post-it note.
2. Look for ideas with similar themes.
3. Group the ideas with similar themes together.

Bring the Requirements Together

The existing system, procedures and processes must be thoroughly documented as the as-is model, discussed earlier. The as-is model should include the current data collection, workflows, decision points, resources and responsibilities.[13] The as-is model, with identified gaps, is useful in understanding requirements for new capability.

Once the functional and nonfunctional requirements for the new system are identified, they should be ranked in order of importance and classified as:

- Must-haves
- Want-to-haves
- Not-criticals

For example, in an EHR system, a component like electronic prescribing (e-Prescribing) that is required for European Institute for Health Records (EuroRec) certification would rank higher than an optional requirement like self-scheduling for the patient.

The functional and nonfunctional requirements should be combined into a future view – the to-be model with projected data collection, workflows, decision points, resources and responsibilities. The as-is model should be compared with the to-be model and the gaps between them documented.

The to-be model should come to life with the EHR implementation, and the identified gaps should be closed when the system goes live.[14] The to-be model should reflect the provider's goals and the functional and nonfunctional requirements for the new EHR system.

Bottlenecks and Workarounds

Poor system design can result in both bottlenecks and workarounds that can create patient safety risks. Lack of clear requirements may result in bottlenecks. For instance, not stipulating the number of client devices needed in an inpatient setting may result in a bottleneck where users have to wait for access to a computer device. Or, not stipulating volume and performance requirements for an implementation where hundreds of users may be logged on at a single time may create longer than acceptable wait times for a screen to appear. Or, possibly designing a process requiring consecutive steps when steps could have been processed simultaneously may also cause bottlenecks.

Inadequate requirements may also result in design where users employ a workaround and don't use the system as intended. A workaround is a method of accomplishing a task when the usual or planned method either does not work or is unacceptable to the user.

Studies have shown that workarounds circumvent built-in safety features. Koppel and colleagues describe the use of barcode medication administration (BCMA) in the United States (U.S.), purchased to reduce medication errors.[15] Unexpectedly, because of workarounds, the new system actually facilitated new types of medication administration hazards.

As Koppel et al. stated that it is important to "understand how BCMA systems are actually used in the challenging reality of hospital practice, why BCMA workarounds are so common, and what hospitals can do to find them and to address their causes and unintended consequences".[16]

In this example, nurses created a workaround. They made extra copies of bar-coded medication labels to avoid having to push the heavy and awkward 70-pound WOWs into a patient's room. Instead, they scanned the extra labels from their pockets. This defeated the purpose of bar code scanning in the first place. The bar code should be on the medication and on the patient's arm band so that the label and the drug could be scanned and matched to assure that the right drug is being given to the right patient.

"Extra" labels in the pocket are just an accident waiting to happen. A lack of a full user-centered approach including deep evaluation with the user base, in the design of the "solution" created new problems. This is an example of unintended consequences of health IT designed with good intent, but with insufficient evaluation.

General Project Considerations

No two projects are identical. The project team will decide how the project is planned, monitored, and controlled, as determined by the nature of the project. There is a wide variety in health IT projects. Some are focused on selection of new capability; some are focused on enhancing existing systems; some are aimed at developing interface; others are focused on meeting reporting/analysis requests from the end user community. Other examples might include:

- Creating a dataset that can be used repeatedly to understand physician volumes and revenues.
- Developing interfaces for a health information exchange (HIE) and/or integration with an HIE.
- Developing a database to store information utilized for chronic disease.
- Developing capabilities that extract information from multiple sources for studies and research.

Once the project is approved and initiated and a project charter exists, the planning process can begin. A project charter authorizes the existence of the project, designates the project manager and provides the project manager with the authority to acquire resources and lead the project.

Planning is a crucial step in project management. Without planning, it is difficult to ensure a project's success. It is unwise to undertake a project of any size or complexity without taking the time to plan the approach to how the project objectives will be accomplished. No project should be started without planning the work that must be performed, including things such as scheduling and budgeting.

Some of the activities that take place during project planning include collecting and validating requirements, defining the scope of the project, developing the project management plan, defining the activities that must take place during the project, creating a work breakdown structure; developing a schedule, identifying and assessing risks, developing risk response plans, developing a test plan, developing an implementation plan and developing a communications plan including education for end users.

Often, project managers will document critical success factors so that both the development team and the end user audience understand the criteria for a successful project. Success factors might include:

- Proper project documentation
- Clearly defined and assigned roles and responsibilities
- Senior management or executive support (note that this is always a key factor, because without the support of senior management, most projects will not succeed)
- Stakeholder buy-in documented with signed approvals for project artifacts
- Completion of training by super users
- Periodic team meetings and periodic meetings with stakeholders

Factors that can lead to project failure include:

- Unnecessary and/or unapproved scope changes
- Lack of control over new requirements
- Lack of change control management
- Not following the project management plan
- Poor project monitoring
- Poorly defined requirements or poorly understood requirements
- Undefined or poorly defined scope
- Overly optimistic or unrealistic assumptions
- Unclear project roles and responsibilities

Project managers plan, lead and control project activities. Their responsibilities include but are not limited to identifying and documenting project requirements, identifying team members, establishing clear and obtainable project objectives, understanding stakeholders' expectations, preventing unnecessary scope changes, monitoring and measuring project progress, communicating project performance and progress, ensuring that the team understands project objectives and working with the team in developing project plans.

Project Management Plan

After a project is initiated, the project manager and team will begin the planning phase. Based on the scope of the project and product, which can be gathered from the project charter and stakeholder register, the manager can develop a project management plan. The project team uses this comprehensive document as a master plan to guide them through project execution. Although it is finalized and approved during the planning phase, the manager continuously updates the project management plan when new information is acquired during the project's life cycle.

A project management plan is a comprehensive and essential document that provides a justification for the project being undertaken, captures key project objectives, describes the approach for managing the project, summarizes what the project must accomplish, and details how the work will be performed, who will perform the work and how the work will be measured, monitored and controlled.

The project management plan involves a collaborative effort between the project manager, team members and executive sponsor(s). The team's participation in developing the plan helps strengthen their commitment to the project.

Information regarding project scope is obtained from the project charter and from project stakeholders. After creating the work breakdown structure, often referred to as the scope baseline, the scope boundaries are established.

The scope statement is prepared after collecting the project requirements. It provides a description of the project scope that includes major deliverables, project assumptions and constraints and descriptions of work. It also provides a documented basis for making project decisions and developing a common understanding of the project scope. It is a key input into creating the work breakdown structure. Constraints on health IT projects could include global privacy instruments like China's Cyber Sovereignty (wangluo zhuquan), the European Union's General Data Protection Regulation (GDPR), Health Insurance Portability and Accountability Act (HIPAA) requirements in the U.S. or any organizational privacy standards specific to the project.

For communication purposes, and to set end user expectations, the team may also clearly document what capabilities, documented originally as requirements, will not be included with the project.

Terminology

Project management is laden with terminology. Some important project management terms to know include:

- **Schedule management plan.** Document that contains information on how the schedule will be developed and controlled, how schedule processes will be measured and what scheduling tool will be used.
- **Duration.** Total number of work periods, as in days or work weeks that are required to complete a scheduled activity.

- **Effort.** Amount of work or labor hours necessary to actually perform a scheduled activity.
- **Project schedule network diagrams.** Schematic depiction of scheduled activities and dependencies, which are logical relationships of activities. They model sequenced activities.
- **Activity relationships.** Diagramming technique that illustrates the activity's logical relationships: finish-to-start, start-to-start, finish-to-finish and start-to-finish.
- **Schedule.** Documents when the project activities will be completed.
- **Critical path.** Longest path of activities through the schedule network; it establishes the earliest date by which the project can be completed.
- **Float (sometimes referred to as slack).** Amount of time an activity can be delayed and not push back the early start of a successive activity.
- **Scheduling tools.** Computerized project management software applications that help the project manager develop the schedule and provide information to manage the project.

Estimation Techniques

It is important for the project management team to estimate the likely number of work periods required to perform an activity, and there are a variety of estimation techniques. The project manager and the project management team can use the following estimating techniques in order to achieve this.

Analogous techniques determine the estimate by using resource duration estimate information from similar past projects; this type of technique is often used in project initiation or early planning when detailed project information is lacking. A project manager may use such expert judgment techniques as acquiring estimate information from individuals with historic information or experience related to similar prior projects. It is not uncommon to bring in someone with expert judgment to help perform project estimation.

Quality Management

During project planning, the team identifies and documents quality requirements, standards and metrics to measure quality performance for the project and product and then develops a quality management plan.

The quality management plan is a document within the project management plan. This document addresses project quality control, quality assurance and continuous quality improvement.

Human Resource Management Plan

A good human resource management plan describes how training requirements of team members will be accomplished and provides project organizational charts and position descriptions. A common tool for project management and human resource management is a responsibility assignment matrix.

Request for Proposal (RFP)

If requirements have been clearly documented for new health IT capability, the organization may decide to evaluate vendor products that have the potential to meet those requirements.

As discussed in Chapter 4, an RFP, and its precursor, the request for information (RFI), uses a specific outline to tell prospective vendors what they need to know about a healthcare organization in order to provide useful information about their products. This will help ensure that the responses received from vendors can be easily compared.

After receiving responses to the RFP, the next step is to query provided references to ensure customer references are satisfied with the product and customer support. Vendor responses have to be evaluated, often using a predefined method to force-rank products in order to ensure that the system selected meets the most important requirements. After vendors have been selected, they are invited to provide demonstrations of their products.

Normally, if this purchase represents a major investment, involving a multiyear effort, the selection team will travel to one or more customer sites to see the system in use at a site similar to their own.

Hardware and Network Implications

In most cases, the vendor will recommend hardware that will optimize performance of a system. When the vendor returns the RFI, the vendor also stipulates what hardware is required, including servers if they are to be run locally, requirements for client devices and requirements for other peripheral devices.

With this information, the IT department is in a position to:

- Inventory current servers, client workstations and mobile technology devices to determine the level of investment needed to support the new system.
- Evaluate the impact of the new system on the hospital network. In larger, complex environments, the network has to be formally evaluated to determine if the existing network can handle the new system or application without deterioration in response times.

Standards in Electronic Health Records

Development of electronic health records (EHRs) worldwide is being guided by a number of initiatives, programs and projects. The broad goals of these plans are to keep healthcare costs low while ensuring and increasing quality. The EHR can support these efforts by facilitating the collaboration of all members of the healthcare team, allowing the patient to take a more active role in his/her medical treatment and foster a high level of quality in patient care. Whether we are considering global, country-wide, regional or organizational interoperability, the problem becomes the establishment of a common view of EHR quality. Quality is defined by the ISO as the degree to which a set of inherent characteristics fulfills requirements and while a global consolidated set of characteristics does not currently exist, there are a number of organizations defining functional characteristics of EHRs based on national preferences and associated quality indicators.[17] Some of these groups include the Certification Commission for Healthcare Information Technology (CCHIT) in the U.S., the European Institute for Health Records, the international Integrating the Healthcare Enterprise (IHE) organization and the European open EHR foundation.[18]

Implementation and Data Migration

Once an organization has committed to making the change from one EHR to another, or from paper records to an EHR, the organization will need to develop a strategic plan for migrating the data from paper to EHRs, or from one EHR to another. A clear plan will help the implementation team effectively manage the process of change and efficiently develop goals.

Several key people are necessary for a successful EHR implementation. At the top of the organization, the chief executive officer (CEO) should be a strong leader invested in the process of change. An experienced transformational leader is important in steering the organization through the process of EHR selection and implementation. In a hospital setting, the chief information officer (CIO), chief medical information officer (CMIO) and chief nursing officer (CNO) with expertise and training in clinical informatics are also essential to the change process.

Physician and nursing champions with an interest in clinical informatics can play key roles. Often, these clinicians are early adopters of technology in their work settings and are able to persuade colleagues of the benefits and potential advantages of an EHR. Physician champions can act as leaders and promote the benefits of EHRs to the physician community by sharing information about use of the system, and in some cases, training their peers. They can also act as liaisons with the IT staff and can play a key role in planning for future enhancements and integration with an HIE or regional health information organization (RHIO).

The organization will need to determine what existing capabilities should be integrated into the new EHR. For example, if an organization wishes to keep its practice management software used for registration and billing, it must ensure that the software interfaces with the new EHR. Additionally, an organization may want to ensure that data stored within its legacy clinical information system can be transferred to its new system prior to the go-live of the new system.

There are several types of implementations, each with its advantages and disadvantages. The "big bang" approach involves bringing multiple applications live at one time and usually has a shorter implementation time. A staged implementation, on the other hand, brings up applications gradually. The implementation team will do analysis of pros and cons of each of these approaches as part of implementation planning.

Gap Analysis

A useful tool for preparing for the migration to an EHR is a gap analysis. This type of analysis compares the conditions that currently exist within an organization with those that will exist after implementation of the EHR. The difference between the two sets of conditions is the "gap".

A gap analysis can help determine the steps needed to transition from paper records to an EHR. By listing current characteristics, noting future objectives and mapping factors required to make this transition, gaps can be identified and help the organization understand and define exactly what is needed to make the change to an EHR. If implementing an EHR in an inpatient setting, special attention has to be given to medical records requirements. After an EHR implementation, medical records must be able to easily access information and documents needed for analysis and completion of charts, coding and release of information. A system designed to support clinical workflow will not necessarily meet the requirements for medical records departmental workflow.

Functional Requirements of Software, Hardware and Network Solutions

What are functional requirements? Functional requirements describe what a system should do, while nonfunctional requirements, also known as quality attributes or informally as "ilities", do not actually "function" but are important attributes nonetheless. Examples include scalability, usability, reliability and security.

For example, your phone must respond to touch input. This is a functional requirement.

A related nonfunctional requirement would be if you place your phone in your pocket, the phone should then **not** respond to touch input (usability).

Let us examine some functional requirements for software. For example, the scheduling system should be able to create an appointment for the patient with a doctor. Our related nonfunctional requirement would be the patient should only be able to make one appointment with the same provider for the same date.

An example of a hardware functional requirement would be that your laptop should be able to perform as a video conferencing tool, while a nonfunctional requirement might be its battery life.

Business Continuity Planning (BCP)

When there is an interruption to a business caused by fire, flood, hurricane, system crash or some other unexpected event, it can result in a loss of the ability to function as a business. The interruption may impact patient safety parameters supported by impacted systems, business income or security protections. BCP helps protect against disruption by creating plans of action to be followed in case of any event that could negatively impact business operations. One important component of a business continuity plan is the IT service continuity (ITSC) plan which focuses on restoring IT infrastructure and operations after a disruption. Some components of an ITSC plan are described below.

Business Impact Analysis (BIA)

- Predicts the consequences of disruption of a business function and process and gathers information needed to develop recovery strategies.

Recovery Time Objective (RTO)

- Targeted duration of time and service level within which a business process must be restored after a disruption.

Recovery Point Objective (RPO)

- The point in time in the past to which you will restore data transactions patient records.

Less impactful disruptions of business that occur more frequently are classified as scheduled and unscheduled downtime. Downtime refers to periods when the computer system in an organization is unavailable. A scheduled downtime is planned in advance and may be put on the calendar in anticipation of system maintenance, software/hardware upgrades or to install and test incremental upgrades know as software patches. These scheduled downtimes usually occur overnight and last for a very short period of time. While unscheduled downtimes are often due to environmental factors like a hurricane, flood, fire or earthquake, more commonly companies will experience internet service provider service malfunctions or power outages. The duration of an unscheduled downtime is usually unknown.

Scheduled Downtime Procedures

Some EHR vendors supply "read only" versions of the user data during a scheduled downtime to allow limited organizational functionality. Overall strategies need to be defined by the organization for scheduled downtime.

Unscheduled Downtime Procedures

Some EHR vendors allow business continuity access (BCA) web intranet access to various patient forms required during downtime from any enabled PC. BCA PCs are usually identifiable by a red tubing around the wiring and allow the printing of downtime reports and patient care documents.

Data Management

While the last decade of health information technology's focus has been on the implementation and optimization of EHRs, and the capture and sharing of data, our efforts are shifting now to using that data to improve individual healthcare quality. Without appropriate management of the data, we will have difficulty achieving this objective.

According to ngdata.com, data management is "an administrative process that includes acquiring, validating, storing, protecting and processing required data to ensure the accessibility, reliability and timeliness of data for users".[19]

In order to effectively manage data, one must understand concepts associated with the validating, storing, protecting and processing of data.

Types of Data in a Database Environment

Data types specify the values of data that the field or object can hold. Examples of data types are:

Real Number

- The number Pi is a real number that goes on forever even though 3.14 is between 3 and 4 we would need an infinite number of numbers to accurately represent Pi. The real number data type approximates the number Pi to 4 bytes or 7 digits of precision (the number of digits to the right of the decimal point) in database structures.[20]

Integer

- Represents the numbers between 1 and 10.

Date and Time

- There are many different ways to represent dates and time in a dataset. The examples below all represent the same day:
  - 1/10/2024
  - 01/10/2024
  - 01-10-2024
  - 01102024

- 1/10/24
- Wednesday, January 10, 2024
- Wednesday, 10 January 2024

- Time may also be formatted in a variety of ways. The examples below all represent the same time.
  - 14:28:21
  - 14:28
  - 2:28 PM
  - 2:28PM
  - 2:28pm
  - 2:28 pm
  - 14:28:21 CST
  - 14:28 CST
  - 2:28 PM CST
  - 2:28PM CST
  - 2:28pm CST
  - 2:28 pm CST

Character Text Data

- Represents a collection of letters in a database. The characters may be words, abbreviations or codes.

Metadata

- Metadata is a data summary which makes tracking and analysis of data easier. An example of metadata include data about Tumors and Oncology (Cancer treatments)
  - Tumor images (type of image)
  - Tumor size
  - Treatment used on tumor
  - Patient demographic data
  - Outcomes data

Data Dictionary

- A data dictionary is also known as metadata repository or a data definition matrix. The IBM dictionary of computing defines a data dictionary as "a centralized repository of information about data, such as the meaning relationships to other data origin usage and format".[21] This is a key portion of a database management system (DBMS) that allows a data structure to be known and queried.

Field Formats

Data dictionaries cannot be created, nor can a database be functional without documented field formats. The field format defines and enforces a database field helping to ensure that every entry into a database will format correctly and that the data obtained is in an expected format.

Summary

Implementing a new system requires a thorough analysis of current processes and workflow, documentation of requirements and future-state workflow, with careful consideration given to usability and end user acceptance. Project planning and control helps to ensure the project will meet objectives and be completed on time and within budget. In some cases, requirements will lead to the generation of an RFI and a system selection process. Planning for the implementation is a critical step and must factor in migration, either from paper or from one system to another. If the project involves an

EHR, the IT staff must remain abreast of both regulatory and technological developments to ensure that the clinical system remains current to achieve goals of improved efficiency, quality and patient safety, increased patient engagement, improved care coordination and better measures of population health management.

References

1. Chew, Sara, Mei Lai, Pauline Siew, & Ng, Chirk Jenn. (January 2020). Usability and utility of a mobile app to improve medication adherence among ambulatory care patients in Malaysia: Qualitative study. *JMIR mHealth and uHealth*. https://www.ncbi.nlm.nih.gov/pmc/articles/PMC7055750/ (accessed 15 December 2020).
2. Stecklein, Jonette M., Dabney, Jim, Dick, Brandon, Haskins, Bill, Lovell, Randy, & Moroney, Gregory. (4 November 2014). Error Cost Escalation Through the Project Life Cycle. Wiley Online Library. https://onlinelibrary.wiley.com/doi/abs/10.1002/j.2334-5837.2004.tb00608.x.
3. Baecker, Ronald, Grudin, Jonathan, Buxtin, William A. S., & Greenberg, Saul. (1995). *Readings in Human-Computer Interaction: Toward the Year 2000*. Elsevier Science. https://www.semanticscholar.org/paper/Readings-in-human-computer-interaction-%3A-toward-the-Baecker/94ce530ac467e66d402ce05c6a4975393812c7f2.
4. Ledel Solem, Ingrid Konstanse et al. (2020). A user-centered approach to an evidence-based electronic health pain management intervention for people with chronic pain: Design and development of EPIO. *Journal of Medical Internet Research*, 22(1): e15889. https://pubmed.ncbi.nlm.nih.gov/31961331/.
5. Plomondon, Mary et al. (2007). Primary care provider turnover and quality in managed care organizations. National Library of Medicine. https://pubmed.ncbi.nlm.nih.gov/17685827/.
6. International Organization for Standardization (ISO). https://www.healthcareusability.com/article/iso-9241-and-healthcare-usability.
7. Holcomb, Richard, & Tharp, Alan L. (23 September 2009). What users say about software usability pages. *International Journal about Human-Computer Interaction*, 23: 49–78. https://www.tandfonline.com/doi/abs/10.1080/10447319109525996.
8. Pfister, Helen R., Ingargiola, Susan R., IHealthBeat. (20 February 2014). ONC: Staying focused on EHR usability. https://www.healthcareusability.com/article/onc-staying-focused-ehr-usability.
9. Koppel, R. P., Wetterneck, T. M., Telles, J. L., & Karsh, B. (July–August 2008). Workarounds to barcode medication administration systems: Their occurrences, causes, and threats to patient safety. *Journal of the American Medical Informatics Association*. https://www.ncbi.nlm.nih.gov/pmc/articles/PMC2442264/.
10. How to Define Measurable and Traceable Requirements for SharePoint Projects. August 2010 Dux Raymond Sy. https://www.cmswire.com/cms/enterprise-cms/how-to-define-measurable-and-traceable-requirements-for-sharepoint-projects-008223.php.
11. Ibid.
12. Ibid.
13. Spohr, Mark H. Health Informatics Series, Software Selection. https://www.pitt.edu/search/google/Health%20Informatics%20Series%2C%20Software%20Selection (accessed October 2020).
14. Ibid.
15. Koppel, R. P., Wetterneck, T. M., Telles, J. L., & Karsh, B. (July–August 2008). Workarounds to barcode medication administration systems: Their occurrences, causes, and threats to patient safety. *Journal of the American Medical Informatics Association*. https://www.ncbi.nlm.nih.gov/pmc/articles/PMC2442264/.
16. Ibid.
17. ISO 9000. (2005). *Quality Management systems. Fundamentals and vocabulary*. https://www.iso.org/standard/45481.html.
18. Hoerbst, A., & Ammenwerth, E. (2010). Quality and certification of electronic health records: An overview of current approaches from the US and Europe. https://www.ncbi.nlm.nih.gov/pmc/articles/PMC3632276/.
19. NG DATA. https://www.ngdata.com/dictionary/data-management-definition/ (accessed October 2020).
20. SQL Tutorial & Training / Computer Science Courses, SQL Data Types: REAL, FLOAT & DOUBLE. https://study.com/academy/lesson/sql-data-types-real-float-double.html.
21. Dictionary of IBM & Computing Terminology. https://www.ibm.com/ibm/history/documents/pdf/glossary.pdf.

Chapter 6

Selection, Implementation, Support and Maintenance

Learning Objectives

At the conclusion of this chapter, the reader will be able to:

- Facilitate solution selection activities and documentation (e.g., evaluating functional requirements vs proposals, demonstrations, site visits, reference checks)
- Understand characteristics of various training and support methods (e.g., computer-based learning, classroom training, train the trainer, at-the-elbow support from superusers)
- Understand the interrelationships between scope, schedule, budget and quality for solution implementations
- Maintain healthcare information systems (e.g., operate, upgrade)
- Gather, input and help analyze data for problems and trends (e.g., error reports, help desk logs, performance metrics, network monitoring)

Introduction

Whether it is a first-time implementation or an upgrade of a current system, selecting and implementing a health information technology (health IT) system such as an electronic health record (EHR) is one of the most critical projects a healthcare organization (HCO) can undertake.

Although much is mentioned about EHRs in this chapter, these guidelines can be applied to any technology system selection, implementation and maintenance across the healthcare ecosystem (telehealth, laboratory, radiology and imaging, public health, etc.).

Implementation of technology systems in healthcare require significant financial investment both in software or system development cost and the resources and time commitment involved in its implantation in the organization. Comprehensive planning and ongoing assessment are necessary steps throughout all stages of the system selection and implementation process.

Even after system selection and initial implementation, the required maintenance, which continues through the life of the system, determines the ultimate success of the system, return of investment and value.

System Selection

The selection of an EHR system requires that healthcare change leaders develop an organized selection effort that will ensure a successful system adoption. Planning includes evaluation of the organization's needs and an evaluation of the vendor system's features.

DOI: 10.4324/9780429443862-9

The system selection plan includes several steps. Although not all steps are required in every decision, below are the activities commonly observed in the selection process:

1. Identify key stakeholders and decision-makers
2. Establish system selection committee
3. Conduct a thorough requirements analysis
4. Determine which requirements are "must-haves" and "nice to have" and rank based on the importance
5. Conduct vendor market analysis
6. Create a request for proposal (RFP)
7. Invite eligible vendors to respond to RFP
8. Review RFP responses
9. Attend vendor demonstrations
10. Check references
11. Rank vendors
12. Conduct site visits
13. Select a finalist
14. Quantify the total cost of ownership
15. Negotiate the contract
16. Implement selected system

Before starting the system selection process, healthcare change leaders and executives must determine organizational change readiness. In determining change readiness, key stakeholders must be involved in the discussion about the strengths, weaknesses, threats and opportunities of the current system and critically appraise what changes are necessary to achieve long-term and short-term business goals.

The new system should improve limitations and expand efficiencies, helping the organization to accomplish its mission more closely. Once there is a conscientious decision about the strategic direction of the organization, then a system selection committee should be established. The selection committee should involve representatives from all impacted departments. The selection committee will then work with key stakeholders to conduct a thorough requirements analysis.

A critical step toward purchasing any health IT system is performing a requirements analysis of the environment.[1] Functional requirements can be defined as those processes that users want in a system. The more granular one gets with requirements, the better overall understanding one will have of how the system will work and the impact implementation will have on workflows and processes. During requirements analysis, stakeholders identify and prioritize crucial features of the system and categorize them as "must-have" and "nice to have" features. The purpose of this step is to identify business requirements, user requirements and system requirements, including hardware, software, data and network. After the organization determines the required features, then leaders must conduct a market analysis to determine if there are vendor products available in the market to fulfill these requirements. In cases where details about vendor offerings are unknown, a request for information (RFI) is first conducted. After identifying viable vendors, the organization must develop and issue a RFP document. Vendors who respond to the RFP are reviewed and invited to attend a product demonstration meeting with the organization. Other activities included in this process are site visits and reference checks. After the finalist is selected, the organization quantifies the total cost of ownership and then both parties engage in contract negotiation.

An important consideration during the system selection process is the make-or-buy decision. This is the act of choosing between accepting the product offerings of a vendor or making the product in-house. Sometimes the vendor products available on the market do not meet the organization's needs leading to the decision to make the health IT system in-house.

Additional Considerations for Successful System Selection

When implementing health IT systems, it is important to consider existing governance and interoperability standards locally and internationally. Implementing technology systems will enable an organization to capture data but often no one technology system will meet all the information needs of the organization. Therefore, it is not unusual for an organization to implement system based on specific department needs. For example, EHRs will fulfill most of the clinical documentation needs for routine patient care.

However, it is not unusual to have more than one EHR in an organization that is limited by department such as surgical information system, emergency room system. Even outside an organization, healthcare data sharing needs spans states, government agencies, healthcare stakeholders and across countries. When planning for a new system selection, it is important to consider whether the architecture and technical capabilities exist in the vendor system to support interoperability.

Certification of EHR – Authorized Testing and Certification Bodies

In the United States (U.S.). The Office of the National Coordinator for Health Information Technology (ONC) is empowered by the U.S. Department of Health and Human Services (HHS) to provide a certification program for EHR systems.[2] The ONC Health IT Certification Program enhances oversight for safety and health IT developer's accountability. ONC authorized the American National Standards Institute (ANSI) to certify authorized testing and certification bodies (ONC- ATCBs), which grant certification to the products and vendors of EHR systems and modules. ONC-ATCB certification of an EHR system verifies that the EHR technology has the capabilities necessary to meet the goals and objectives of providing valuable data and knowledge to support the healthcare ecosystem.

In Europe. For each EU Member State (and Norway), a specific country report is available, containing the legal requirements applying to EHRs. These reports are not only focused on the current state of affairs, but also take into account potential future legislation. The national reports are used to perform a comparative analysis resulting in concrete recommendations, on a broad range of issues, for both national and EU actors.[3]

The Purpose of EHR System Certification in the U.S.

According to the ONC, health IT certification programs provide assurance to purchasers and other users that an EHR system, or other relevant technology, offers the necessary technological capability, functionality and security to help them meet the meaningful use criteria established for a given phase. Providers and patients must also be confident that the electronic health IT products and systems they use are secure, can maintain data confidentially and can work with other systems to share information.

Certification of EHR systems accomplishes four major goals:

a. Reduces the financial risks to investment in EHR systems by providing additional assurance that the system is worthwhile.
b. Facilitates interoperability between EHR systems, as each system would adhere to the same set of standards.
c. Establishes a prerequisite for Medicare and Medicaid incentive payments, among other stimulus incentives.
d. Requires EHR systems and networks to protect the privacy of personal health information.

Providers who are evaluating EHR systems can feel assured that each certified software product achieves basic functionality, interoperability and security, allowing providers to focus on their own specific and unique needs. Caution must be exercised when choosing a certified EHR software system solution. Certification does not ensure the vendor's service history or its financial solvency. Organization must exercise due diligence in all aspects of the system selection process. Certification standard may have some variations by countries, so it is necessary to consider the standards that are specific to your region or country.

Interoperability and Data Exchange Standards

Health Level Seven International (HL7)

Health Level Seven is a not-for-profit ANSI-accredited standards developing organization dedicated to providing a comprehensive framework to support exchange, integration, sharing and retrieval of electronic health information that supports clinical practice and the management, delivery and evaluation of health services.[4] HL7 has also documented the following capabilities that should be evaluated during a selection process. Many of these characteristics, like reliability and performance, should be assessed during reference check and site visits.

a. **Usability.** The ease with which a system can be learned and used. An example would be that the end user can navigate to any page in the EHR in five clicks or fewer.
b. **Reliability.** The degree of uptime the system must perform for the users. An example would be that the EHR system will have redundant backups allowing for 99.5% uptime.
c. **Performance.** How well the system works for the user in measurable degrees. Examples of performance would be response time and capacity.
d. **Supportability.** The application's ability to be easily modified or maintained to accommodate typical usage or change scenarios.
e. **Scalability.** The ability to increase the number of users or applications associated with the system.
f. **System requirements.** Minimum and recommended required operating systems, commercial-grade software development tools, specific hardware or platform requirements and any environmental requirements such as redundant environmental controls.
g. **Legal and regulatory requirements.** Including telecommunication requirements, compliance, etc.
h. **Security.** The ability to provide confidentiality, data integrity and data availability, as mandated by HIPAA, for example.

Vocabulary and Terminology Standards

Vocabulary and terminology standards allow for the common meaning of a concept being communicated through code sets and classification systems.[5] Common examples are:

- **Current Procedural Terminology (CPT®).** Use for office procedures and outpatient billing in the U.S.
- **ICD-10 and ICD-11.** The International Statistical Classification of Diseases and Related Health Problems (ICD) is a medical classification list by the World Health Organization (WHO). It contains codes for diseases, signs and symptoms, abnormal findings, complaints, social circumstances and external causes of injury or diseases. The 11th revision will replace the ICD-10 in January 2022.
- **Logical Observation Identifiers Names and Codes (LOINC®).** A universal code system for identifying health measurements, observations and documents. These codes represent the "question" for a test or measurement. LOINC codes can be grouped into laboratory and clinical tests, measurements and observations.
- **National Drug Code (NDC).** Maintained by the U.S. Food and Drug Administration, NDC provides a list of all drugs manufactured, prepared, propagated, compounded or processed for commercial distribution.
- **RxNorm.** A terminology used to normalize names for clinical drugs and links its names to many of the drug vocabularies commonly used in pharmacy management and drug interaction software. By providing links between these vocabularies, RxNorm can mediate messages between systems not using the same software and vocabulary.
- **Systematized Nomenclature of Medicine-Clinical Terms (SNOMED-CT).** A comprehensive clinical health terminology product. It enables the consistent, processable representation of clinical content in EHRs.
- **The Unified Code for Units of Measure.** A code system intended to include all units of measures used in international science, engineering and business to facilitate unambiguous electronic communication of quantities together with their units.

Transport Standards

Transport standards address the format of messages exchanged between computer systems, document architecture, clinical templates, user interface and patient data linkage. Standards center on "push" and "pull" methods for exchanging health information.[6]

- **Digital Imaging and Communications in Medicine (DICOM®).** The standard for the communication and management of medical imaging information and related data. DICOM enables the transfer of medical images across systems and facilitates the development and expansion of picture archiving and communication systems.

- **Direct Standard™.** Defines a set of standards and protocols to allow participants to send authenticated, encrypted health information directly to known, trusted recipients over the internet. Two primary specifications are the Applicability Statement for Secure Health Transport v1.2 and the XDR and XDM for Direct Messaging.
- **Fast Healthcare Interoperability Resources (FHIR®).** An HL7 standard for exchanging healthcare information electronically. The basic building blocks of FHIR are "resources," which describe exchangeable health data formats and elements. FHIR also provides standardization for application programming interfaces (APIs). FHIR provides a number of benefits and improvements as a modern healthcare standard including facilitating interoperable exchange with legacy standards, lower overhead, shorter learning curve, an ability to transmit only the necessary pieces of information, potential for patient mediated data and an energized community of supporters and implementers.
- IHE provides a number of specifications that can be used in the exchange of health information. For example, Hong Kong's Electronic Health Record Sharing System (eHRSS) (manage patient data on care episodes, lab results, radiology studies and drug items); European reference networks (virtual network of healthcare providers in Europe); Argentina's national interoperability network enable communication between participating health information systems (HISs); Canada Health Infoway (manages ePrescribing services).

Vendor-Specific Considerations

Hardware

As part of the RFP, each vendor is asked to list the minimum and recommended hardware and software requirements for installing their version of an EHR. Choosing the right hardware is important to ensure that the EHR's performance potential is fully realized and to minimize installation and performance issues down the road.

Prior to solidifying a contract with a vendor, the organization should take an inventory of the current server, workstation and mobile technology hardware (such as laptops and mobile devices), as well as the current operating systems and applications being deployed. Use this guiding question when assessing hardware compatibility, do the vendor's specifications align well with the organization's current technologies?

Vendor Selection – Narrowing the Choice

With numerous EHR systems currently available on the market, the task of narrowing down to the right one is difficult. One way to find those EHR systems most relevant for a given organization is to ask the following questions:

1. Will the software interface with other systems in the HIS environment, and what is the vendor's experience in exchanging patient data with other systems, including a health information exchange (HIE) or regional or national health information organization?
2. Is the EHR currently under consideration typically marketed to practices similar to the HCO that is looking to purchase a new one?
3. Does the EHR have favorable published ratings? Several excellent sources for EHR ratings are available. Also, trade shows such as HIMSS Global Health Conference can provide opportunities to evaluate options.
4. Does the EHR meet the purchasing organization's needs in terms of function and affordability? Each system under consideration should be assessed using a checklist and rankings to determine which ones should receive an RFP.

The Selection Committee will be comprised of the organization's stakeholders and experts, and they will be tasked with narrowing down the EHR candidates based on the established vendor selection criteria and matrix.

When ranking the products, the committee should formally weigh priorities in the following areas:

1. **Functionality.** How well does the product perform to your specifications?
2. **Total cost.** How much will the product cost, including all the needed hardware, software and implementation?
3. **Vendor services.** What services will the vendor provide in terms of service, training and initial implementation support?

Vendor Selection: Demos and Reference Checks

The next task is to set up vendor demonstrations with each of the systems having the highest rankings. For the demo, it is important to prepare scenarios that will demonstrate important functional requirements the organization has documented. For instance, a scenario might include showing how the physician would document a subjective, objective, assessment and plan (SOAP) note or how a physician might create a new documentation template. During vendor demonstrations, the organization will use a standardized rating form that will ensure consistency.

Actual users of the system should be included in this step of the process. The provider should check at least three references for every vendor that is being considered. Ideally, references should include one or more physician users, an IT person and other management roles. This step should include an evaluation of system characteristics and capabilities not seen in a functional demo. For instance, the provider might ask how well the vendor supports the product, how responsive the vendor is in resolving issues, response times, end user satisfaction in terms of usability and so forth.

The vendor will provide a list of references, but if it's a small list, these are usually the vendor's most satisfied customers. The RFP may request that the vendor provide a larger list of references that can be checked. The larger the reference list, the more confidence the selection committee will have in terms of selecting this vendor. If possible, it is also important for a provider to use references that are like the provider's organization.

Have a prepared list of questions for the reference phone calls. Consider asking questions of each reference centered around the following topics:

- Background
- Provider usage
- Training and support
- Implementation and hardware
- Satisfaction
- Any problems experienced with implementation or adoption

Vendor Selection: Site Visits

After reviewing the RFPs, reviewing vendor demos and doing reference checks for the top choices, the next step is to narrow the field to two or three vendors.[7]

Once these final contenders have been selected, the selection team will plan site visits to see how the systems perform. Site visits are usually limited to two or three because these visits can be challenging to organize, time consuming to conduct and expensive if travel is involved. The organization should conduct site visits at sites that are similar in size and configuration as the one in which they are working. Clinical users and staff who will use and support the system are in the best position to participate in a site visit where they can discuss system use with their peers. Depending on the type and size of provider, a typical team might include physicians, nurses, members of the administrative staff, IT professionals and representation from senior management.

After each site visit, the team will review the original vendor rankings to see if they still agree with the findings during the site visit. The team will select the system with the highest rankings and a runner-up. If negotiations don't go well with the number one choice, it might be necessary to fall back on the runner-up. Current and future costs should be clearly stated in negotiations, as should the role the vendor will play and the amount of time the vendor will commit to the implementation process.

Implementation

System implementation follows contract negotiation. Implementation consists of converting from the old system to the new system and include a conversation about hardware, software and workflows. There are five stages in the implementation process: exploration or adoption, installation, initial implementation, elaborations and continuous improvement or optimization.

Exploration/Adoption. During the explorations or adoption stage, decision is made about the organization's commitment to adopting the system and supporting the successful implementation.

Installation. During installation, the infrastructure is set up for the implementation. Activities included in this stage are the acquisition of resources, establishing the implementation team, preparing the organization human resources and data systems for the change, and developing the implementation plan.

Initial implementation. Initial implementation is the stage at which the system is pilot tested, allowing users an opportunity to interact with its features and functionalities. Additional activities include working out technical and workflow issues necessary for the successful adoption. Project leaders must maintain a comprehensive issues list to keep track of problems and resolutions.

Elaboration. Elaboration is the stage at which the system is implemented in additional locations across the organization. During this stage, issues identified in the initial implementation are resolved or a suitable workaround identified. These changes are incorporated in future implementations. For example, training plans and scenarios may need to be adjusted or network load adjusted to improve performance.

Critical Installation Considerations

Testing and training are two essential activities that must be done well to ensure successful implementation. After system acquisition, the system must be configured to facilitate the completion of future state workflows. Following this step, the system is thoroughly tested to ensure that users can complete daily activities. Testing occurs through the implementation process. Comprehensive user training follows successful user acceptance testing.

Testing

Please refer to Chapter 7 on Testing.

User Training

End user training and support are critical to the successful implementation and/or upgrade of a system. The implementation effort requires a comprehensive and well-constructed training plan. The training must be delivered at the right time – in time to practice but not so early that they will forget what they have learned.

The design, configuration, and implementation of a large-scale EHR system can cost an HCO tens of millions of dollars. End user training has often been considered an optional feature of the EHR system implementation, but experience shows that it must be an integral part of the implementation. Efficient and safe use of the system depends on high-quality training delivered on a timely training schedule. The acceptance of a new EHR system often depends on how well end users are trained.

Effective trainers must be able to analyze and assess instructional needs and then develop and deliver instruction by a variety of methods, including classroom sessions, online modules, individual tutoring, reference materials and laboratory simulations. The selection and deployment of superusers from the organization's staff is also a common and effective way to support an EHR implementation.

Training for end users is critical for a successful software rollout.[8] The initial training session should also be used to identify expected changes in workflow the user may need to address. It's only natural for people to not retain many of the details during the initial training session, so the initial session should be followed up with additional sessions as the rollout date approaches so the user feels reasonably comfortable operating the system without being totally dependent on the rollout team. Final training should occur as close to the go-live as possible.

Initial training must factor in user characteristics and utilize methodology most appropriate for types of users. Some skills will apply to every user group, and these should be covered thoroughly in the initial training. Specialized groups such as nurses, physicians, receptionists and records personnel will benefit from training customized for them.

Training Strategies and Methods

Several strategies for providing user training are available. A train-the-trainer approach has the system vendor train a small group who in turn train the remaining users. Standard classroom-style training, where the vendors create in-person courses, can also be efficient in training large numbers of users. Web-based training is often self-paced and convenient, but care must be taken to ensure that training is effective. One-on-one training is often the most effective but the most expensive for time and resources. This type of training is often utilized for physicians.

Sometimes a variety of training methods can be engaged to better reach the workplace staff, each with his/her own preferred style of learning. EHR training time will vary depending on each user's responsibilities. For example, at least one institution raised their training allocation from 4 hours to over 10 for physicians after identifying comprehension issues surrounding different forms used for documenting and prescribing medications and completing other tasks.

The workflow and pre-implementation training should be adequate to enable the staff to retain enough information to comfortably use the EHR with minimum support from the implementation team who will be busy mitigating other technical issues. In an ideal situation, the HCO will support end users at the point of use. Many EHR systems are packaged with a set of training demonstrations that can be played as the user needs them.

Training with ADDIE

One popular instructional system design model is analysis, design, development, implementation and evaluation (ADDIE).[9] ADDIE is a cyclical, reiterative process that can be used to develop effective training.

ADDIE Analysis

In the analysis stage, the instructional problem is clarified. Instructional goals and objectives are established, and the learning environment and the learners' existing knowledge and skills are identified. Some of the questions that are addressed during the analysis phase of the ADDIE model include:

- Who are the learners and what are their characteristics?
- Are the learners physicians, nurses or staff?
- Are there any language barriers?
- What is the training and learning culture in the clinic?
- What is the new behavioral outcome?
- Has the management clearly defined the goals or the outcomes of the training?
- What types of learning constraints exist and what are the delivery options?
- Which will work best: classroom training, one-on-one coaching, standalone web-based training, a written training manual – or maybe all of these or a combination of just a few?
- What are the online pedagogical considerations? Can you use video and audio? Will the computers in the clinic be able to handle them?
- What are the methods to facilitate discussion and feedback?
- What are the adult learning theory considerations in designing the material?
- What is the timeline for project completion?
- How much time and money has been allocated to the project?

ADDIE Design

This stage requires creating learning objectives and lesson plans, selecting content and media, developing exercises for the learner to apply their knowledge, and creating assessment instruments to test the learners. The design stage should be systematic and specific with a logical, orderly method of identifying, developing and evaluating a set of planned strategies that match the project's goals.

The steps involved in the design stage:

- Document the project's instructional, visual and technical design strategies.
- Apply instructional strategies according to the intended learning outcomes, be they effective, cognitive or psychomotor.
- Design the user interface if technology will be used for training.
- Create a prototype of the lesson and apply the visual designs, images, graphics, sounds and video.

ADDIE Development

The development stage is where instructional designers and content specialists, programmers and graphic designers create and assemble the content assets that were defined in the design phase. In this phase, storyboards and graphics are designed. If e-learning resources are used, programmers develop and/or integrate the necessary technological requirements. Quality assurance testers debug and proof the content of the application. Finally, the project is reviewed and revised according to the feedback received.

ADDIE Implementation

During the implementation phase, a procedure for delivering the training has been finalized and put into action. In some cases, the IT professional may be called upon only to design the training, but not to conduct the training. In these situations, facilitators should train the trainer on the course curriculum, learning, outcomes, method of delivery and testing procedures.

Preparation for training includes the creation or upgrading of a training environment and provisions for any needed documentation, hands-on equipment, computers, teaching labs, and software. The key is to ensure that the learning environment is completely functional.

ADDIE Evaluation

The final stage of a training cycle is evaluation. The evaluation phase consists of two parts: formative and summative. Formative evaluation is present in each stage of the ADDIE process to ensure that the training is sticking to the original plan. The summative evaluation consists of testing the learning objective and providing opportunities to gather feedback from the learners.

Initial Implementation/Elaboration Go-Live

There are multiple conversion strategies when implementing a new system. During the planning phase of the implementation, leaders decide about which approach is right for the organization.

Big bang. Going live with all functionalities of the system in all locations at the same time. Big bang go-live replaces the old system as a whole in one step.

Parallel. Going live with the new system while still operating the old system. In parallel go-live, the old and the new system are in operation side by side until the organization is confident that the new system is meeting its needs.

Pilot. Going live with one location or one functionality of the new system first before engaging in a companywide implementation.

Phased/incremental. Going live with one location, feature or functionality at a time until the system is completely implemented in the organization.

In large HIS adoptions, there is debate about whether it is better to take the big bang approach or to use a staged approach to introduce new technology and processes at an organization. With the big bang implementation strategy, the goal is to reduce the implementation time by bringing up multiple systems in a single go-live. In a phased approach, systems are brought up incrementally, giving the organization more time to adjust to new processes and resolve problems.

The implementation strategy selected will depend on several factors including the complexity of the system being implemented, the new system's relationship to other systems and applications in the environment, and an analysis of impacts associated with both approaches. If workflow processes are interdependent within components of the HIS, it is often difficult to utilize a phased-in approach. For instance, a computerized provider order entry (CPOE) implementation would likely include implementation of pharmacy because of the interdependencies between modules.

A successful implementation depends on many factors including the following:

- Creating a strong implementation team
- Creating an implementation plan
- Anticipating the impact of the new system and developing a change management plan

Working with the vendor, IT members of the team play a major role in the implementation process. The team's knowledge of the software development life cycle and the purpose for different testing processes contribute to a successful implementation, as well as to post-implementation monitoring and planning.

There are several factors that determine whether an implementation is successful. Critical success factors for implementation generally fall into one of these three categories:

- User characteristics
- System design characteristics
- Organizational characteristics

No two users are alike, and neither are the difficulties they will encounter in adoption. Some of the factors include individual differences in cognitive styles, personality and demographics like age. A user's expectations of what the system can do for them, and his or her attitude toward change, technology and their job are also factors.

System design characteristics are another aspect that can determine whether a new system achieves end user acceptance. Some of the critical success factors that originate from design include:

- How easy is the system to learn?
- How usable is it?
- How well does the graphical user interface (GUI) support the end user's workflow?
- Was it designed with the user in mind?

Organizational characteristics can also greatly influence adoption. If management does not buy into the new technology, it is unlikely that the rest of the organization will embrace it very easily. Planning for change management should identify cultural or organizational risks and identify strategies for addressing these.[10]

To successfully anchor the change in the organization, culture change must be considered first. For instance, if the nursing organization is resistant to the effort involved in implementing a new clinical system in a hospital, the project plan must include time for embedding the change in the culture and a plan for gaining support from nursing administration and staff. Ultimately, the organizational culture has a great impact on the health IT adoption process.

Contextual Implementation Model

The contextual implementation model (CIM) is a way of examining how one should approach health IT implementations. Given that such implementations are ongoing and iterative, it is important to take into consideration three contextual levels of differences. These include organizational, clinical unit and individual contextual differences.

When analyzing the context at the organizational levels, implementation teams should look at:

- The organization's mission and strategic plan and where IT fits into that vision
- Organizational culture
- Available resources
- The experience the organization has with IT implementations
- Size and complexity of the organization
- Existing structures and policies related to the use of health IT

The implementation team should then analyze work practices at the clinical unit level. They should assess the culture of the team, the engagement level of unit leadership, any experiences the unit may have had with IT, the clinical profile of the unit, its size and user attitudes related to use of IT. Differences in these areas can then be planned for and included in the implementation project plan.

Finally, the implementation team should look at the diverse ways of working, thinking, communicating and collaborating with individual users, as well as their computer literacy and keyboard skills. During implementation, the implementation team should focus on contextual differences at individual and clinical unit levels and how these differences could be accommodated within the use of the information system. This requires detailed analysis of the functionality of the system and how different clinicians' needs could be accommodated.

Computer literacy and keyboard skills would require targeted training programs. Team cultures that are constructive and supportive of innovations should be a goal. Implementation teams should devise strategies to modify team cultures into ones that are receptive to change and supportive of the change process.

Interventions can be devised to improve information sharing among team members, encourage support for innovation, provide a clear vision and objectives for staff and thus promote a constructive culture that is receptive to innovations.

Implementation Challenges

There are several common challenges to adoption and integration of health IT that warrant discussion. When health IT is being implemented, change from the normal way of doing things is inherent. Getting people to change the way they work must be factored into the implementation plan. For instance, many clinicians favor recording notes in free text. Encouraging them to enter documentation in templates that provide structured data essential for reporting and analysis may present a challenge.

Beyond changes to existing process and workflow, other challenges to successful adoption and integration of health IT include the following:

- Total cost of the system including ongoing maintenance and support
- Feared loss of physician productivity and loss of revenue
- Concern for how the patient/provider relationship will be affected by use of the EHR during a patient visit
- Ongoing training required in an environment with high staff turnover

Implementation Support

There are many ways in which implementation support can be crafted. For smaller organizations, most software vendors either provide or can recommend, external consultants to assist with implementation support or training support. Larger organizations generally find that it is better to cultivate internal consultants.

Many organizations rely on external consultants to provide training and go-live support. These individuals have expertise in use of the software application being implemented, are experienced in implementing that system in a wide variety of settings and have the dedicated time to support the implementation. The downside to using external consultants is their lack of familiarity with specific organizational policies and workflows and the fact that this option is usually more costly than using internal personnel.

Clinical personnel, usually nurses, often termed superusers who have training and knowledge beyond the usual end user for the given software application, can be very valuable in supporting a system implementation. These clinicians serve as "bridgers" or links between the clinical world and the IT world. They have a deep understanding of clinical workflows and have credibility with other users, since they understand the problems that users face in the clinical environment. They can also help translate the needs of the end user to the IT technical teams. These internal experts are known by a variety of names, depending on the role that they play in their organizations. These roles may be informal or formal.

Internal consultants assist with training and implementation, and many of them have ongoing roles well beyond system implementation. Most often their primary responsibilities include serving as champions and promoting IT adoption, assisting with and reinforcing training, assisting with policy and procedure development, and serving as liaisons between clinical and IT personnel. In some instances, their roles extend to ongoing competency testing and quality oversight of use of the EHR.

IT support may be hired and developed in-house or may be outsourced to provide support on an as-needed basis. If an in-house staff is chosen to provide partial or full technical support for the EHR system, there are several different organizational staffing models to choose from depending upon the institutional needs and support responsibilities.

For larger institutions, the chore of maintaining a large EHR infrastructure, combined with the need to interface with (perhaps) hundreds of users daily, becomes a more daunting and costly task, typically requiring an additional in-house IT staffing component.

The production support team should provide highly available, highly usable and expedient support to address user service issues as they arise. In today's healthcare environments, EHR downtime can potentially have a negative effect on patient outcomes – a reality that necessitates access to skilled IT support during all operational hours. The IT department must devise an efficient method of ensuring user requests are processed and resolved in a timely manner with the goal of minimizing productivity loss and any patient safety issues.

Responsibilities of the support team might include tasks such as managing user access to the EHR system, monitoring an interface activity, or scheduling jobs that need to be run periodically, like a system-generated file with aggregate patient data needed for outcome analysis.

Performance Baseline Measurement Post Go-Live

Once a system implementation has occurred, a performance baseline is generated after completion of performance baseline testing and shows the normal operating parameters of a system under normal load conditions. It is used to gauge the overall health of the system and to assist with isolating performance issues.

Baselines are used to help confirm normal system operation (say, for instance, automated monitoring systems) when an anomaly in the system is suspected and to assist in pinpointing where to begin looking for a root cause.

Performance baseline testing, also referred to as benchmark testing, is typically performed by the test engineer to compare the performance of a new server, application or system to a known standard of reference, such as existing measurements or software specifications.

To take a performance baseline, begin by taking performance measurements at regular intervals when the system is functioning within normal parameters. Then begin comparing each set of measurements to the ones taken earlier. Over time, get a gauge of normal system performance, which will vary based on time of day, amount of system usage, etc.

The following areas affect the performance of many systems and should be considered part of a baseline strategy:

- System resources, including server and system hardware
- Network architecture
- Operating system
- Database applications
- Client applications

There are many tools on the market to assist with establishing baselines for the system's components. Work with the vendor to determine which set would be most appropriate for the environment and what methods are best suited for baseline testing the EHR database.

At a minimum, baseline measurements should be used to determine:

- When peak and off-peak hours of operation take place
- The organization's average production-query or batch-command response times
- How long it takes to complete a database backup and restore jobs

After completing and establishing a server performance baseline, use that baseline on a day-to-day basis to compare the baseline statistics to the current server or system performance. When performance numbers deviate too far above or below baseline statistics, there is cause to investigate further. For example, if it takes longer to execute a set of queries, then it may be time to decide if the queries need to be rewritten or new database indices added.

Support and Maintenance After Go-Live

During the implementation, the support organization needs to develop processes that give end users a sense that their feedback is being factored into the plan.[11] It is also important to set realistic expectations for how fast users should expect to receive IT help from the help desk. IT support may be in-house staff or outsourced personnel, or a combination of both.

Whenever possible, the support organization should centralize the first point of contact and have that person prioritize requests to minimize disruption of busy technicians. Support processes should include a definition of what constitutes an emergency (such as an outage) as well as the standard process for contacting support technicians if needed or possibly contacting the vendor. Publish these expectations and be consistent about meeting them.

Goals should be to maximize reliability and productivity. Make every attempt to resolve problems as quickly as possible, be respectful of the end users' time when they are needed in the process and communicate any status changes promptly.

Support Team

The production support team should provide highly available, highly usable and expedient support to address user service issues as they arise. In today's healthcare environments, EHR downtime can potentially have a negative effect on patient outcomes – a reality that necessitates access to skilled IT support during all operational hours. The IT department must devise an efficient method of ensuring user requests are processed and resolved in a timely manner with the goal of minimizing productivity loss and any patient safety issues.

Responsibilities of the support team could include tasks like managing user access to the EHR system, monitoring an interface activity, or scheduling jobs that need to be run periodically, like a system-generated file with aggregate patient data needed for outcome analysis.

The support team includes staff with a variety of skill sets. Common roles include:

- **Help desk staff.** Triage incoming requests and process basic diagnosis and administrative requests.
- **Applications and operations team.** Respond to issues surrounding the use of applications, including EHR software issues. They are also responsible for oversight of upgrades.
- **Networking team.** Diagnose and resolve issues regarding connectivity and data exchange including network administrative tasks.
- **Workstation support team.** Respond to inquiries regarding workstation usage, including potential hardware malfunctions or local application support, installation and troubleshooting.

Each IT department must find the balance between workload and available resources that best suits their organizational needs.

In larger organizations that often need to support multiple clinic sites, a tiered support approach might be used to maximize support productivity. In this tiered approach:

- The first tier consists of superusers and/or help desk staff.
- The second tier is staffed with workstation and networking specialists. Technical analysts are deployed when the cause of the issue is deemed to be related to the workstation or network.
- The third tier is usually made up of application support specialists and support consultants. They evaluate issues specifically related to the application software.

Superusers

Superusers are usually members of clinical teams who are experts in the application and who are positioned to teach and coach other users in the use of the system. They are strategically located at practice sites or departments to provide frontline user support to commonly asked questions and to promote proper security and confidentiality practices. Superusers serve as liaisons between the EHR support team and the provider organization. Superusers are also good at identifying problematic EHR and workflow issues and recommending potential improvements to the development team for consideration.

Troubleshooting

Each EHR system and networking environment is different. However, there are some standard troubleshooting practices that ring true no matter what system is being used.

Tips for troubleshooting complex EHR problems include:

- Identify the problem. Be sure to contact the user personally and listen closely to the symptoms of the issue. Whenever possible test the application from the user's workstation and attempt to duplicate the problem.
- Determine the size and scope of the issue. Does the problem appear to be localized to one computer or user? If so, start the troubleshooting there. Ask the user if any changes were recently made to the system, computer, EHR access privileges or profile and have them recreate the error again and watch for abnormalities.
- Check localized application and hardware. Do this before looking at the system as a whole. If there are multiple complaints or if the issue appears to be related to the database or server, begin to expand the search.
- Ask questions. Has anything changed recently? Are there any new upgrade patches or procedures implemented? Has any new hardware been added to the network, system or server? Are there any commonalities between the affected users? Often, the most complex problems are the result of a single failure. Start simple.
- Remember to communicate. Provide regular updates to users and stakeholders describing what actions are being taken to find a resolution. However, it's also important that key staff don't become overburdened with communication efforts. They need time to do their work.
- Use the EHR application, system and security logs to diagnose an issue. Understand where these logs are stored, as well how to access and decipher them. The logs can provide additional insight about where things went wrong and usually offer some sort of explanation as to the cause.
- Develop a timeline of events leading up to the issue. This is particularly useful for issues resulting from a series of events occurring over a period.
- Watch the time. IT staff sometimes get tunnel vision. They can become so engrossed in solving a problem that they lose track of time. Have an escalation plan in place to bring in other resources and stick to it.
- Stay focused on resolving the problem at hand. A major outage is not the time for finger-pointing or for egos to get in the way of completing the task. Once the outage or problem has been resolved, there will be time to analyze the root cause and make procedural changes to help prevent similar issues from reoccurring.
- Monitor the system closely after resolving the problem. Another tendency is to immediately declare an issue resolved as soon as the issue returns to normal. Generally, it is wise to monitor the issue perhaps 24–48 hours after the issue has been resolved.
- Remember that problems and outages are just part of the job. Don't stake a professional reputation on one problem; base it on how the entire IT team responds, evolves and improves over time.

If an issue turns out to be more widespread in nature, it may be necessary to look at the EHR server components themselves. If the server infrastructure is in-house, with help from the vendor and/or server administrator, determine:

- Is the memory or hard drive space on the server due for an upgrade?
- Was the server recently upgraded, tweaked or configured differently?
- Is connectivity to the server itself operating optimally?
- If the organization is using a software as a service (SaaS) or an EHR hosted by a vendor, work with the vendor to determine if their data connection is failing or if there is a problem with the EHR design or code.

Options for additional diagnosis will depend on the EHR system used by the organization.

Working with Vendors

Building and maintaining a good relationship with the EHR vendor is essential – for both a successful implementation and continued success throughout the product's life cycle. Successful business partnerships are built on mutual goals and trust; the knowledge that both entities are "in this together" and that the success of the vendor goes hand-in-hand with the success of their product.

Purchasing an EHR system brings about a long-term commitment between an organization and the vendor. These relationships become quite complex once the EHR system becomes fully embedded into the organization, which, in turn, then becomes completely dependent on its capabilities. The type and nature of the relationship with the vendor will no doubt vary depending on the organization's size and the scope of the implementation.

Upgrading

Upgrading system components is crucial for extending EHR functionality and overall system lifespan. However, improperly planned or managed upgrade procedures can severely damage the system, reducing performance or even bringing down the entire system. Most vendors publish at least one major upgrade a year, and patches throughout the year may be needed to repair issues and improve performance glitches.

Before moving forward with an upgrade, leaders should ask these questions:

- What new functionality or benefits will be added as a result of the upgrade?
- Will additional hardware or software upgrades be needed to ensure the upgrade's success?
- Is the recommended hardware or software compatible with existing components?
- How will the upgrade affect users?
- What can be done to minimize downtime and educate users?

Upgrading any major critical production system should take a highly structured approach, as outlined below:

1. The upgrade team reads over the upgrade documentation and analyzes functional enhancements and configuration decisions, being sure to work with the vendor to address any unknown variables in documentation or due to system customization.
2. If the upgrade involves more than one application, the upgrade team develops a plan for integration and testing of the affected applications.
3. If a test environment is not already in place, the technical team will develop an alternative environment closely mimicking the production environment for testing purposes.
4. The upgrade team then compiles a preinstallation and installation checklist and accompanying documentation and determines how much downtime will be needed for the upgrade process to complete.
5. After the first testing is completed in the testing environment, logs are reviewed and any errors or discrepancies are reported to the vendor for resolution. Working with the vendor is crucial for successful upgrade implementations.
6. The vendor then completes any needed improvements, and the upgrade team performs another install test, being careful to follow upgrade documentation and coordinating testing with the affected application teams. Additionally, special attention is given to ensuring preservation of data integrity.
7. Specialized software, capable of simulating standard workflows and number of users, can help to paint a clearer picture of network performance during and after the upgrade. A unified spreadsheet for recording, prioritizing and documenting issues, along with their resolutions, can be very useful for managing problems as they arise and communicating with the vendor.
8. Once testing has been completed and the upgrade process approved, final documentation is prepared and training is scheduled. The installation team is also finalized and assigned various roles.
9. Upgrade windows should be scheduled during off-peak times to minimize issues. Additionally, a shadow copy of the EHR – in other words, a read-only copy without real-time interfaced results – would ideally remain available for access during the upgrade window.
10. Begin testing the upgrade immediately after completion. Once testing is complete, the help desk is notified and systems are brought back online.
11. After the upgrade has been completed, a dedicated team should be available over the next few business days to resolve any issues the upgrade could have created.
12. Similar processes should be followed for upgrades to the server OS, workstation OS and databases.

Providers must stay up to date in terms of vendor communications regarding patches or upgrades. Additionally, providers should take advantage of any available training, particularly regarding new EHR upgrades.

Summary

An EHR implementation project begins very much as a research project. To ensure a successful outcome, both an organization's current system and a range of available alternatives should be thoroughly vetted. It's important that an organization pursues a defined selection process and then develops a thorough and comprehensive plan for the implementation, including training and support.

References

1. Centers for Medicare & Medicaid Services. Health IT Certification Programs. (2020). www.healthit.gov/poliScy-researchers-implementers/health-it-certification-programs.
2. The Office of the National Coordinator for Health Information Technology. Health IT Playbook. www.healthit.gov/playbook/electronic-health-records.
3. European Commission. (2016). Overview of the national laws on electronic health records in the EU Member States. https://ec.europa.eu/health/ehealth/projects/nationallaws_electronichealthrecords_en.
4. Health Level Seven International. (2021). Introduction to HL 7 Standards. https://www.hl7.org/implement/standards/.
5. Interoperability in healthcare. https://www.himss.org/resources/interoperability-healthcare.
6. The Office of the National Coordinator for Health Information Technology. How to select a vendor. https://www.healthit.gov/faq/how-do-i-select-vendor.
7. Dennis, A., Wixom, B., & Roth, R. (2019). *Systems Analysis and Design* (7th ed.). Danvers MA: John Wiley & Sons.
8. Longhurst, C. A., Davis, T., Meneker, A., Eschenroeder, H. C., et al. (2019). Local investment in training drives electronic health record user satisfaction. *Applied Clinical Informatics*, 10, 331–335.
9. Branch, R. M. (2009). *Instructional Design: The ADDIE Approach*. New York, NY: Springer. doi: 10.1007/978-0-387-09506-6.
10. KotterKotter, J. (1996). *Leading Change*. Boston, MA: Harvard Business School Press.
11. Hebda, T. L., Hunter, K., & Czar, P. (2018). *Handbook of Informatics for Nurses & Healthcare Professionals* (6th ed.). London: Pearson.

Chapter 7

Testing and Evaluation

Learning Objectives

At the conclusion of this chapter, the reader will be able to:

- Identify and differentiate accepted testing methodologies (e.g., unit test, integrated test, stress test, acceptance test)
- Identify and differentiate internal controls to protect resources and ensure availability and integrity during testing (e.g., security audits, versioning control, change control)
- Verify deliverables against contractual terms or design specifications
- Gather and compile data to support that expected outcomes have been realized (e.g., return on investment, benchmarks, user satisfaction)

Introduction

Selecting and implementing a new health information technology (health IT) system is a painstaking process requiring attention to an array of critical details. The health IT professionals responsible for ensuring successful outcomes will not know whether or not their job is actually complete until the system has been tested in a variety of ways.

Testing, of course, is critical to understanding whether the system will perform according to expectations, and those expectations are shaped by the many ways in which a health IT system is called upon to store, transfer and analyze health information in today's multifaceted healthcare organizations.

The fact is that many people are expecting to utilize a health IT system in seemingly countless ways, so health IT professionals must ensure that the system they've implemented is up to the challenge. That means understanding a broad range of testing methodologies that test a system under a variety of circumstances and with a variety of purposes in mind. It also means understanding the steps necessary to ensure that the system is protected and maintained so that its capabilities are always available. Finally, it means understanding the range of financial, clinical and user-oriented benchmarks that are involved in ensuring a system is ready and able to deliver the necessary outcomes.

Testing

Most system development methodologies used today require iterative development with frequent evaluation at each stage. Types of testing vary according to the stage of development. When unit testing and integration testing are complete, system testing can be performed. The testing process can be summarized as follows:

- Create the test plan
- Determine test cases and set up test data for input

DOI: 10.4324/9780429443862-10

- Execute the test cases, which includes the building of a testing environment, automation of test cases (where applicable) and creation of scripts to run the tests
- Implement test controls
- Fix identified bugs
- Retest the code and repeat as necessary

Good testing includes the creation of a test plan to ensure all situations have been tested, successful conditions are recognized and all problems are mitigated. The test plan is developed at the same time that the system is designed, which ensures that all of the features and functionality are fully tested, and that all of the requirements are met. A thoroughly tested system helps ensure a successful installation and deployment.

Test Cases

A test case is a formal or informal set of conditions or variables under which a tester can identify issues and determine if the application or software system is working correctly. In formal testing, there must be at least two test cases for each requirement – one positive test and one negative test – to determine that all requirements of an application are met. Keeping track of the link between the requirement and the test is frequently done using a requirements traceability matrix.

Types of Testing

Written test cases include a description of the functionality to be tested and the preparation required to ensure that the test can be conducted. A formal test case is characterized by a known input and an expected output. The known input should test a precondition, and the expected output should test a post-condition.

For applications or systems without formal requirements, informal test cases are written based on the accepted normal operation of programs of a similar class. Sometimes test cases are not written at all, but the activities and results that are reported after the tests have been run validate that the system is performing as expected.

Scenario Testing

Scenario testing uses hypothetical situations to help the tester consider a complex problem or system. They can be as simple as a diagram or can take the form of a written description. The ideal scenario is a story that is credible, complex and easy to evaluate. Scenario testing, for instance, is very useful in testing a clinical user's interaction with the system when the user's workflow spans multiple functions. In an electronic health record (EHR), a common test scenario would be to review patient data, review new results and order medications using computerized provider order entry (CPOE). Each piece of the scenario shows the tester what must be checked or evaluated through testing.

Unit Testing

A unit is the smallest piece of testable code and is tested by itself to be sure it behaves as expected. Unit testing identifies and eliminates run-time or execution errors that make the program stop abnormally and logic errors (incorrect results) that might not have been caught during the design phase.

The main purpose of unit testing is to take the smallest piece of testable software in the application and isolate it from all other code to determine whether it acts as expected on its own and whether its functionality meets the requirements.

Integration Testing

Integration testing occurs right after unit testing. Two or more previously tested units are combined into a component, and their integration is tested. More units are combined and tested together until the full product is tested at once.

System Testing

System testing focuses on the system as a whole and is often performed by a dedicated testing team. System testing may also utilize real-life scenarios to ensure all functions and features of the system will work when it finally goes live. System testing includes verification and validation of both the business requirements and the application architecture. It is intended to assure users, developers and managers that the programs meet all specifications and that all necessary features have been included and function as expected.

System Integration Testing

System integration testing extends system testing to include testing the system in the environment where it will run. This includes running the system along with other software. System integration testing leads to user acceptance testing (UAT) where the system is finally tested by the users against the requirements defined in the analysis and design phases.

Usability Testing

Usability is described by the International Organization for Standardization (ISO) as "the extent to which a product can be used by specified users to achieve specified goals with effectiveness, efficiency and satisfaction in a specified context of use".[1] Usability testing evaluates the system through observational studies, surveys and focus groups and should be a part of all stages of the systems development process. User input to the beginning planning stages is crucial; initial prototypes and designs can also be evaluated by users. Once the system is implemented, it should be evaluated thoroughly by different types of users for the different tasks they need to perform to ensure that the system is effective, easy to use and limits errors.

Accessibility Testing

Accessibility describes the degree to which a product, service, device or environment is accessible by as many people as possible, such as those with limited eyesight, dexterity or other physical or learning challenges. Accessibility testing covers the government requirements such as the Americans with Disabilities Act (ADA), Section 508 of the Rehabilitation Act and the Web Accessibility Initiative (WAI). Accessibility testing evaluates the system for meeting these requirements.

The European Accessibility Act is a directive that aims to improve the functioning of the internal market for accessible products and services, by removing barriers created by divergent rules in Member States.[2]

Ad Hoc Testing

Ad hoc testing is testing performed without planning and documentation. These on-the-fly tests are intended to be run only once unless a defect is discovered.

Exploratory Testing

Exploratory testing is used to find out how the software actually works and to ask questions about how it will handle both difficult and easy cases. The quality of the testing is dependent on the tester's skill of inventing test cases and finding defects.

Installation Testing

Installation testing is a type of quality assurance work in industry that focuses on what customers will need to do to install and set up the new system successfully.

Load Testing

Load testing refers to testing the system under high load conditions where there are several applications running with many network and memory demands. Determining the maximum load for an application without errors is part of the testing. Load testing helps also identify bottlenecks.

Stress Testing

Stress testing is similar to load testing, but the capacity is pushed beyond what would ever be expected for the system. Like load testing, stress testing is used to determine the breaking point of the system and to observe what occurs within the system when that point is reached.

Maintenance Testing

Maintenance testing is performed during the maintenance phase of development. This type of testing can be used to identify new problems or confirm that software updates are effective.

Recovery Testing

Recovery testing shows how well an application is able to recover from crashes, hardware failures and other similar problems. During recovery testing, the system is deliberately made to fail and is then evaluated in its response to the failure. A simple example of recovery testing: In the middle of downloading a file from the Internet, turn off the computer, then turn it back on. Does the download resume or must the process be started over?

Reliability Testing

Reliability testing tries to discover the specific point at which failure occurs. When reliability is considered from the perspective of the consumer of a technology or service, the actual measures may differ dramatically from the perceived reality. When a bad situation is magnified in the mind of the customer, it may inflate the perceived unreliability of the experience, but that perception becomes their reality. For example, one plane crash where hundreds die immediately instills fear in a large percentage of the flying population, regardless of actual reliability data about the safety of air travel.

Regression Testing

Regression testing uncovers software errors by partially retesting a modified program. It provides a general assurance that no additional errors were introduced in the process of fixing other problems. Regression testing methods include rerunning previous tests and checking whether previously fixed errors have reemerged. Without regression testing, it is difficult to find or see how a change in one part of the system affects other parts.

Sanity Testing

A sanity test or sanity check quickly evaluates whether a claim or the result of a calculation can possibly be true. The point is not to catch every possible error but to rule out certain classes of obviously false results. In computer science, a sanity test is a brief run-through of the functionality of a computer program, system, calculation or other analysis to assure that the system or methodology works as expected. This is often done prior to a more exhaustive round of testing.

Scalability Testing

Scalability testing measures the capability to scale or increase the user load, number of transactions, amount of data, etc. Performance, scalability and reliability are often considered together by software quality analysts.

Security Testing

Security testing evaluates the security measures of an information system. It ensures that only authorized users can access the system or the specific components or functions of the system to which they have been granted permissions.

Smoke Testing

Smoke testing refers to the initial tests completed after a repair to a system to determine if the system is repaired enough to withstand further testing.

Volume Testing

Volume testing tests how a system reacts to a specific amount of data. The system's functionality and performance are then evaluated.

Benchmark Testing

Once a system is deployed, system performance is tested to ensure that the system is meeting requirements and goals. System performance is measured with benchmark testing that uses a set of standard tests to evaluate system performance and capacity. Common metrics include response time, bandwidth, throughput and turnaround time.

Additional Monitoring

In addition to the above tests, the health IT administrator will be required to monitor other elements of the system, including:

Response time. Response time is the overall time between a request for system activity and the delivery of the system's response. Users expect an immediate response and are frustrated by apparent lags or delays. Response time is what users notice and frequently complain about when it does not meet their expectations.

Bandwidth. Bandwidth describes the amount of data the system can transfer in a fixed time period and is expressed in kilobits, megabits or gigabits per second (Kbps, Mbps, Gbps).

Throughput. Throughput measures actual system performance under specific circumstances and is affected by network loads and hardware efficiencies. It is also expressed as a data transfer rate in Kbps, Mbps or Gbps.

Turnaround time. Turnaround time applies to centralized batch processing operations such as customer billing or credit card statement processing. It measures the time between submitting a request for information and the completion of the request.

Capacity planning. Capacity planning monitors current activity and performance levels and plans for anticipated future activity. First, a current model based on the system's present workload and performance specification is developed. Then capacity or demand is projected over a given time period. Analysis of the model shows what is needed to maintain satisfactory performance and meet requirements. The "what if" analysis allows the varying of one or more elements in a model to measure the effect on other elements. The main objective of capacity planning is to make sure the system can handle anticipated future demands.

User Acceptance Testing

In the world of software development, there are two types of software acceptance testing. The first, conducted by the system vendor, ensures the product meets defined requirements. The second, UAT, is conducted by the healthcare organization to ensure that functionality meets the acceptable institutional requirements.

UAT is the final stage of testing performed and involves using the software product prior to rollout. UAT is usually a contractual agreement between the healthcare organization and the vendor during negotiations. It gives both the end users and the software manufacturer one last chance to be sure that the product being delivered fully meets their expectations and project objectives and is free of any defects. UAT also provides another opportunity for further debugging since the end user often uses the product from a perspective different than that of the manufacturer or even others from their own organization who may have been involved in prior rounds of testing.

Steps to UAT

- Planning UAT
- Designing UAT cases
- Selecting a test team
- Documenting the identified defects
- Resolving issues
- Signing off

Early on in the project timeline, a list of baseline requirements should have been generated and mutually agreed upon by the organization and the vendor as "must-haves" for software implementation to be considered successful. Testing strategy should be based, at least in part, on validation of these requirements.

As stated earlier, UAT is usually the final step before the general rollout process begins, so the software product should be fully developed before it begins. Because of the critical nature of health record systems, UAT should always be completed before initial rollout or any upgrade to the system.

Since the focus of user acceptance is on the system's functionality, the vendor should have rectified a majority of the technical glitches in the product prior to UAT. This would be the equivalent of a manufacturer doing product testing after a part comes off the assembly line to ensure the product functions to its specifications.

UAT for the software should be carried out in a test environment that mimics the actual work environment as closely as possible in which the product will be used.

Several important terms related to UAT:

- **Test strategy.** Includes who will be involved, any special equipment or software will be needed, procedures to be followed and any other support mechanisms that will be needed to ensure successful testing.
- **Test scenarios.** The events or workflows that require testing by users.
- **Test scripts.** Step-by-step instructions, including specific inputs that will be used for each test, as well as the expected results.

There is a difference between test scenarios and test scripts. Test *scenarios* give a broad interpretation of what you are testing, while test *scripts* are the step-by-step instructions associated with running the actual test and recording outcomes. For example, a scenario could say, "When you enter a prescription that could cause an adverse reaction for the patient, a warning message should appear". The corresponding script might include click-by-click instructions for opening a test patient's chart, entering a new specific prescription, signing the order and includes the exact wording of the error message the user is expected to encounter for this scenario.

Closeout Meeting

When all the testing is complete, hold a customer acceptance meeting with the vendor. Sometimes called a *closeout meeting*, this can be an opportunity to summarize UAT and finalize customer service agreements.

Planning

The planning stage is the most important part of creating an effective testing strategy and is critical to a successful UAT process. The planning stage defines the key focus areas, along with entry and exit criteria. Since this is functionality testing, focus areas targeted for testing should be roughly defined by the expected overall product deliverables.

Typical elements to include in the planning process are:

- Objectives of this testing effort
- Entry and exit criteria for testing
- **Schedule** (testing date or range of dates)
- **Location** (where is testing taking place?)
- **Participants** (who are involved with the testing?)

The testing environment will also need planning. Be sure to include the following in the plans:

- **Test environment.** Explain, in detail, the environment used for testing. For example, will there be a separate testing environment and, if so, what are instructions for logging in and what data will populate the system prior to testing?
- **Equipment needed.** Identify all of the equipment required for testing and its setup requirements.
- **Data.** Identify the data required for the testing. For example, 100 test patient records will be accessed spanning visit dates from 2015 to 2020.
- **Backup requirements.** Define when data backups should occur and who will be responsible for backups. Determine the duration needed for backup retention.
- **Restoration.** Additionally, determine which events warrant a restoration or refreshing of the test data along with who can authorize such restores and whose responsibility it will be to complete them.
- **Implementation strategy.** Once testing is complete, a healthcare organization will need to have a process in place to process errors once they are discovered by testers. Identify who will be responsible for collecting identified errors and ensuring they are handled appropriately.
- **Sign-off.** For each event tested, a process should be in place to determine when it is appropriate to sign off or accept that element of the testing activity. Signing off usually occurs after retesting has been completed and it has been determined that any identified defects have been adequately mitigated.
- **Test management and performance management software.** List any specialized test management software to be used to document the testing, record discovered issues and manage the mitigation process.
- **Testing software.** This would include any specialized software needed to generate the testing environment or perhaps automate some repetitive testing functions. Outline any software that will be used during the testing process.

Designing Test Cases

The next stage involves designing the test cases, or scenarios and/or corresponding scripts. Once testing strategies and scenarios have been developed, the testing team begins working on user test cases, or scripts, to test the focus areas defined during the planning process. Often test cases are created at the time the software requirements are being ironed out or as part of the workflow analysis.

Once the focus has been defined, the test team manager is often responsible for matching the skill sets of each team member to the specific tasks needing to be accomplished. This includes utilizing subject matter experts and more experienced testers to define testing scenarios.

Test scenarios broadly define the scope of each test along with the output expected upon completion. They are used to develop detailed scripts for end user testing. In addition to test cases developed by the team, business analysts or other subject matter experts may be involved in developing testing scenarios or scripts for implementation. If use cases or scenarios were developed as part of the system selection process, these can also be utilized in testing.

As stated earlier, a test script is a step-by-step instruction set for conducting the actual test and recording outcomes. The script also defines the data to be entered, provides a section for the tester to record the output generated by the test, and contains instructions for forwarding any erroneous findings to the appropriate team members for resolution.

Creating specific test scripts can vary, however. More often than not, a test script will contain:

- A column indicating the set number in the process
- A column for the step-by-step instructions to perform
- A column indicating the expected test result (expected output to be generated and what it should look like)
- A column for the tester to document the actual result
- A column for any additional comments the tester would like to note

Sometimes it is advantageous for the testing team to go beyond manual user testing and actually create code to automatically perform some of the testing procedures. Programmers take the testing scripts and devise a program to run the input using a tool called an interpreter, which mimics the end user's input and records the result.

Test Controls

System controls are implemented to protect the confidentiality, integrity and availability of data and the overall management of a system across environments during design, development, testing and deployment. Some of the most common types of test controls include version controls (also called revision controls), security audits and change controls.

Version control (or revision control) tracks and provides control over changes to source code. Software developers and testers sometimes use version control software to maintain documentation and configuration files, as well as source code. As teams design, develop and test software, it is common for multiple versions of the same software to be running in different sites and for the software's developers to be working simultaneously on updates. Often bugs or features of the software will be present only in certain versions due to the fixing of some problems and the introduction of new ones as the program develops. Therefore, for the purposes of locating and fixing bugs, it is vitally important to be able to retrieve and run different versions of the software to determine in which version(s) a problem occurs.

Security audits are manual or automatic systematic, measurable technical assessments of a system or application. Manual assessments include interviewing staff, performing security vulnerability scans, reviewing application and operating system access controls and analyzing physical access to the systems. Automated assessments include system-generated audit reports and software that monitors and reports changes to files and settings on a system. Systems that require security audits can include personal computers, servers, network routers and switches.

Change control is a formal process used to ensure that changes to a product or system are introduced in a controlled and coordinated manner. It reduces the possibility that unnecessary changes will be made to a system without forethought, introducing faults or undoing changes made by other users. Typical activities that would call for change control are patches to software products, system configuration changes, installation of new operating systems, upgrades to network routing systems and changes to the electrical power systems supporting the infrastructure. Change control is also a means by which the number of changes in an environment at any one time is controlled.

End User Testing Process and Acceptance

When determining end user testing, it's important to draw testers from an entire cross section of the end user environment to ensure that all workplace elements have been represented. This diversity will help draw out any hidden workflow or functional obstacles not previously discovered. Once the end users have been selected, testing begins in earnest. End users should execute each of the test scripts and thoroughly document the outcomes experienced.

Users can find all sorts of ways to break things if left to their own devices. Be sure to allow some "free range" time for the testers to randomly explore their environment. They will often find errors on their own that will need resolution.

Once each tester has completed a testing cycle, the documentation should be quickly collected and forwarded to the testing team for resolution. The team meets with subject matter experts and the vendor to iron out a plan of attack for completing the necessary software revisions, and work commences to resolve the issues. A system defect may require development of an alternate process or workaround until a software change is made by the vendor.

When all issues are resolved and end users are confident in the product's abilities, the team acknowledges acceptance of the application. All known issues have been satisfactorily resolved or mitigated. The organization's sign-off on acceptance testing is often a milestone that represents payment to the vendor.

Pilot Testing

As the rollout date approaches and internal testing winds down, at some point real users must be allowed to interface with the new system, take it through its paces in a production environment, and provide feedback. This process, known as pilot testing, is designed to catch and correct potentially costly errors before they are magnified through full deployment. Pilot testers not only put the system through its paces at a technical level but also reaffirm that efficient workflow practices have been adequately modeled during development.

Developing and using a readiness assessment prior to the pilot testing phase can be beneficial for assessing staff abilities and to identify technological shortfalls for each department that may need addressing prior to the rollout process. The readiness assessment can also help devise a final rollout strategy by identifying which departments are more willing and capable of more ambitious rollout schedules and which departments will need additional readiness efforts prior to implementation.

Soliciting user feedback is a critical component of pilot testing. Pilot users can identify potential problems or workflow issues. It is important that the organization listens to pilot user feedback to isolate and resolve potential glitches in the system or make interface adjustments to resolve severe workflow issues that may have arisen.

Evaluation and Feedback

Once the system implementation has occurred, it is important to listen to user feedback to document, track and resolve newly identified issues. Effective implementation teams actively solicit feedback so as to implement improvements before problems arise. Slow resolution may demoralize users and result in low adoption and dissatisfaction. Surveys are helpful for collecting user feedback, and they can address such topics as:

- Workflow changes
- User interface problems
- Enhancements users would like to see in future releases

Data errors the users have noted and requests for enhancements should be documented in a repository that will serve as a source for future requirements.

As part of a system evaluation after go-live, a project review meeting should be held with all the key stakeholders and implementation players, often referred to as a "Lessons Learned" session. The group should discuss what went smoothly and where things went wrong and develop a plan that will make the implementation of future releases or software updates go more smoothly.

Once the system is live, the maintenance phase of the product life cycle begins. Maintenance of the system involves running a variety of tests to determine potential shortfalls associated with increased system or network use. Please refer to Chapter 6 which addresses maintenance.

Summary

"Test and test again" might be one way of summing up what needs to take place after a new health IT system has been implemented. Healthcare systems support workflow for a variety of clinical users and clinical specialties and may be deployed across a complex healthcare network, so testing can be complex and time consuming but is, nevertheless, essential to ensuring consistent performance that supports the delivery of safe and efficient patient care.

References

1. Usability. Definition from International Organization of Standardization. http://en.wikipedia.org/wiki/Usability.
2. European Commission. Employment, Social Affairs and Inclusion. https://ec.europa.eu/social/main.jsp?catId=1202.

Chapter 8

Privacy and Security

Learning Objectives

At the conclusion of this chapter, the reader will be able to:

- Describe the organizational policies and procedures to ensure confidentiality, privacy, security, integrity and availability of data
- Use specific procedures and tools to identify, escalate and mitigate potential privacy/security risks and breaches
- Administer user access controls according to established policies and procedures
- Audit physical, technical and administrative controls to ensure safeguards are in place to protect assets (e.g., servers secured, unattended computers, two-factor authentication)
- Identify and differentiate organizational roles (e.g., information security, physical security, compliance) responsible for managing vulnerabilities
- Maintain data management controls (e.g., data ownership, criticality, security levels, protection controls, retention and destruction requirements, access controls)

Introduction

As health information technology (health IT) becomes more prevalent across the healthcare security, ensuring the privacy and security of health data continues to be a top priority. The proliferation of health data has great potential to improve public health, but with it come controversy and concerns for patient privacy rights that are yet to be resolved. Healthcare organizations are under increasing pressure to guard against security breaches, and the advent of "bring-your-own-device – BYOD" to hospitals makes security more difficult for health IT professionals to ensure.

Given the gravity and ubiquity of health information privacy concerns, it is important for health IT professionals to understand the legal context of health data security and steps that should be taken to ensure that a provider organization's data systems are secure as well as the range of security concerns and the array of safeguards and processes that can be put in place. These may include, though are not limited to firewalls, encryption, virus and malware protection and programming.

Privacy, Confidentiality and Security

Privacy refers to the right of an individual to be left alone and to keep his or her personal information secret.

Confidentiality pertains to sharing information on a "need to know" basis. In healthcare, the patient may share personal information with the physician, but the physician must keep that information confidential.

Security refers to the use of mechanisms, tools, technologies and techniques to assure the safety of data and the systems in which it resides. Thus, if health information needs be kept secure, mechanisms must be in place to ensure that only those who need it can access. Security does not only refer to electronic information, though most recommended security

DOI: 10.4324/9780429443862-11

practices are sometimes easier to implement and monitor for electronic information, but health information also resides in paper and hybrid (paper plus electronic) formats with the same implications for security.

Before implementing an electronic health record (EHR), whether a commercial off-the-shelf (COTS) or one developed in-house, it is important to look for software glitches that may compromise security and frame policies and establish reasonable safeguards to prevent abuse and security breaches.

The famous five pillars of health information security are as follows: confidentiality, integrity, availability, accountability and nonrepudiation. The trio of confidentiality, integrity and availability are commonly referred to as the CIA of security.

Types of Security

Several security aspects need to be considered for protecting the health information and the health IT systems and include physical security, network security, application security and user security.

Physical Security

The physical security implies protection of physical assets, such as computer systems, network hardware and storage media. This aspect of security is not just protection from intruders, but also form natural disasters such as fire and floods. For this type of security, physical access to premises must be strictly controlled and each entrance equipped with appropriate security device such as identification (ID) badges or biometric scanning systems. To secure computer and operating systems (OSs), locks, backups, tracking software and stringent passwords help guard servers, desktop computers and notebook, laptop and tablet computers as well as access to information residing on them.

Network Security

The data in transient on the network should be encrypted (encoding of data so that it cannot be read without authorization). The wireless networks should use strong authentication to access. Firewalls and network intrusion detection tools should be deployed. For remote access to organizational network through public network (internet), virtual private network (VPN) technology should be employed. Ports not in use should be blocked, and services not required should be stopped.

Application Security

Application security requires an understanding of services, hardening, permissions, input validation techniques, software patches and updates and software logs.

Security hardening (keeping security patches and hot fixes updated, installing firewalls, closing certain ports, disallowing sharing among applications); correct configuring of security-related components; developing applications that can prevent, block or mitigate different forms of attacks and removing unnecessary accounts, services and features would be great ways to enhance application security. Beside these measures, printing and copying to external storages should also be disabled.

User Security

User security involves identification, authentication and authorization of users. Identification identifies the user (by username), authentication proves that user is the same who she/he claims to be (by password, token, biometric feature) and authorization implies what the user can access and do (permissions). Identity management pertain to the controls and procedures for the identification of legitimate users.

While user passwords will help keep a system secure as long as they are strong (complex), kept private and changed often, procedural or operational security assures that procedures and controls are in place to ensure secure operations.

The corporate culture should be aware of the importance of security and following the procedures to maintain that security. Regardless of other security precautions and features, security ultimately depends on the system users and their habits, practices and willingness to support the security goals of the organization. For this, the employee training should be conducted regularly.

When considering both threats to data and its protection, it is important to identify threats to network security and devise a mitigation plan before allowing data onto a network to minimize the damaging effects of the data breaches. The mitigating measures can include creating and implementing a security policy; authenticating users; using firewalls; installing antivirus software; using an intrusion protection system (IPS); encrypting communications; and auditing adherence to security policies.

The mitigating measures can include creating and implementing a security policy; authenticating users; using firewalls; installing antivirus software; using an IPS; encrypting communications; and auditing adherence to security policies.

The security policies contain provisions related to security definition for the organization, possible security concerns and ways to address them. Enforcement of the security polices implies as to how users are expected to comply with the rules listed in a policy. Policies also address user access to the network, devices, software and data; password management; email and internet use; antivirus software use; backup and recovery procedures; intrusion detection; auditing; and other security-related aspects.

Measures for Mitigating Security Threats

Authentication

Users typically input their credentials in the form of a *username* and *password*. In this case, authentication involves something that user knows. Authentication can also involve something that user has – for example, a smart card, a badge, a token or something that is a part of the human body such as fingerprint, retinal scan, palm print or voice (biometric authentication).

Combining authentication types is known as *factor* authentication. Three levels of factor authentication used to enforce security policy are: one-factor, two-factor and three-factor authentication. Common example of one-factor authentication is password and is the simplest form of authentication; a two-factor authentication requires another authentication type also such as a smart card or a fingerprint beside password or personal identification number (PIN). The three-factor authentication requires all three authentication types: a username and password combination, a smart card or badge and some kind of a biometric authentication like a fingerprint or retina scan.

Access Control

Two types of access controls are: *logical* and *physical*. Logical access control is used for managing access to data files, programs and networks. Methods for controlling logical access include access control lists (ACLs), account restrictions and authentication. The physical access controls are mechanical means to control access to systems and devices by locks, keypads and ID badges.

Four access control models are:

Discretionary access control (DAC) means that it is completely up to the owner of the objects to determine who can access them and to what extent.

Mandatory access control (MAC) is where an owner or administrator cannot decide who has what access. Access is controlled by a numeric access level. This is used in the military. For example, if a document is classified as *top secret*, only those users with clearance to top-secret documents will be able to access the document. Even if the creator of a document, or an administrator, thinks that someone without top secret clearance should have access to that document, she/he cannot give this authorization.

Role-based access control (RBAC) is access based on the role that a person plays in an organization. Access is given to a particular role in an organization and is available to all users with that role. For example, we might create a role of receptionist in a medical practice and then figure out what access to what resources a receptionist needs and assign that access to the receptionist role. Then, we would associate all the receptionists with that role, and they would now have all the access that we gave to that role. If a receptionist leaves the practice, we simply disassociate him/her from that role, and he/she now has no access.

RBAC is based on rules to allow or deny access to a resource. It is usually configured on routers as ACLs to allow or deny access to the network based on the configured rules.

Firewalls

Yet another way to mitigate security threats is implementation of a firewall on the network.

A firewall is software or hardware that blocks unauthorized to and from communication from a computer or a network. The Windows OS provides a "Windows firewall", which should be enabled to protect a home or small office desktop computer system.

A firewall works by filtering incoming and outgoing traffic based on a set of user-defined rules. It inspects each piece of inbound and outbound communication (packets) and then permits or denies that traffic from entering or leaving the system based on the configured rules. Firewalls can be configured based on the source or destination computer/network addresses or types of communication packets.

The Windows firewall and an internet service provider (ISP) router will adequately protect a home office. However, larger networks require more extensive protection through the use of a more robust firewall or multiple firewall devices.

The Windows firewall can prevent hackers or malicious software from gaining access to a computer through the internet or external network. The green shield indicates that the firewall is functioning. The firewall is set to block all connections to programs that are not on the list of allowed programs. It can also be configured to allow a program or a feature through the Windows firewall, called "punching a hole in the firewall".

Antivirus Software

Requiring all devices to have antivirus software installed is yet another way to mitigate security threats. Antivirus software detects and removes malware. It can also protect against unauthorized installations of adware and spyware on computer and network systems.

A virus is a computer program that can harm a computer and make it inoperable. Some viruses disable important OS functionality such as the ability to back up a hard disk and some even can reformat a drive or disk. Many viruses only cause annoyance by making computers/network slow or forcing computers to reboot and usually do not make copies of themselves. Removing such virus usually cleans the computer, assuming it is the only virus on the computer. However, some viruses do make copies of themselves, and if one copy of the virus is removed, the remaining copy replaces the removed virus, making it difficult to clean the system. Beside traditional viruses, other malware types include worms (do not multiply with each click like viruses) and Trojan horses (look like real software but performs ill functions, like viruses). Any antivirus software should include the three types of malware cleaning functionality.

Macro viruses usually infect Microsoft Office files and install themselves when users click Microsoft Office files. A Macro is a small program written in Visual Basic for Applications (VBA). In fact, all Microsoft Office files have the ability to have VBA code written inside them for functionality. VBA code itself isn't harmful, but if written for bad intentions can cause harm. They can also delete files and disable Windows functionality.

Finally, it is important to be aware of the risks when receiving external files and/or emails. If the sender is not known or trusted, it is best not to open files and click on the email, especially not open the email associated attachment as most malware hides inside them.

Intrusion Protection System (IPS)

In corporate or healthcare environments where security of data is paramount and cannot be compromised, employing a hardware device called IPS is advised. The IPS is similar to a firewall but provides much more protection. The IPS monitors all network traffic in real time for malicious activity. It examines every packet passing through the network and then determines if that packet has bad intent. The purpose of the IPS is to stop intrusions and then alert network administrators to the threat.

Encryption

Encryption is another mechanism used to improve security of electronic information. Encryption (encoding information to make unreadable) makes the electronic information unreadable by unauthorized viewers.

Encryption uses private and public keys to encrypt (encode) and decrypt (decode) information. In case of private key, the same key (formula or algorithm) is used to encrypt the information by the sender and to decrypt it by the receiver. In the public key, the publicly available key of the sender is used to encrypt the information, but the receiver must use his/her private key to decrypt the information. The public key thus acts as master key for encrypting the message while the receiver must use his/her private (secret) key to decrypt the information. The former is considered less secure as the private key needs to be sent to receiver over the network which can be intercepted than the public key, which need not be sent to the receiver. A typical example of encryption is password.

Most healthcare emails and text messages are now encrypted for security using the public key. The hard drives as well as the removable storages are also encrypted. Documents requiring password to read are encrypted.

Even if all of these mechanisms are established to protect an organizations' network and data, it is still necessary to ensure that users follow the rules outlined in the security policy document.

Security Audits

It is important to audit security policy practices at an organization. An audit reveals whether an organization is actually putting into practice its security policy.

For example, if nurses have been instructed to log off a nursing station when they leave the station, an auditor would observe the nurses and then record their actions. Another example is ensuring that a database server is kept up to date with critical updates. An audit report of the database servers would show when critical updates to the OS or other software were released and when applied.

Other audit aspects to consider are:

- Is all access to medical records being logged?
- Are backups being done regularly and stored according to the security policy?
- Do employees adhere to security policies?

Additional steps that organizations should take to improve the security of their assets and data include educating employees and establishing a security culture in an organization. Employees should be taught to never open unsolicited email attachments or from unfamiliar sources, lock screens while away, log off computers when leaving, never divulge the log in credentials and report any strange activity to the IT department.

Finally, only authenticated and authorized use of software should be permitted, and the applications should contain logs to record the user of the software. For example, an organization may have a customized database program that allows users to enter patient information in a database, but it was later learned that information recorded in a patient's record was not entered correctly. The software should show who entered that data and when.

Nonrepudiation

When a system proves that a user or a program performed an action beyond a reasonable doubt, this is known as nonrepudiation. Therefore, the user cannot deny having entered data in a database, removal of an item from inventory or any other action.

Password Policies

Password policies usually revolve around password complexity. A complex or strong password is usually at least eight characters in length and includes at least one uppercase character, one lowercase character, one number and one special character.

A password policy may state that passwords must be changed every 90 days and that the current password cannot be used for 365 days or that passwords never be written on paper. Hackers usually look for passwords on sticky notes on the monitor or under the keyboard. Hackers are quite aware of the myriad ways people attempt to remember their usernames and passwords, especially writing and hiding them. The only person allowed to write a generic password and store along with other company credentials in a secure place is the network administrator so that it is not forgotten and render the organization functionless.

Domain-Based Network Environment

Implementing a domain-based network environment is another good security measure. In a domain-based network, a server, called domain controller (DC) manages users, devices, software and domain policies. The DC manages all objects within its domain and enforces set access policies on network assets. Different users in an organization are provided different levels of access rights, called permissions, to view, edit, delete or create objects within a domain based on their roles and responsibilities that are monitored and enforced by DC.

Advisable Security Measures for a Domain-Based Network Environment

- Restrict the number of network or domain administrators to only those who need to perform network administration functions.
- Make sure that all servers and other devices on the network are equipped with uninterruptible power supply (UPS) and provided power-surge protection all times to protect data integrity.

GDPR, HIPAA and Risk Analysis

General Data Protection Regulation (GDPR)

Few companies rely on personal data to a greater extent than healthcare organizations (HCOs), which are already required to abide by a long list of data privacy regulations. GDPR holds import for the healthcare industry, which is no stranger to sweeping regulations.[1]

In the United States (U.S.), most of those regulations are tidily packaged in the Health Insurance Portability and Accountability Act (HIPAA). Throughout the rest of the world, prior to GDPR, it's mostly been a patchwork of different and confusingly overlapping governance frameworks cobbled together over decades.

GDPR is similar to HIPAA in that it requires tight security measures govern the use of medical technologies[2] and clinical assets. GDPR differs in its demand that data breaches be reported within 72 hours of discovery. Under HIPAA, HCOs have 60 days to report breaches. When it comes to GDPR in healthcare, a critical component of compliance is the implementation of a wholesale cybersecurity strategy,[3] complete with technological solutions that help insulate HCO networks.

The Health Insurance Portability and Accountability Act of 1996 (HIPAA)

HIPAA is a multipart act designed to help workers maintain health insurance when they move from one job to another, to protect group health insurance policyholders with preexisting conditions from being denied coverage and to improve the overall effectiveness of the U.S. healthcare system. It establishes standards for the electronic submission of claims and for protecting the privacy and security of health information.

Title I of HIPAA addresses healthcare access, portability and renewability. Title II addresses the prevention of healthcare fraud and abuse, administrative simplification and medical liability reform. This section also sets policies for privacy and security of all forms of health information and requires that national standards be set for electronic healthcare transactions and dissemination of health information.

The part of HIPAA that addresses privacy concerns is the administrative simplification which aims to make the handling of health information more efficient. Title II of HIPAA contains five rules pertaining to administrative simplification:

1. Privacy Rule
2. Transactions and Code Sets Rule
3. Security Rule
4. Unique Identifiers Rule
5. Enforcement Rule

It is important to understand that these rules complement each other. Standard codes for health information help protect the privacy of that information and enable it to be transmitted readily and securely. Unique identifiers for users of health information also protect the privacy of that information and help ensure that the right users are accessing the right information. Although complex, it is possible to format health information in a way that maximizes both its privacy and security.

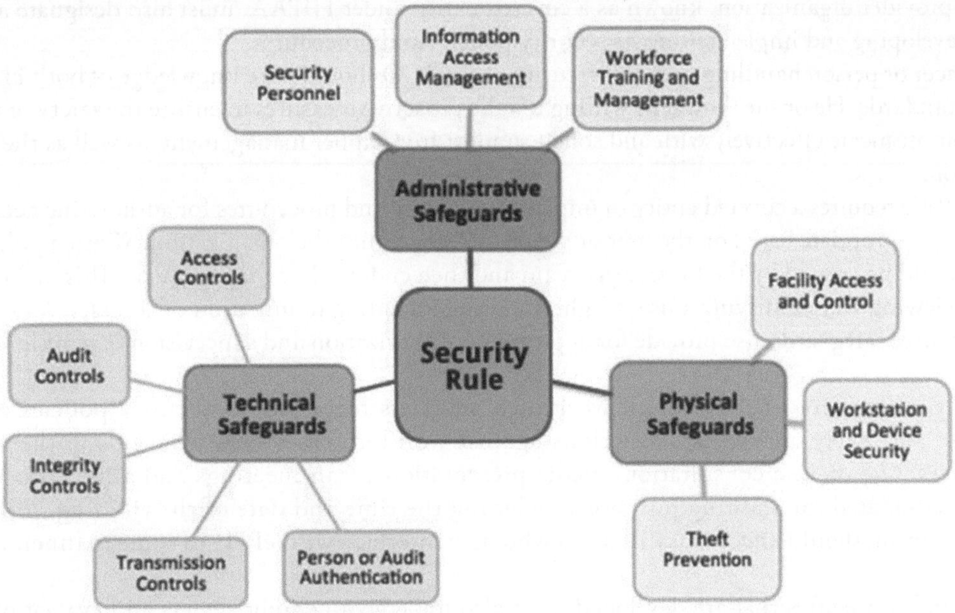

Figure 8.1 Model for healthcare entities' administrative, physical and technical safeguards.

Source: CC-BY by CAST.

As technology continues to evolve, the protection and accountability of protected health information must progress with it. Since the breach notification requirement was implemented under the Health Information Technology for Economic and Clinical Health (HITECH) Act (2009), many breaches have been reported. The revision of current acts and the enactment of new acts strive to protect patient information and make covered entities and business associates (BAs) accountable. This is a complex process of protecting patient information while technology evolves to increase quality, efficiency and effectiveness of healthcare services.

The HIPAA Privacy Rule establishes national standards to protect individuals' medical records and other personal health information and applies to health plans, healthcare clearinghouses and those healthcare providers that conduct certain healthcare transactions electronically. The Rule requires appropriate safeguards to protect the privacy of personal health information and sets limits and conditions on the uses and disclosures that may be made of such information without patient authorization. The Rule also gives patients' rights over their health information, including rights to examine and obtain a copy of their health records, and to request corrections.

The HIPAA Security Rule defines administrative, physical and technical measures that covered entities must have in place to protect electronic health information. The Rule does not require the use of any specific technology, but the intent is that organizations should be free to keep up with the rapid changes in electronic communications and security technologies. The Rule emphasizes that security is an ongoing process rather than a one-time goal. The HIPAA Security Rule seeks to reduce risks posed by, for example, unlocked doors, natural disasters, untrained employees, lack of firewalls and computer systems that are not backed up. In some states, the law may require more rigorous safeguards, and if so, covered entities must follow the state law or more stringent of the two.

Covered entities must always identify, review and modify their security measures to continue to protect electronic health information. Most healthcare entities use a combination of administrative, physical and technical safeguards, as shown in Figure 8.1.

Administrative Safeguards

Administrative safeguards address the process an organization has for administering the security of the electronic protected health information (ePHI) system. Each organization is required to identify and analyze potential risks to its ePHI, and it must implement security measures that reduce those risks and vulnerabilities to a reasonable level, usually done using a risk analysis.

Risk analysis should be an ongoing process. Regular reviews should be performed to evaluate the effectiveness of the security measures put in place, and newly identified potential risks to ePHI should be addressed in an ongoing fashion.

A healthcare provider organization, known as a covered entity under HIPAA, must also designate a security official responsible for developing and implementing its security policies and procedures.

A security officer or person handling network security at an HCO should have knowledge of both HIPAA guidelines and IT security standards. He or she should be willing to take proactive measures to ensure the safety of the ePHI system and be able to communicate effectively with and solicit support from upper management, as well as the staff at all levels of the organization.

The Security Rule requires a covered entity to implement policies and procedures for authorizing access to ePHI only when such access is appropriate based on the user or recipient's role within the organization. Written policies for granting access to ePHI should be created by the IT security team and then endorsed by management. This includes establishing, documenting, reviewing and modifying a user's right of access, including termination of access.

The administrative safeguards also provide for appropriate authorization and supervision of workforce members who work with ePHI.

A covered entity must routinely train all workforce members regarding its security policies and procedures, and it must have and apply appropriate sanctions against workforce members who violate them. Training can include newsletters, one-on-one consultation, media presentations, staff meetings and alike. This training should be adequately documented for auditing purposes, including the time and date of the training, topics covered and who attended. Training should encompass all users who may interface with ePHI in some manner, including upper management.

Any policies and procedures that are developed must also undergo a periodic review and evaluation process. Since the regulatory environment may change with new legislation or newly identified best practices, older policies may be out of date or no longer appropriate.

Additionally, onerous or poorly implemented policies may cause development of security bypassing "workarounds" from personnel that bypass critical security features. If these bypasses are used to "get the job done", then the procedures bypassed need to be restructured so that the requirements of the Security Rule remain fulfilled.

Steps for Risk Analysis

- Evaluate the likelihood and impact of potential risks to ePHI.
- Implement appropriate security measures to address the risks identified in the risk analysis.
- Document the chosen security measures and, where required, the rationale for adopting those measures.
- Maintain continuous, reasonable and appropriate security protection.

Access Policies Should Address These Questions

- Who gets access to ePHI data?
- What level of access is needed?
- Who is the agent authorizing the access?
- Is this authorization adequately documented? Is the access periodically reviewed?
- Is there a process for rescinding access once it's no longer needed?

Types of Hacking

There are many ways in which a system could be breached, allowing compromising sensitive data. Here is a list of the more common ways systems are hacked, as outlined by the Microsoft TCP/IP core networking guide:

The Insiders

An overwhelming majority of network security issues center around the organization's own workforce. Not understanding policies, laziness or disgruntlement among workers are always threats. Training employees on the hazards of mishandling sensitive data and the importance of following both legal regulations and organization's policies will help mitigate this risk.

Social Engineering

Social engineering is the process where someone is tricked into divulging information that allows an attacker to infiltrate a network. The most common attempt centers around pretending to be a network administrator needing the user's password to repair something in the system.

Brute Force

Brute force attacks are just what they imply. An evildoer identifies a server on the network – perhaps by scanning for the remote desktop port – then attempts to break into the system using the administrator account and runs specialized utilities that will try an endless number of passwords until it cracks the password.

Eavesdropping

The majority of network communications occur in an unsecured or "clear text" format. An attacker who has gained access to the network can "listen" to the traffic, called sniffing or snooping. Eavesdropping is generally the biggest security problem that administrators face in an enterprise environment. It has become more common in wireless networks being implemented by most healthcare facilities. The wireless communication traveling through the atmosphere is more prone to interception. Enabling strong encryption services on sensitive data as it traverses the wired or wireless network can mitigate this risk. While access to wired network requires more physical control measures for accessing computers, routers, wired transmission media, access to wireless network requires more logical control measures, such as requiring network ID and password.

Identity Spoofing

The hacker impersonates another device or user on a network in order to steal data, spread malware or bypass access controls. The most common forms are IP spoofing, email spoofing and Domain Name System (DNS) spoofing. Most networks and OSs use the IP address (logical address) of a computer to identify a valid entity. In certain cases, it is possible for an IP address to be false or spoofed. Try not to use IP addresses as a method of ensuring connectivity to a particular device, rather use MAC addresses (hardware address) instead.

Password-Based Attacks

Failure to use strong passwords or multifactor identification requiring more than one method of identification to authenticate to a network can lead to account compromises.

Application Layer Attacks

Application layer attacks are designed to attack the applications, focusing on specific vulnerabilities or issues, resulting in the applications not being able to deliver content to the user. Most common targets are web services and the most common attack is Denial-of-Service (DoS) attack whereby a server is bombarded with too many requests for information that it cannot function anymore and serve legitimate clients.

Breach Events

Each potential security breach must be thoroughly investigated to determine if it is intentional or not, and the HCO must immediately work to mitigate the risk and/or implement the IT contingency plan to address the event. Attempted or successful breaches of patient data are usually detectable. Table 8.1 provides some examples of the indicators the HCO must monitor.

Physical Safeguards

Physical safeguards address issues regarding facility access control, workstation use, workstation security and device and media controls. This includes limiting physical access to work facilities without impeding access to those

Table 8.1 Example of Indications of Potential Branches

Indication of Potential Breach	*Description of the Indication*
Failed user logins	Excessive number of failed logins may indicate an external break-in attempt
Crashed web server	Server crashed because a hacker found a way to bypass the security firewall
Unusual network traffic	Dramatic increase or decrease in network traffic could indicate an attempted breach
File name with odd characters	An email with a file attachment that has a file name containing odd characters may be a sign of an attempt to infect
Auditing configuration change in log	An unexpected audit log change may be a successful hacker concealing his or her tracks
Confidentiality breach	A reported confidentially breach is an incident that must be resolved
Worm-infected host	A worm is a definite breach and must be isolated and promptly resolved
Stolen laptop	A stolen laptop is a security incident that may become a breach depending on who stole it and how that person uses it
Slow internet access	Slow internet access could indicate an attempt to infiltrate or block system access
Threatening message	A threatening message may be a security or privacy breach or an attempt to send a virus
Bounced email	If all email sent to an organization is being returned, it indicates some type of incident

requiring access. This is particularly true in areas where ePHI may be present, such as work areas, server rooms and backup media storage units. These areas require an extra level of protection to limit access to authorized users only. There should be special access logging mechanism for the maintenance staff, who may require entry into these locations but are not considered routine in nature.

Additionally, keeping a reliable hardware inventory along with its value and locations is also an important safeguard to preventing theft of a system, which may contain ePHI.

Policies should also exist for the acceptable use of workstations, devices or media potentially collecting or storing ePHI. These include physically locking workstations in public areas which may store ePHI and requiring devices and EHR software to use strong passwords that are difficult to guess. For this reason, there are many recommendations to increase password strength, such as length, inclusion of upper- and lower-case letters, numbers and special characters besides changing passwords frequently and not using past 12 months' passwords. A password should not have any relevance to the person himself/herself (date of birth, license plate, family member name) and any dictionary word.

Additional restrictions to increase password security include:

- Not reusing passwords from a previous login or system.
- Encrypting all storage media containing ePHI.
- Whenever possible, the strongest methods for encryption should be used, preferably 256-bit or higher encryption.
- Backup media should be kept locked away in a secured environment with tight access controls.
- Policies should be implemented prohibiting the storage of ePHI on workstations, laptops, or any other unapproved device.
- Measures should be taken to routinely examine these devices for compliance.
- When disposing hard drives or other connected media from these devices should be rendered completely useless after being thoroughly wiped a minimum of seven times in a manner consistent with the U.S. Department of Defense DoD data destruction specifications. There are several freeware tools available for this purpose: DBAN (Darik's Boot and Nuke) being the most popular.

Technical Safeguards

HIPAA requires that sufficient measures be put into place at the technical level to guard healthcare data from all reasonable means of attack and unwanted disclosure. Technical safeguards address access controls, audit controls, integrity controls and transmission security.

The technical access control requirement mandates that "a covered entity must implement technical policies and procedures that allow only authorized persons to access electronic protected health information". From a technical perspective, there are several tools that assist administrators with administering this process.

Effective security practices embrace a layered approach to providing security to a network. That is, several different technologies are employed concurrently to protect the network instead of relying solely on one approach. That way, if an attacker finds his/her way through one layer, he/she still must overcome additional obstacles before being successful.

This would be the equivalent to adding a security alarm and watch dogs at one's home besides the deadbolt lock to dissuade intruders.

Active Directory

Active Directory (AD) is a database of the network resources (users, computers, printers, databases) and is used to assign policies, deploy software and configure access privileges for roles based on users and user groups. AD being very flexible can be used in small to large networks with few to several hundreds of objects (users, computers, printers) with the same degree of usefulness.

AD uses Lightweight Directory Access Protocol (LDAP) to manage its objects. In healthcare settings, a common example would be to use AD for an EHR system. For instance, when a new physician begins at an organization, his/her access would be partially governed by the AD group to which his/her account was assigned. When added to the physician group account with already configured privileges, he/she would inherit all parameters configured on the group account. AD makes network management easy and more secure.

Audit Control

Audit Control tracks user activity with respect to logging in, accessing resources, adding, deleting and modifying data. These user actions are logged in the system's log files and records events based on user access privileges and what is required to be logged. The common logged features include:

- Who accessed or tried to access what and when?
- What data or databases were accessed and the changes made?

All Certification Commission for Health Information Technology (CCHIT) certified EHR systems mandated by the government for Medicare and Medicaid reimbursements must support logging user access in terms of data accessed, sign-on failures and any changes to the data. In particular, CCHIT checks each EHR system for users' authentication mechanism, auditing every access to ePHI and controlling access based on the user role.

Proactive audits should be performed periodically by sampling datasets to look for possible inappropriate use or activity. Proactive audits can sample from the entire log population or from areas known to be of higher risk. For example, when reviewing access logs to patient records, it may be appropriate to intentionally sample from the population of employee patients, as well as from the patient population as a whole. Proactive auditing can serve as a deterrent to would-be hackers. Therefore, it is important that system users be aware that proactive auditing takes place.

Reactive audits are performed whenever a defined event triggers the need for an audit. An "event" might be a patient or employee complaint or a security system alarm.

It is also advisable to audit appropriate logs when unusual or extreme situations occur, such as a highly publicized accident involving victims treated at your facility, an illness of an employee known to coworkers with access to systems containing the employee's PHI, or the involuntary termination of an employee.

Electronic Controls

EHR systems must have policies, procedures and electronic controls to ensure that ePHI is not improperly altered or destroyed. This should be automatic and verifiable.

The electronic control measures may be implemented at the (a) network level through network security, (b) OS level through authentication and authorization controls or (c) patient information level through database authentication and data integrity control, but preferably a combination of all three.

Since ePHI is transmitted over networks, security measures must be in place to guard against unauthorized access to those networks and protect the data in transient.

Off-site access to ePHI poses a great risk. Although the use of off-site access can be disallowed many healthcare institutions maintain a network of outside physicians who work in collaboration with the healthcare facility and need access to patient's record remotely. However, the off-site access should be strictly controlled, and any data being transmitted from the facility site to off-site location should be adequately protected through the use of encryption and VPNs.

A VPN makes a tunnel through the public network, such as the internet, and uses encryption, authentication and authorization to protect data in transit. Common VPN connections protocols are OpenVPN, PPTP (Point-Point Tunneling Protocol), L2TP/IPSec (Layer-2 Tunneling Protocol/Internet Protocol Security), SSTP (Secure Socket Tunneling Protocol) and IKEv2 (Internet Key Exchange version 2).

By using the internet as a connection medium, VPN can adequately protect data while saving the cost of long-distance phone service and hardware costs associated with using dial-up or leased line connections.

Another tool is the virtual local area network (VLAN). This is an administrative division on network equipment to separate devices and data, such that the data cannot be intercepted by a device on a separate VLAN. Modern telephones that operate over IP networks (IP phones or VoIP phones) often are configured and managed on a separate VLAN. Additionally, non-sensitive data for appointments, internet access and general office use can be on a VLAN with less onerous controls than a VLAN with ePHI data. Lab devices that require network communication can be separated from employee workstations to reduce the risk of computer virus transmission.

Intrusion detection system (IDS), also discussed previously, is a useful tool for preventing unwanted access. An IDS is a device or application that monitors the network (or the system it is installed on) for malicious activities based on predefined patterns or policies. It reports the malicious activities to the network administrator who can intervene to control the damage. Some systems actually take it a step further by stopping the detected activities for a certain amount of time, or until the administrator intervenes. These systems are known as intrusion prevention systems (IPS). A combination of both IDS/IPS could provide a great protection to network security.

Security Baselines

It is advisable that health IT administrators create a security baseline for their servers. The security baseline is a periodic record of system parameters (like software versions and configuration details) that can be compared to determine if any vulnerabilities have been newly discovered. These lists should be updated periodically and compared against publicly known exploits and vulnerabilities.

For windows deployments, Microsoft has a tool called "Microsoft Security Baseline Analyzer – MBSA" designed for the creation of security baselines specific to the server software. MBSA determines security state by assessing missing security updates and less-secure security settings within Microsoft Windows and Windows components – Internet Explorer, IIS web server and Microsoft SQL Server, and Microsoft Office macro settings.

Database applications need additional safeguards. Be sure to research the particular database applications and remember to install all patches as recommended by your vendor.

Summary

Wherein health IT is leveraging a host of benefits in terms of health data collection, storage and processing to improve the healthcare delivery, it also brings with it the traditional data security issues. The health data both in stationary and transient forms can be accessed by hackers and unauthorized users and warrant protection and mitigation in line with the HIPAA Security Rule.

Health organizations thus should protect both the systems and the health information stored in them through the implementation of physical (access to buildings, server rooms and systems through locks, numeric keypads, ID badges), technical (strong passwords, encryption, firewalls, IDS/IPS) and administrative (policies and procedures) controls as well as procedures for mitigation of any man-made damage or natural disasters.

Healthcare organizations may consider employing a security officer to ensure that the organization complies with the HIPAA Security Rule requirements as well as other privacy and security guidelines.

References

1. Vashkover, Amir. After the Dust Has Settled: GDPR in Healthcare. https://www.cybermdx.com/blog/after-the-dust-has-settled-gdpr-in-healthcare.
2. Vashkover, Amir. How Cybersecurity Enables Medical Device Regulatory Compliance. https://blog.cybermdx.com/cybersecurity-as-a-broad-spectrum-tool-for-streamlining-medical-device-regulatory-compliance.
3. Orinski, Safi. Cybersecurity: A Key Component of the Hospital Strategic Planning Process. https://blog.cybermdx.com/blog/cybersecurity-a-key-component-of-the-hospital-strategic-planning-process.

MANAGEMENT AND LEADERSHIP

IV

Chapter 9

Management and Leadership

Learning Objectives

At the conclusion of this chapter, the reader will be able to:

- Assess the organizational environment (e.g., corporate culture, values and drivers)
- Understand components of an IT strategic plan (e.g., process maturity and growth, gap analysis, quality improvement, organizational alignment, roles and responsibilities, performance measurement)
- Gather and compile metrics to monitor and assess specific organizational performance indicators
- Monitor, assess and report on key performance indicators of systems effectiveness
- Comply with legal and regulatory standards
- Understand and comply with the organization's ethical business principles
- Prepare and deliver business communications (e.g., presentations, reports, project plans)
- Maintain awareness of emerging industry trends
- Identify and recommend strategies to mitigate organizational risk
- Maintain effective and ethical working relationships with internal and external stakeholders (e.g., clinicians, vendors, partners)
- Identify and provide data to support recommendations for decision-makers
- Understand and support organization change management processes
- Understand individual and team roles, responsibilities and job descriptions

Introduction

The list of objectives for this chapter on management and leadership has been gleaned from healthcare leaders, not only in health information technology (health IT), but also from leaders and influencers across various healthcare settings. These skills are vital to effective managers and leaders and are applicable in any healthcare setting and in any department. It is important to note that each manager and leader must find his or her own style and then find a way to make that style the most effective as it relates to these key skill areas:

Communication. Can you have those critical conversations with multiple stakeholders and get your point across using multiple formats and media?

Team building. What role will you play in not only recruiting good team members, but also training and retaining good team members?

Critical thinking. Will you not only be able to think through various situations yourself, but empower your team to think critically as well?

Project management. Can you not only guide a team, but are you able to be an effective member of a team?

Adaptability. The adage, "the only thing that stays the same is change" is no truer than it is in health IT. New technologies, mergers, acquisitions, ever-changing rules and regulations … enough said.

DOI: 10.4324/9780429443862-13

Ethics. This can be a chapter on its own, but if not on its own, ethics should be included in all chapters and especially in health IT management and leadership.

Quality assurance and performance improvement. The focus on transparency in healthcare does not exclude health IT. Are the right data available in the right format at the right time in a secure way? Lastly, as managers and leaders, we are constantly being asked to do more with less.

In short, managers and leaders may approach things tactically from different perspectives, but if you focus on the key areas listed above, the results should be the same, no matter your personal management style.

Leadership Style

The way leaders manage their responsibilities to the team is their leadership style. Some leaders are considered autocratic, some democratic, while others would be considered laissez-faire. Each style of leadership can be effective in different situations:

Autocratic or authoritarian leaders. Autocratic or authoritarian leaders make all the decisions for the team and expect the team to carry out orders as described. This style can be effective in situations where creativity is not required. For example, a leader might assign chores to each member of the team so that they can spend one hour quarterly to clean up the break room. Autocratic leadership can be difficult for experienced or creative people to work with because these team members do not feel engaged in the process if their experience and creativity are underutilized.

Laissez-faire leaders. Laissez-faire leaders are more hands off, allowing the team members to operate as they see fit. This type of leader does not give specific assignments or feedback. For example, a laissez-faire leader might assemble a team for the task of training staff on new software, checking in only to make sure that the goal is met. This type of leadership should be used only with team members who are capable and confident working independently.

Participative or democratic leaders. Participative or democratic leaders try to engage all parties and determine a mutually agreeable solution. This type of leadership is better at engaging diverse and creative teams, but the process is more time intensive. For example, a participative leader may ask the team to brainstorm solutions to a workflow problem and then work with the team to identify common steps that should be included in the new workflow. This type of leadership requires that the team participate in the decision-making process with the leader.

The Importance of Emotional Intelligence

Effective leaders and managers have high emotional intelligence. Emotional intelligence, often defined as the ability to monitor or understand one's own or other people's emotions, is a greater predictor of workplace success than is IQ. In a study by Talent Smart, a consultancy that provides emotional intelligence test and training, 90% of top workplace performers scored high in emotional intelligence, whereas only 20% of the worst workplace performers scored high in emotional intelligence.[1]

Daniel Goleman, a psychologist, author and science journalist, states that emotional intelligence has multiple components: self-awareness, social awareness or empathy, self-management or internal motivation and social skills.[2] These four competencies are explained more fully below:

- **Self-awareness.** Self-awareness relies on an individual's ability to assess his or her own emotional state as well as accurately identify and state those emotions. Self-regulation is a characteristic of self-awareness. Individuals with excellent self-awareness think before acting. Self-aware individuals are open to change, can deal with ambiguity and are trustworthy. Self-aware individuals can realistically assess their personal strengths and weaknesses.
- **Social awareness or empathy.** Social awareness is the ability to recognize and understand the emotions of others. Socially aware managers are adept at working with people and their emotions and emotional reactions. They are comfortable working with employees from many cultures. Socially aware managers also tend to be more service oriented. Empathy does not necessarily mean compassion. Understanding and accurately assessing the emotions of others is a powerful skill for managers, but it is not necessarily associated with compassionate responses.
- **Self-management or internal motivation.** Internal motivation describes a desire to achieve beyond intrinsic rewards such as money and recognition. Self-management attributes include patience, orientation toward specific

goals and creativity. Health IT managers with good self-management skills are better able to manage change. Optimism, even in difficult circumstances, as well as commitment to the organization, are self-management characteristics.

- **Social skills.** Social skills include adeptness in establishing relationships and networks. Socially skilled individuals readily find mutual areas for collaboration. Socially skilled health IT leaders are persuasive and are effective change agents. Socially skilled leaders are expert at building and leading teams.

Communication

Healthcare teams often must work to overcome the challenges of communication in the workplace. In the healthcare environment, many issues – such as communication between people with different expertise; changing demands on time and resources; and the dynamic, high-stakes environment – can interfere with effective communication.

Consider a patient who is presenting at a rural emergency department with signs of a stroke. The clinical staff are going to work quickly to assess the patient's symptoms and medical history, then perform any diagnostic tests that might be recommended. They may call on outside specialists for consultation, and those specialists will not be able to physically see the patient, so a shared language will help both parties share information quickly and efficiently. Many clinicians will be involved in executing procedures ranging from recording patient data to diagnostics and treatment plans, and the workflow for each of these processes must be executed quickly. As clinical decisions are made, they may be communicated using different language with the patient's family.

In this example, there are many types of and purposes for communication. Healthcare workers operate in an overwhelming and distracting environment. They provide increasingly complex care, with declining visit times and coordinate with a greater number of providers. They are frequently interrupted by alerts, errors, messages, pages and requests, which can lead to cognitive overload. This busy environment makes it challenging to discern which messages are most important and to make clear choices with that information.

There are many approaches to supporting effective communication in the healthcare workplace. A standard language is one method that is commonly used to prevent confusion, and this language ranges from Current Procedural Terminology (CPT) codes to medical terminology. Standard language supports communication between healthcare workers but can be difficult for patients or nonclinical staff to parse. Because clinical staff share information with so many others – from specialists and care staff to patients who usually need information translated from clinical to common terms – communication is an essential skill set for those in the clinical environment. Regardless of the use of health IT tools in the workplace, good communication remains essential for teams in the healthcare and health IT environment.

Electronic health record (EHR) systems were initially introduced to support communication of health information to different providers. However, EHR systems cannot overcome problems caused by inadequate or dysfunctional communication. Health IT can amplify problems in communication or workflow by perpetuating the use of poorly designed existing processes. Health IT should always be viewed as *supporting* communication and workflow rather than *replacing* it. The implementation of new technology will always reflect the existing communication process and workflows in its design, implementation and adoption. It is much easier to improve those processes before they have been ingrained in a technology solution, which will require a new implementation process to resolve. Health IT professionals should be particularly sensitive to the relationship between communication processes and the technology they work with.

Communication is derived from social norms and cultural cues. When technology is introduced without accommodating these factors, it can directly alter those social norms and cues, creating unexpected consequences for providers and patients. Consider this narrative from a nurse after an EHR rollout:

> We just implemented a provider order entry system, and it is not going well at all. Before computers, when the docs wanted a drug given STAT, they would tell the nurse first, then write the order. Now that they can enter in orders from anywhere, they don't talk to us anymore. The computer system does have a red flag when a stat order is entered, and our docs think that the red flag lets us know immediately about the new order. Hello … I'm taking care of patients here, not watching the computer system![3]

As the nurse's comments demonstrate, the impact of technology on social norms has a direct role in the behavior and function of teams using health IT. Members of a team should be aware of how technology might change the way their message is received, particularly in terms of timing and tone. Team members may also choose to use different media, such as a phone call in place of an email, to deliver types of messages. One of the challenges for teams that rely heavily on technology, especially virtual teams, is not to allow the technology to get in the way of their collaboration. Health IT can support or inhibit the work of healthcare teams, and health IT professionals should strive to make sure that the technology always helps.

Here is how one hospital demonstrates how data and communication of that data to the appropriate end users can improve patient care. Tan Cher Heng, Assistant Chairman Medical Board (Clinical Research and Innovation), Tan Tack Seng Hospital and Deputy Clinical Director, Centre for Healthcare Innovation, shared during the HIMSS APAC Digital Dialogue Series, Episode 2 (May 2020) the approach taken in Singapore to address COVID 19. The successes in Singapore can be directly tied back to lessons learned dealing with SARS. "Based on our experience, (it's important to share) numbers (and data) not just with leadership, but staff as well. Because staff experienced SARS, they know what to do with COVID". By capturing and sharing real-time data with care givers who relied on it for clinical decision support, "I was able to separate anyone who had not been confirmed yet (with COVID). From those who had been confirmed. This meant that they could be separated (in a COVID hospital) from patients in our general hospital".

Communication Modes

When considering what type of communication system is most appropriate for a specific message or team, communication can be broadly divided into two modes: synchronous and asynchronous. Both modes can and should be used by health IT teams, depending on the circumstances. Technology exists to support both modes of communication.

Synchronous Communication

Synchronous communication is any type of communication that occurs simultaneously for all parties. Typical examples are face-to-face conversations, phone calls and broadcast announcements. As the examples suggest, synchronous communication is always two-way communication, which relies on both parties being available for communication at the same time. Synchronous communication is important for exchanges that are meant to build interpersonal relationships, when decisions need to be made quickly or when tone may otherwise be misinterpreted, such as in negotiation.

Asynchronous Communication

Asynchronous communication is communication that occurs at different times for each party. Examples of asynchronous communication are voicemail, email and other digital records. Asynchronous communication is not limited by the availability of the parties: these messages can be read when it is convenient for the recipient. Asynchronous communication is good for communicating messages that are not urgent or that may take some time to process.

Selecting Tools for Communication

When selecting a tool for communicating, it is always best to first determine the type and urgency of the message for which the tool will be used. Technology should never be used where it is not needed, and sometimes the desire to use technology can obscure the message.

Another consideration is the audience for the message. Determining how the recipient will understand your message should direct the choice of mode. Will recipients understand the tone of your message? Will they be able to quickly understand and respond, or should you avoid putting them on the spot? Confirming an appointment can be done asynchronously, as can sharing the hospital's strategic plans for feedback, whereas passing an urgent message about a server failure to the support staff should be done synchronously. Expectation is another consideration regarding audience. If a nurse is standing at a patient's bedside waiting to hear from the pharmacist about how to manage the patient's pain, that information should not be relayed via the EHR system or another asynchronous route – it should be delivered directly to the nurse.

Finally, consider whether text-based tools should be used. Some messages can be difficult to interpret without nonverbal clues such as tone of voice and body language. However, text-based tools offer several advantages if they are used appropriately. Text-based tools often create their own record, such as notes left in an EHR, emails and other documents that might be shared. In addition, text-based communication is easy to transmit and can be more easily understood by those who do not speak English natively or who do not hear well.[4] Text-based tools can be used in combination with others as well. Some teams take meeting minutes, which can be shared with those who are absent or kept as a record. Some people follow up important phone calls with an email that summarizes the key points of the conversation to confirm and record those points.

Business Communications

It is critical for leaders and managers to possess excellent written and verbal communication skills and to have the ability to organize and manage business meetings. Organized meeting preparation helps the attendees to understand the goals and objectives of the meeting and the importance of the time invested. Well-prepared documents outline the topics and time to be spent on each issue. An example of a comprehensive meeting agenda helps to keep track of points of discussion.

A meeting agenda template for all meetings and minutes of the meeting will help meeting facilitators. Use of these tools creates a uniform method of communication that allows the staff to learn how to identify issues, actions and decisions in a consistent way.

Leaders and managers should always be prepared to present and deliver different types of business communications. Depending on what you wish to communicate, different delivery formats may be used – whether that be a presentation, report or project plan. There are many ways to deliver these; whether in a Word document, Excel spreadsheet, PowerPoint, project management tools, etc. Utilizing the most appropriate tool or program along with clear and concise communication will help your team understand the goal you have in mind.

Healthcare leaders (and other industry leaders) need to stay current with emerging industry trends. Reading trade magazines and blogs, networking with peers, earning certificates and becoming a member of an association are some of the ways managers can learn about industry trends. Staying current will not only help your organization but your team will also benefit.

Team Building

To achieve the ambitious goals of health IT programs, teams are a central operating unit. There are many definitions of a team. The *Harvard Business Review* defines a team as "a small number of people with complementary skills who are committed to a common purpose, performance, goals and approach for which they hold themselves mutually accountable".[5]

The World Health Organization (WHO) defines a team as "two or more people working interdependently towards a common goal. A team develops products that are the result of the team's collective effort and involves synergy".[6] Both definitions describe a higher level of cooperation and collaboration than a group of people who have overlapping tasks. Especially in healthcare, teams are often made of diverse people who represent different areas of expertise that come together to address complex issues ranging from chronic disease management to billing and operations of a clinic.[7]

One way to think about the operation of a team is to consider three main functions: the input, throughput and output of the team (see Figure 9.1).

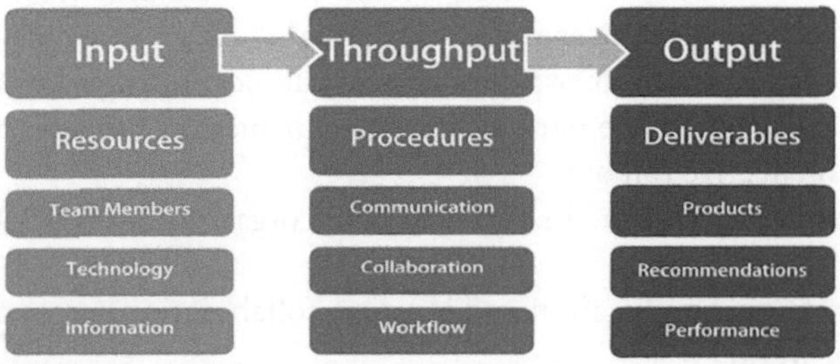

Figure 9.1 Three functions of teams.

Source: CC-BY by Sandlin Seguin/CAST.

Input

The input for a team consists of the resources available to that team, including tools, technology, information and, most important, the human resources – or team members. Recall from the definition of a team that the team members must agree to work together toward a common goal. Having a shared commitment is essential for the function of the team.[8]

In early stages of the formation of a team, it can be helpful to identify the skills each member brings to the team and the tools that are available. Several technology tools can be used to help teams work together virtually, such as through sharing documents, having virtual meetings or organizing team operations. However, technology should be applied only where there is a need; technology can be a distraction for the stated purpose of a team if not applied appropriately.

Throughput

The team's throughput describes any essential processes or procedures for the team. Throughputs can include how the team communicates, collaborates and works through problems. When possible, the team should establish procedures for key tasks such as decision-making and recurring action items. For example, in an outpatient clinic, the medical assistant knows that he or she should check a patient's vital signs and record a patient history for the physician without the specific request of the physician at each visit.

In some cases, the clinical team must be flexible and cannot rely on established workflows. For example, emergency medicine teams respond to diverse patient needs that often are unpredictable. However, they have established routes of communication and methods of collaboration that allow them to identify and manage patient care. Ensuring that the team has effective throughput is essential for effective collaboration and can greatly improve the outputs of the team.

Output

The output of a team is its deliverables. Deliverables include products, such as a computed tomography (CT) scan image; recommendations, such as a treatment plan; and performance, such as a patient physical. Especially for healthcare teams, these outputs can take a variety of shapes and forms. On health IT teams, the outputs are more commonly things like computer systems or customer support and training. The output is usually the goal or shared mission of the team.

It is tempting to think of the output as the primary purpose of the team, but without proper inputs and throughputs, the outputs of a team will not meet the team's goals. If the outputs are criticized, it is often because of issues with the input or throughput. For example, if a patient's rash is misdiagnosed by the primary care team, it may be because the team does not have specific expertise in dermatology or because team members failed to communicate with a specialist about the diagnosis.

Healthcare has always used collaborative teams to accomplish care goals for patients and organizations. During a typical outpatient visit, a patient sees the primary care team, who may consist of a medical assistant, physician and billing staff. A patient in a hospital interacts with many nurses, specialists, pharmacy staff and a hospitalist who works to coordinate the patient's care while he or she is admitted. Healthcare teams can be a way to share labor and specializations, which can help to resolve complex or large problems. It is not surprising, then, to see health IT teams that pull together the expertise and efforts of a variety of personnel.

A health IT team must operate as more than just a group with a similar goal, such as supporting users. A group's success is determined by the performance of each individual, and a team's accomplishments are measured in the shared production of those team members. Teams in health IT should share best practices, support team members in their efforts to meet their goals and seek ways to meet their shared goals.[9] As an example, an EHR implementation team should include both clinical practitioners and software, database, and network specialists. All of these specialists rely on each other to provide insight and action on the parts of the implementation process that are outside their own area of expertise, which is essential to an effective roll out.

Strong teams and teamwork offer many benefits to a healthcare organization (HCO):

- Teams break down barriers to communication and improve collaboration across departments.
- Teams improve the pace of work.
- Teams encourage commitment of team members by increasing their accountability.
- Teams make an organization more adaptable to change, both internal and external.[10]

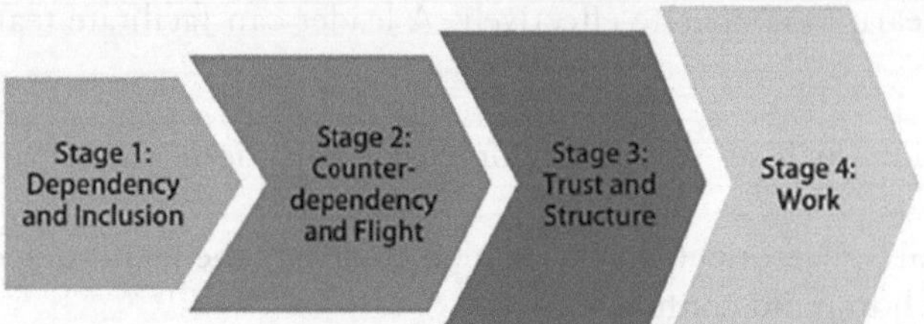

Figure 9.2 Wheelan's four stages of team development.

Source: CC-BY by Sandiln Seguln/CAST.

Wheelan Model of Team Development

One model of team development is described by Wheelan, who lays out four stages of team development (see Figure 9.2):[11]

- Stage 1 – Dependency and inclusion
- Stage 2 – Counterdependency and fight
- Stage 3 – Trust and structure
- Stage 4 – Work and productivity

Stage 1 – Dependency and Inclusion

In this stage, members rely heavily on a leader or strong team member to provide guidance and set the tone for the work. Team members are unfamiliar with the work and work environment and will follow the queues of others while working toward feeling included. Wheelan described team members who engage in pseudo-work, such as discussion of their personal lives or other topics not relevant to the team's work. Pseudo-work helps to build a sense of inclusion for team members. During this stage, team members are reluctant to challenge or express opposing viewpoints while they are still learning how the team operates.

Stage 2 – Counterdependency and Fight

Once individuals are ready to become independent of the leader, conflict can arise. At this stage, team members are willing to express opposition to team goals, procedures or processes. This conflict should be viewed as a healthy part of the development of the team because it supports trust and confidence among team members.

Stage 3 – Trust and Structure

As the team develops trust, their commitment and cooperation toward the team's goals increases. This stage shows an increase in productivity and more effective communication as roles and tasks are clarified.

Stage 4 – Work and Productivity

During this ultimate stage, the team does not need to expend energy on efforts that are not part of the team's goals. Communication patterns, processes and procedures are all determined, and conflict is minimal at this stage.

Critical Thinking

Although team development may happen naturally as groups work together, this process can be slow and may not yield the best, most efficient team. For example, if a team becomes stuck in one of the early stages of development because of a conflict, the team may never learn to cooperate effectively. A leader can facilitate team development through several approaches:

- Set clear rules for behavior, such as standards for communication, participation, contribution and conflict management.
- Start with immediate performance-oriented goals, which challenge the team to operate quickly and give the group some early success on which to build confidence.
- Give the group new challenges and information, which keeps the group engaged and can support continuous improvement.
- Spend time together as a team, which reinforces interpersonal bonds and increases commitment to the team.
- Use positive feedback, recognition and reward to provide incentives for the team to operate well and perform together.[12]

Compiling metrics to monitor and assess organization performance indicators is important to not only measure team productivity but also your team's morale. Some examples to monitoring these indicators might be the time it takes for a staff person to finish checking in a patient or finding a more productive way for a process. Staff surveys are an excellent way to measure employee morale or improve a process. Be sure to include everyone in the survey, especially those frontline workers who are involved in day-to-day operations of the organization.

What Do Health IT Customers Want?

In the healthcare arena, it is important to ask what the customer wants. Services provided by the health IT professional vary by the customer being served. Some basic commonalities exist in health IT customer needs: All customers want adequate privacy and security protections as well as on-demand EHR system and data access.

Clinical end users expect to be fully engaged in the health IT system implementation decision-making process. Consultant, vendor or other external or temporary staff must be considered, particularly if they are direct caregivers and if they provide services associated with or use data taken from the EHR.

Meetings with health IT customers may need to be scheduled and rescheduled at the clinicians' convenience. Physicians and nurses are engaged in treating patients, and that sometimes means life or death. Health IT professionals must be flexible and realize that access to clinical customers will often be impacted by unpredictable patient demands.

Hospital, clinic and physician practice administrators have their own concerns with the patient community. Health IT system implementation problems that become visible to the patient community, such as an apparently small problem in the billing process, could create havoc if they become visible to the patient. The costs of rectifying such mistakes can spiral out of control.

Health IT professionals must attend to such a complex and myriad set of customer service requests that they cannot all be presented here or even fully anticipated. However, some customers have very specific needs that relate to their responsibility or role, including:

- Physicians
- Nurses
- HCO administrators
- HCO staff
- Patients and their families

Skills for Excellent Customer Service

Customer service skills are applicable regardless of the specific responsibility, industry or type of customer served; they are transferrable to any professional endeavor. Achieving excellence in customer service requires health IT professionals to acquire a challenging combination of traits and skills, including:

- Personal traits
- Professional skills
- Customer service skills
- Follow-up skills

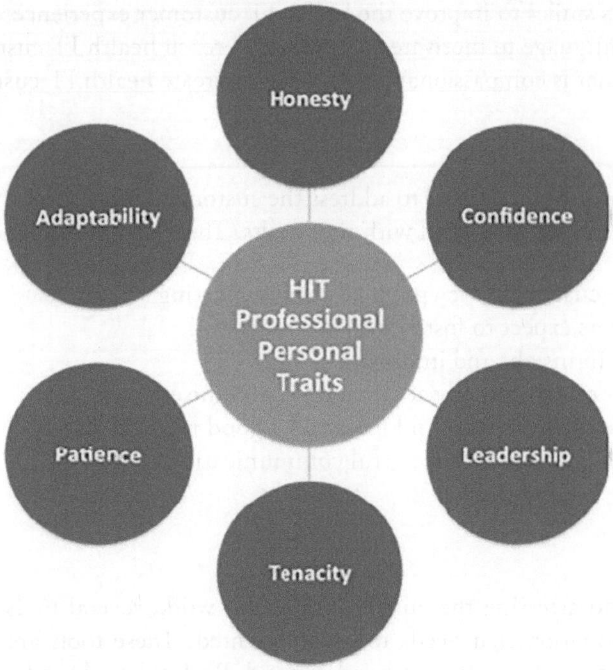

Figure 9.3 Health IT professional's personal traits.

Source: CC-BY by CAST, adapted from eyecandyinfographic.

Personal Traits

Health IT professionals must demonstrate certain personal traits essential to excellent customer service, as shown in Figure 9.3.

Reflecting the traits in Figure 9.3, some things to consider:

- Honesty demonstrates sincere concern for health IT customers.
- Confidence inspires health IT customers to accept the solutions offered.
- Leadership is demonstrated by providing new and innovative solutions.
- Tenacity is a determined focus on representing the customers' goals.
- Patience and calm response show respect to even disgruntled or confused health IT customers.

Professional Skills

Health IT professionals also need certain professional skills to succeed in their customer service efforts, including the following:

- Keeping promises so health IT customers receive up-to-date solutions.
- Gaining expertise in products and services to provide best solutions for health IT customer.
- Knowing people to genuinely connect with and influence health IT customers.
- Handling pressure with composure to demonstrate professionalism.
- Honing PC skills for quick communication with health IT customers and colleagues.
- Gaining knowledge of the business for effective collaboration and satisfied health IT customer.
- Managing time well to support superb service and avoid missed deadlines.

Customer Service Skills

Interactions with customers require that health IT professionals demonstrate customer service skills, such as:

- Listen intently to demonstrate concern for the solution that's right for the health IT customer.
- Demonstrate good communication skills to simplify interactions with health IT customer.

- Use body language such as smiles to improve the health IT customer experience.
- Speak positively and use language to motivate, persuade and reach health IT customer.
- Display positive attitude that is compassionate and caring to create health IT customer friendly atmosphere.

Follow-up Skills

Finally, health IT professionals must take actions to address the customer's issues, to bring the interaction to a successful conclusion and to ensure the customer is satisfied with the results. These actions include the following:

- Gain perspective from the customer's viewpoint to achieve a fitting solution.
- Do more than the customers expect to foster loyal customers.
- Learn from mistakes to gain insight and improve service.
- Negotiate and persuade to reach mutually acceptable compromises.
- Check on customer satisfaction to ensure and maintain a good reputation.
- Close the deal and finalize the issue for successful communication.

Project Management

When it comes to managing and assessing the quality of a team's work, several tools can be used to measure quality depending on the type of information that needs to be represented. These tools are often associated with a specific methodology, so a tool and a methodology often go hand in hand. Both the tools and methods for measuring quality on a project should be specified in the quality management plan. Two quality management tools and methodologies that pertain to quality measurement are as follows:

- Pareto principle and Pareto chart
- Root cause analysis (RCA) and Ishikawa (or fishbone) diagram

In essence, the Pareto principle (also known as the 80–20 rule) holds that the majority of quality issues can be resolved by addressing just the major causes. In other words, a small number of causes are responsible for the majority of quality issues. A Pareto chart is used to easily identify these causes, as illustrated in Figure 9.4.

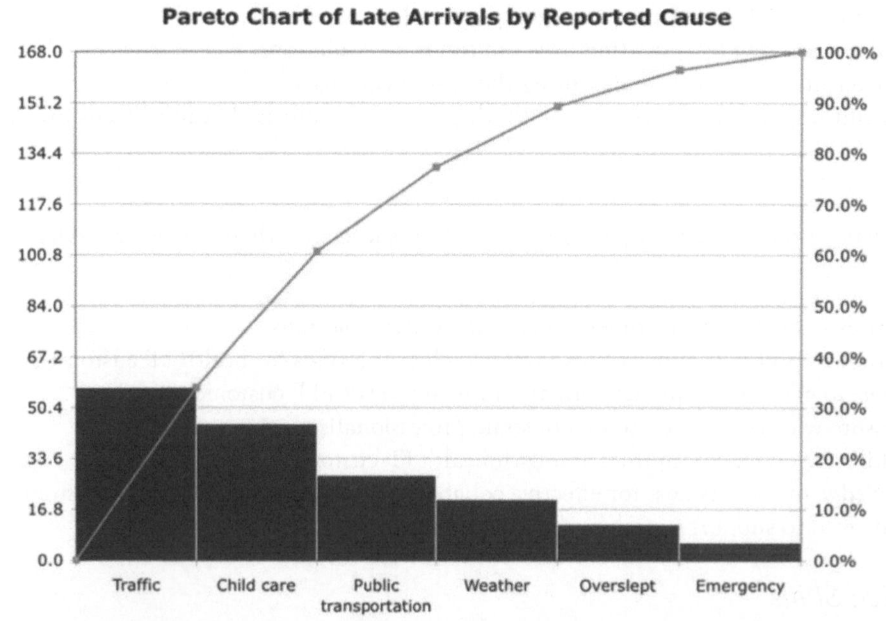

Figure 9.4 Pareto chart.

Source: CC BY-NC-SA by ONC.

Traffic and childcare together cause 60% of employee late arrivals to a particular organization. Addressing just these two causes could reduce 60% of all late arrivals. Add public transportation, and the number jumps to 80%. As shown in the figure, a Pareto chart uses bars and a line graph to display the relationships between similar chunks of data. Bars typically depict monetary value or rate of occurrence. Pareto charts make it easy to isolate the most significant causes of quality issues, which is especially useful in quality control (QC) in fixing instances of flawed products. It is important to note that the 80–20 rule behind the Pareto principle is merely a generalized way of saying that most problems result from few causes. This rule should not be taken literally and use of the Pareto principle and Pareto chart typically reveals that only a few causes can account for approximately 60–90% of problems.

RCA is a problem-solving approach that seeks to identify the root causes of problems. Once the causes of problems are identified, they are addressed through an iterative approach (continuous improvement). Applied in this way, RCA is a reactive approach because it is conducted after problems have already occurred. However, it is possible to use RCA to predict problems and therefore proactively prevent them from occurring in the first place or at least prepare a contingency plan to address them if they do occur. This tool is useful for exploring all actual or potential causes of a single problem.

Leadership and Change Management

Effective mangers and leaders are critical to healthcare and health IT. Health IT projects hinge on effective leadership. Competent management ensures that details are attended to, and problems are corrected.

One key attribute of successful health IT leaders is vision. Visionary leaders are always looking for opportunities for their organization to succeed, while at the same time realistically assessing its strong and weak points.

Leaders and managers who are entrusted with the responsibility of implementing new health IT systems often face several challenges. Cost and time restraints, as well as resistance from key stakeholders, require health IT managers and leaders to have a sophisticated set of skills.

Leaders and managers should have a thorough knowledge of change management – that is, the human side of change that entails convincing workers of the necessity for change and guiding them through the change process. A knowledge of the internal and external motivations of healthcare workers is also necessary, as is a practical knowledge of group dynamics.

Strategic Planning

IT strategic planning is a process that all types of business, including HCOs, use to optimize the use of IT infrastructure in ways that facilitate achieving long-term business goals. The process results in an organization wide understanding of how IT needs are determined; how IT initiatives are developed, prioritized and implemented; and how all stakeholders can benefit.

IT Strategic and Tactical Planning

Today, almost all businesses and organizations rely to some extent on IT to facilitate their daily operations. This is especially true of HCOs, which rely on IT for everything from storing patient EHRs, ordering supplies, scheduling patient appointments and managing room use to organizing staff schedules and staff training. Because of the pace at which IT continues to evolve and expand in its ability to meet the needs of HCOs and patients, HCOs need to develop both strategic and tactical plans to ensure their use of IT fully capitalizes on these benefits now and in the future.

Even though HCOs are in the business of helping people, they are businesses and like all businesses, they need to turn a profit or risk going out of business. Therefore, most, if not all, HCOs have a business strategy to guide and ensure their long-term success.

The purpose of the IT strategic plan is to support the business strategy. Those in charge of developing the IT strategic plan must understand how the IT infrastructure supports current business operations and must be able to predict and plan for the organization's future IT needs in a way that will help achieve the long-term business goals. In other words, the development of the IT strategic plan should be driven by the business needs of the organization rather than by the needs of its IT department.

Risk Management

A key piece of the IT planning process (or any process for that matter) integrates with the organizational efforts to manage risk. Issues of risk can be addressed along two dimensions. The first is magnitude of risk: If the event does occur, how big of an impact will it have on the organization, process or project? The second dimension is the likelihood of the risk: What is the best estimate of the likelihood that the risk event will in fact occur?

Identifying and recommending strategies to mitigate organization risk should be included in your IT strategic plan. Bringing the team together to acknowledge and accept that there are risks will help to identify risks and ways to mitigate those risks. Information is widely available on risk management and risk mitigation within a HCO.

Comparing Strategic Planning with Tactical Planning

All strategic plans are long-range plans that map out where an organization wants to be in the future, generally several-to-many years down the road. They are usually developed to achieve the organization's long-term future goals set forth in mission statements or the long-range vision of those in leadership positions. Therefore, developing a clear and well-thought-out strategic plan that is precisely defined and communicated throughout the organization is vital to the organization's future success.

As important as strategic plans are in describing where the organization wants to be in the future, they do not map out the necessary details of how to actually get there. Those details are outlined in tactical plans. Tactical plans are developed by management and staff who are responsible for knowing the current conditions, operations and factual data of their departments or areas of operational responsibility in the organization. When finished, tactical plans tend to be detailed documents containing specific information that describe daily operations, short-term projects, timelines and budgets, as well as what must be done and by whom. Usually, they extend a year or less into the future and are most commonly developed for the areas of production, marketing, personnel, finance and building facilities.

The Strategic Planning Process

The development of an IT strategic plan is a detailed and often complex process. It involves numerous key elements and contributors and detailed analyses of business and clinical operations. Professionals in the healthcare industry are stakeholders in the IT strategic planning process and must develop a general understanding of the process, how it impacts their work and how they can help facilitate its initiatives.

Industry professionals have developed a variety of methodologies and models for the IT strategic planning process. Regardless of the model used, IT strategic planning is a highly iterative process because plans are frequently revised when the factors that drive them change or when planners gain new information and insight into how to better use technology to facilitate the strategic business plan of the HCO.

This process is analogous to the way a flight crew must periodically update its flight plan while enroute to its destination to account for changing weather conditions, wind speeds and other factors that may throw it off course.[11] In a similar fashion, IT strategic plans must be revised to account for changing business conditions, the development of new and improved IT and health IT capacities and capabilities and so on. For example, an HCO that receives new funding to expand its facilities would need to update its IT strategic plan to account for the requisite increases to its IT infrastructure, health IT department staffing and budget.

Strategic plans have life cycles, often described, for example, as 3-year plans or 5-year plans. The life cycle depends in part on the level of confidence planners have in the predictions on which the plan is based. For example, they might predict significant evolution in hardware and software and only small changes in business conditions. If the planners are confident in these projections, the plan is likely to have a longer life cycle than if the projections are questionable. Because the planning process is so complex, it is often represented as a diagram showing the different phases involved and the actions to be taken in each.

Aligning IT and Business Strategic Plans

Aligning IT strategic plans with business strategic plans is a challenging but necessary endeavor HCOs must commit to in order to stay competitive in today's healthcare environment. Alignment requires a well-organized IT governance structure that can provide the level of oversight and coordination needed to ensure that the IT initiatives included in the IT strategic plan are successfully implemented to their full potential.

Although the alignment process requires a significant investment of finances and resources, this investment confers many benefits:

- Increased level of care provided to patients through advances in technology
- Improved efficiency resulting in lower costs to consumers
- Higher customer satisfaction ratings, including online rating websites such as Yelp
- Greater market share due to reputation for providing a high level of care with a comparatively low level of cost to consumers

Medium- to large-sized HCOs that forego this effort risk losing significant market share and possibly failing as a business.

The Alignment Process

The process of alignment occurs as part of the IT strategic planning process. Because the HCO's mission statement and vision serve as the basis upon which the IT strategic plan is developed, the IT strategic planning committee is responsible for establishing goals for the IT strategic plan that will ultimately serve the long-range goals of the business strategic plan. Setting these goals is the first step in the alignment process.

The next step occurs during the fit assessment phase, when the IT strategic planning committee develops a business case for each IT initiative that was developed during the needs assessment phase. The goal of each business case is to show how a proposed IT initiative will ultimately serve the future business needs of the HCO. The IT strategic planning committee must then prioritize all of the proposed IT initiatives according to which ones best fit the HCO's IT and business needs. The IT strategic plan is then developed, incorporating all of the IT initiatives that have been approved.

Once the IT strategic plan is developed, an IT governance structure must be established to oversee the implementation of the IT initiatives and projects and to monitor their effectiveness in facilitating the business strategic plan throughout the remainder of the IT life cycle.

The Prioritization Process

Prioritizing IT initiatives is a challenging but important task because HCOs, like all businesses, must be profitable to stay in business. Therefore, only the IT initiatives that have the greatest potential to facilitate the business strategic plan can be funded. As the prioritization process has been, and continues to be, carried out by HCOs around the country and throughout the world, researchers have documented several common pitfalls that can have a negative impact on the prioritization process, on the success of the IT strategic plan, and ultimately on the business success of the HCO:

- Using return on investment (ROI) as the primary driver in the prioritization process is a mistake because ROI takes time. Some IT projects may not make an ROI for a year or more but can still be significant enough to warrant approval.
- Lack of an organizational IT decision-making team can result in decisions being made without enough stakeholder input or research to ensure that the best decisions are made. In addition, the decisions may be viewed by the rank and file as having been made unilaterally, resulting in lack of cooperation in executing them.
- Lack of an IT governance structure to ensure proper use of IT throughout the HCO and proper implementation of IT projects can interfere with alignment of the IT and business strategic plans.

Establishing an IT Governance Structure

Of the three common pitfalls, the most important one to avoid is the lack of an IT governance structure. Having an IT governance structure is crucial to the alignment of an HCO's IT strategic plan with its business strategic plan. It establishes a framework for the leadership and organizational structures necessary for the alignment process to happen. It also provides clarification of the roles and responsibilities at every level of the organization so that tasks and deadlines are assigned without ambiguity.

Ethics

Ethics play a significant role in healthcare decision-making and can guide healthcare workers in making decisions for which there is no codified law.

How do ethics differ from codified law? Codified law represents the statutes or legal code adopted by a state or nation, such as the U.S. Code. With codified law, values and appropriate behaviors are written into the legal system and can be enforced through the court system. As such, appropriate behavior is prescribed by law. Ethical standards, on the other hand, are not codified and people sometimes confuse ethical behavior with legal behavior.

An ethical dilemma is a decision in which each alternative has some undesirable consequence, and right or wrong cannot be clearly identified.

The Hippocratic Oath – an oath historically taken by physicians and other healthcare professionals – implies that healthcare professionals will make choices that benefit patients and will protect others from harm. However, medical care decisions often represent a conflict between what the health professional considers is in the best interest of the patient and respect for the patient's wishes.

Care decisions can also involve a conflict between the needs of the individual and the organization or between the organization and society. For instance, a hospital's decision to move to another area may be beneficial to the hospital's profitability, but it may have negative consequences for access to care and the economic well-being of the community.

Ethics and Health IT Professionals

The general standards of ethical behavior and professionalism that apply to healthcare providers such as doctors and nurses also apply to health IT professionals. They are expected to adhere to ethical standards, set by professional organizations and based on a core set of ethical principles, as well as to meet the legal requirements of their profession set forth by federal, state and local governments.

What Is Professionalism?

Professionalism refers to behaving in accordance with generally accepted standards of appropriate conduct within a specific profession. For health IT professionals working with healthcare data systems, professionalism includes staying current with technological changes that affect how systems are used in healthcare. An example of professionalism in health informatics is becoming familiar with the ideas expressed in the ethical codes written by health informatics organizations. Another example is taking continuing education classes to maintain the skills necessary to perform work-related duties.

Sources of Ethics Standards

As in other healthcare fields, the ethical and professional standards of the health IT profession come from a variety of sources (see Figure 9.5).

Figure 9.5 Sources of ethical and professional standards.

Source: CC-BY by Vivian Todhunter/CAST.

Professional organizations. Major sources of standards are the codes of ethics written by health IT professional societies such as the following:

- **International Medical Informatics Association (IMIA).** This organization serves as a bridge organization to bring together other organizations that support the improvement of healthcare, bioscience and medicine worldwide through the application of information science.
- **American Health Information Management Association (AHIMA).** Members of this organization are involved with the management of health information, generally with clinical or public health data systems.
- **World Medical Association (WMA).** The WMA provides a forum for its member associations to communicate freely, to co-operate actively, to achieve consensus on high standards of medical ethics and professional competence and to promote the professional freedom of physicians worldwide.
- **American Medical Informatics Association (AMIA).** This organization includes informatics professionals who are involved with the science of informatics as applied to biomedicine and health.
- **Healthcare Information and Management Systems Society (HIMSS).** HIMSS is a global advisor, thought leader and member association committed to transforming the health ecosystem. As a mission-driven non-profit organization, HIMSS offers a unique depth and breadth of expertise in health innovation, public policy, workforce development, research and analytics to advise leaders, stakeholders and influencers from across the ecosystem on best practices.

In addition, the Project Management Institute (PMI) serves practitioners and organizations with standards that describe good practices, globally recognized credentials that certify project management expertise and resources for professional development, networking and community.

CEOM. The European Council of Medical Orders (CEOM) brings together the Medical Councils and the independent medical regulatory authorities of European Union Member States and the European Free Trade Association responsible for either ethics and professional conduct, registration or licensing procedures, disciplinary matters regarding physicians, recognition of qualifications and levels of specialty, authorization to practice and setting of professional standards.[13]

Federal agencies. In the United States (U.S.), divisions of the federal government such as the Office of the National Coordinator for Health Information Technology (ONC) are also sources of ethical guidelines and professional standards.

Laws. A back-and-forth interaction takes place between the ethical ideals, professional standards and legal requirements that apply to health IT professionals. In the U.S., the privacy and security rules of the Health Insurance Portability and Accountability Act (HIPAA) are part of a law but are also important sources of professional standards. The Health Information Technology for Economic and Clinical Health Act (HITECH) widens the scope of privacy and security protections available under HIPAA and increases the potential legal liability for noncompliance.

In addition, local, state and federal laws set standards that may overlap, exceed or even conflict with ethical duties.

Four Ethical Duties of Health Informatics Professionals

The various professional organizations that set standards for how health informatics professionals perform their work have generated ethical standards, or duties, that can be summarized into four general categories. Although specific to health informatics professionals, the ethical duties apply equally well to other health IT professionals. The four ethical duties of health informatics professionals are to:

1. Represent credentials accurately
2. Protect patient privacy, including the related ideas of confidentiality and security
3. Respect patients, employers and coworkers
4. Respond to unethical practices by others

Duties Owed to Patients

The duties of a health informatics professional to patients are based on the same four core ethical principles that apply to all healthcare professionals: respect for autonomy, beneficence, non-maleficence and justice. As stated in the IMIA code of ethics, the four general principles are defined as follows[14]:

- The principle of autonomy implies that all people have a fundamental right to self-determination. In the healthcare setting, respect for autonomy means that healthcare professionals must recognize that patients have the right to make their own treatment decisions based on their individual preferences and beliefs.
- The principle of beneficence means that all people have a duty to advance the good of others as long as the nature of that good is in keeping with ethically defensible values. This principle simply means that healthcare providers should do things that benefit the patient. This includes both actions meant to prevent problems and actions to address problems the patient is already experiencing.
- The principle of non-maleficence is the principle that all people have a duty to prevent harm to others insofar as they can do so without undue harm to themselves. Non-maleficence is the expectation that healthcare professionals will not intentionally injure a patient. Medical students learn the famous saying that doctors should "first, do no harm".
- The principle of justice is that all people are equal and have a right to be treated accordingly. Distributive justice is the idea that if resources are scarce, they will be allocated in a fair manner. How distributive justice should be implemented is controversial in our society.

The IMIA code of ethics says that patients have the right to know about the existence of electronic records containing their personal medical data. It says informatics professionals should not mislead patients about how these data are used. They should truthfully answer all patient questions about their rights to review and revise their own medical data. In addition, informatics professionals should be helpful when a patient wishes to exercise those rights.

Informatics professionals should ensure that medical data are maintained in a secure, reliable, manner. Further, the code says that medical data should never be used for purposes "outside the stated purposes, goals or intents of the organization responsible for these data". In addition, the data of all patients should be treated with equal care, respect and fairness.

Duties Owed to Employers

According to the IMIA code of ethics, among the general duties that informatics professionals owe to their employers are competence, diligence, integrity and loyalty. In addition, health informatics professionals must ensure that all processes are performed to the highest possible standards and that all requirements and standards regarding security are met. The code also says that informatics professionals should have systems for reviewing their processes and practices to make sure they are current and effective.

Duties Owed to Coworkers

In many workplaces, informatics professionals work with doctors, nurses and other healthcare providers who are their coworkers, not their employers. According to the IMIA code of ethics, healthcare providers have a right to depend on the technological skills of health informatics professionals to help them meet their own professional obligations to patients. Therefore, informatics professionals have an ethical duty to assist healthcare providers "insofar as this is compatible with the [health informatics professionals'] primary duty towards the subjects of the electronic records".

Responding to Unethical Practices

According to the IMIA and AHIMA codes of ethics, it is not enough to simply refrain from unethical behavior. Health informatics professionals have ethical duties to discourage others from unethical behavior, to correct ethical problems when they occur and to expose the unethical practices of others.

Whistleblowers

People who report unethical or illegal practices are sometimes called whistleblowers. The obligation to report unethical practices can result in some challenging situations. The duty to report a coworker's unethical behavior can result in mental or emotional conflicts about difficult issues such as loyalty. Many laws provide protection for people who report unethical practices.

Conflicts of Interest

Another aspect of professionalism is to avoid or report conflicts of interest, circumstances creating a risk that professional judgment or actions regarding a primary interest will be unduly influenced by a secondary interest or motivation. Primary duties include ethical and legal requirements, such as the obligation to keep patient information private. Secondary motivations are personal interests such as the opportunity for financial gain.

Quality Assurance and Performance Improvement

A critical relationship exists between healthcare quality and health IT in advancing the quality of healthcare. Quality standards and performance measures can be applied to health information systems to both assess and improve health quality. Health IT professionals can help establish, monitor and report performance measures and key performance indicators.

Regardless of the size of the HCO, IT systems will be in place and key performance indicators are important in measuring the systems effectiveness. Performance indicators are a popular mechanism for measuring the quality of healthcare to facilitate both quality improvement and systems management.

Healthcare Quality Challenges

Given its size and complexity, the U.S. healthcare system will always be in need of continuous monitoring and improvement. The Agency for Healthcare Research and Quality (AHRQ) is a public health agency responsible for providing evidence that will improve the nation's healthcare system. AHRQ produces annual reports on the current state of healthcare quality and disparities.

In its 2013 National Healthcare Quality Report[15] and the companion 2013 National Healthcare Disparities Report,[16] AHRQ noted that even though there has been progress in improving healthcare quality, many Americans are not regularly receiving the care they need when they need it, and many others are receiving poor-quality care. Further, health services vary widely across populations around the country (Figure 9.6).

Figure 9.6 Quality standards.

Source: This image is by CAST with edited images: © phipatbig/Shutterstock.com, vichie81/Shytterstock.com and Anastasia B/Shutterstock.com, used with permission.

Defining Quality Healthcare

Defining quality healthcare depends to some extent on the point of view. Broadly speaking there are four entities that define quality healthcare:

- **Healthcare providers** typically view quality healthcare as "the application of evidence-based professional knowledge to the needs of individual patients".[16]
- **Patients and families** often view quality healthcare in terms of provider service, such as how the provider interacts with them and how easy (or difficult) it is to see the provider, in addition to whether the provider resolved the health issue.
- **Payers** tend to "value patient satisfaction and use of preventive services rather than focus on clinical outcomes of the patient".[16]
- **Professional and regulatory bodies** set standards and define quality healthcare in terms of how well providers meet those standards.

To assess healthcare quality, performance must be measured against established standards. Of the four entities that define quality healthcare, it is largely the professional and regulatory bodies that set such standards and measure performance. The combined efforts of these bodies help to define and establish consensus on quality improvement issues.[16]

Two of these bodies are AHRQ and the National Committee for Quality Assurance (NCQA).

Quality Improvement and Health IT

Various aspects of the quality of healthcare need to be improved. Consider the number of deaths that occur from medical errors. Studies published between 2008 and 2011 suggest that between 210,000 and 400,000 premature deaths per year occur because of preventable medical errors.[17]

Deaths from medical errors and other healthcare quality issues have long been a problem, and the Institute of Medicine (IOM), in its 2001 publication *Crossing the Quality Chasm: A New Health System for the 21st Century*,[18] outlined the following six aims for healthcare quality improvement to ensure that the nation's health system is:

- **Safe.** Avoiding injuries to patients from the care that is intended to help them
- **Effective.** Providing services based on scientific knowledge to all who could benefit and refraining from providing services to those not likely to benefit
- **Patient-centered.** Providing care that is respectful of and responsive to individual patient preferences, needs and values and ensuring that patient values guide all clinical decisions
- **Timely.** Reducing waits and sometimes harmful delays for both those who receive and those who give care
- **Efficient.** Avoiding waste, including waste of equipment, supplies, ideas and energy
- **Equitable.** Providing care that does not vary in quality because of personal characteristics such as gender, ethnicity, geographic locations and socioeconomic status

Improving the quality of healthcare will improve the overall health of the nation.

Managing Quality in Health IT

Healthcare quality is often defined differently according to one's perspective. With regard to measuring quality in a generic sense, quality is "the suitability of procedures, processes and systems in relation to the strategic objectives".[19] Managing quality is an "ongoing process of building and sustaining relationships by assessing, anticipating and fulfilling stated and implied needs".[19] Managing quality typically involves quality assurance (QA) and quality control(QC), as well as supporting methodologies and documentation tools.

Quality Assurance and Quality Control

The difference between QA[20] and QC[20] is one of process versus product. QA activities are aimed at making sure that the process achieves target objectives during the development and maintenance cycles.

QC activities entail the evaluation of a developed product. These two aspects of quality management are interrelated and should always be carried out in tandem.

An effective QA plan contains both the broad and detailed views of a process and outlines a systematic approach to developing and maintaining the product to meet target objectives. An effective QC plan specifies the products or services to be evaluated as well as how these evaluations will be conducted, including which specific tools will be used. A QC plan might evaluate final goods, intermediate work in progress and/or services.[20]

The ultimate product in healthcare is the health and well-being of patients and all healthcare processes are aimed at promoting that product. Implementing an emergency department workflow that reduces patient wait time is an example of QA in healthcare. Evaluating patient outcomes in an emergency department is an example of QC.

Quality Management and Total Quality Management (TQM)

QA and QC together comprise quality management. These activities entail both planning and improvement. QA and QC activities must be planned in advance in order to be effective. The point of quality management is to develop and maintain the best product possible. When product evaluation reveals less than optimal results, the product and processes that support it must be improved. All the above activities together characterize the essence of quality management.

It might seem obvious that quality management necessarily involves the workers, managers, culture and work environment at an organization. However, quality management programs had come to be seen as lacking strategies for optimizing the "people side" of organizations. TQM programs emerged to address organizational human factors more specifically. TQM can be thought of as quality management plus strategies to optimize the buy-in and participation of an organization's members. The goal of TQM is to maximize customer satisfaction to promote the long-term success of the organization. "If properly implemented, TQM benefits all members of the organization and society in general".[21]

Table 9.1 shows the key elements of TQM. Pay particular attention to how TQM enhances quality management activities.[21]

Table 9.1 Elements of TQM

Key Elements of TQM	*Quality Management Activities That Need to Be Improved*	*How TQM Enhances Quality Management Activities*
Customer focus	Quality management often omits key players when no direct correlation exists between them and the developed product	TQM expands who is regarded as a customer to include suppliers, partners and coworkers
Planning process	Quality management often focuses only on processes that directly support the development and maintenance of products	TQM holds that all processes must be planned and diagrammed before they can be managed and improved
Process management	Quality management often focuses only on processes that directly support the development and maintenance of products	TQM requires that key all processes be monitored and managed
Process improvement	Regarding a specific project, quality management has the tendency to move on after implementing an improvement rather than continuing to look for ways to implement additional improvements	TQM pays constant attention to quality improvement processes to ensure they are continuously improved
Total participation	Quality management often fails to consider organizational buy-in by focusing only on the employees who have a direct connection to a particular product	Under TQM, buy-in from the entire company or organization – from top to bottom – is essential

Creating a Quality Culture

Fully implementing TQM strategies is crucial in creating a quality culture. Likewise, quality experts agree that a quality culture is necessary for TQM to be successfully implemented in an organization.[22] A quality culture is one in which everyone in the organization is committed to achieving and maintaining defined quality standards. Such a culture promotes a positive work environment and pays attention to both workers' and customers' needs. A quality culture balances continuous improvement with workplace ethics.

Successfully creating a quality culture requires an understanding of various components of the organization's culture. Consider the following questions[22]:

From an organizational perspective:

- Does the organization have a change-oriented culture or a change-averse culture?
- What are the organization's core values and mission? Are trust and integrity among the core values?
- Does the organization have a set of unwritten rules (typically enforced by peer pressure) about how things are done?
- If unwritten rules exist, how are they communicated to new employees?
- How does the organization generally communicate its culture, both internally and externally?

From an individualized perspective:

- Who, if any, are the cultural role models in the organization?
- Who actually models the organization's values? This person could be anyone from the chief executive officer down to an entry-level worker.

The answers to these questions provide a good picture of the key components that make up the organization's culture and may well determine the extent to which a quality culture can be supported, as is seen in Figure 9.7.

Health IT professionals can support a quality culture by providing the right information to users in the right time, in the right amount and in the right place. This requires the IT professional to:

- **Provide the right information to users at the right time.** For example, displaying drug alerts at time of order entry is far more efficient than reordering a different prescription upon realizing that the initial prescription will not work for the patient.[23]
- **Provide the right amount of right information to users.** Overuse of system alerts and reminders directly results in alert fatigue. For example, it is not necessary for the chief of cardiology to receive a common drug interaction alert every time he or she opens a patient's EHR. User identification can be used to assign certain messages to certain individuals at certain times. Displaying a common drug interaction alert to the chief of cardiology once might be sufficient, whereas a medical student might need the frequent display of all messages.[23]
- **Provide the right information to users in the right place.** For example, it is more efficient for emergency department staff to be able to view patient status updates in real time from a device anywhere in the emergency department as opposed to the staff having to constantly go to a single room to get this information.

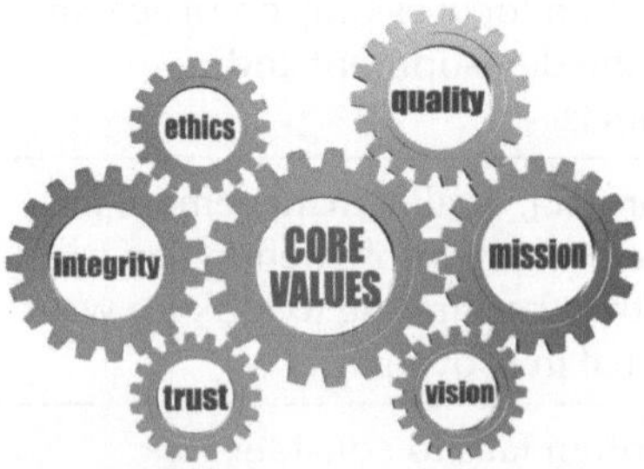

Figure 9.7 Elements of a quality culture.

Source: © marinini/Shutterstock.com, used with permission.

Creating a Quality Management Plan

A useful technique that helps achieve quality on projects is to create a quality management plan. The role of a quality management plan is to outline the activities necessary to deliver and maintain products that meet or exceed customer expectations. The activities outlined in this plan are derived from quality standards defined by the organization.

Regulatory and safety compliance are crucial in achieving quality healthcare. A quality management plan could include a review of the organization's policies and procedures to ensure such compliance. It is much easier to create a compliant system from the outset than it is to rebuild it after it is in operation. For example, "if a procedure states that a certain checklist is used, the system needs to provide that checklist or at least point to where it can be found as part of the system checks and alerts".[24]

An effective quality management plan provides a detailed focus on both project deliverables and processes. This focus helps to ensure that:

- Products meet defined standards.
- Best practices are regularly followed.
- Techniques for identifying ineffective processes and products are implemented.
- QA procedures promote continuous improvement.[24]

A quality management plan must contain clearly defined, high-level objectives. These objectives should be informed by the customer and directly related to a specific project.

The objectives must appear near the beginning of the plan.

After the objectives are outlined, the quality management plan should outline the QC activities, including:

- The products that will be evaluated
- How well the organization's quality standards were followed
- The tools and methods used to measure quality
- The duration and frequency of the quality evaluation activities[24]

A best practice is to document these items in a table or spreadsheet because they are the main focus of the project management plan's QC section.

Another table or spreadsheet can be used to outline the QA activities following the QC section of the quality management plan. These activities assess the effectiveness of processes and workflows in achieving planned outcomes. Such a table or spreadsheet can be used to outline the following:

- The processes that will be evaluated
- The quality standards for the processes
- The tools and methods used to measure how well the processes were correctly performed
- The duration and frequency of the quality measurement activities

Improvement itself focuses on revising process – the series of actions or steps that transform inputs to outputs. Most processes are revised by teams, called performance improvement teams (PITs), established to address a specific process (or issue) ... (effective) PITs follow some form of the Shewhart Cycle of Plan Do Check Act (PDCA). PITs should be made of a team that represents multiple stakeholders within the organization. They approach process revisions by carefully studying the problem or situation with a deliberate effort to identify the most effective solution (plan) then develop an idea or action plan (do) (Figure 9.8). They then test or trial the plan (check) and once approved by the team implement (act).[25]

The PDCA process model is often used as part of Lean. Lean tools are used at all levels of an organization in different ways. One example of a Lean tool that follows the PDCA model is demonstrated below in Figure 9.9.

Lean has been increasingly deployed in healthcare because it focuses on standardizing work, reducing waste, improving quality and solving problems permanently. Lean is derived from the Toyota Production System (TPS), which instilled a strong process in automotive production. As healthcare faces the heightened demands to move from volume- to value-based care, more focus is being placed on the need to generate value at all levels of the organization. Learning Lean is an entire course of its own. Understanding the focus of and the philosophies behind Lean as well as the processes, is a skill

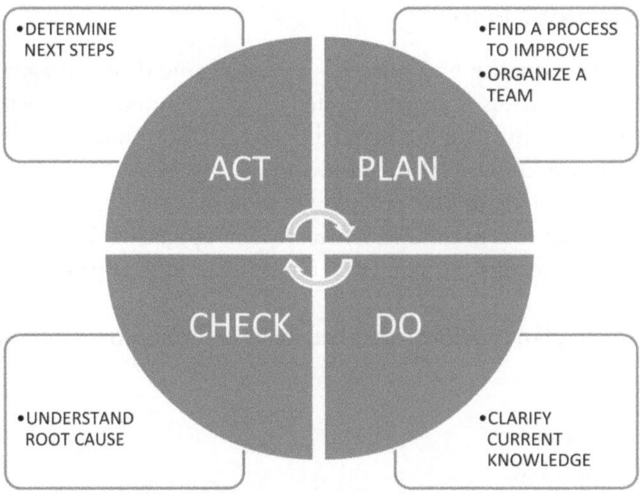

Figure 9.8 The Deming Cycle of Management Methodology: Plan Do Check Act (PDCA) (Courtesy of Wil Limp, Member, HIMSS Emerging Healthcare Leaders Task Force (2020)).

that all health IT managers and leaders must be aware of.[26] The two core concepts of Lean Leadership are: continuous improvement and respect for all people.

Key Quality Management Standards: International Organization for Standardization (ISO) 9000

As is the case with quality management tools, different standards can be applied for quality management. ISO 9000 is just one, but any chosen quality standards should be spelled out in a quality management plan.

ISO 9000 is a group of standards developed and maintained by ISO that reflects many TQM concepts. It is administered by various other certification and accreditation groups.

Plan the Improvement – Set goal for future state. Example: 100 million vaccines in 100 days			
Do the improvement – Action items, data collection Example: Increase production of vaccine			
#	Change Idea (s) / Action Items	Measure(s) /Outcomes / Data Collection	
1	increase staffing	trained staff increase 30%	
2	production increase 25%	doses per day production	
3			
4			
5			
Check the results. Team members should review data and evaluate action plans			
Target	baseline (start)	1 month	2 months
100 FTE	70 FTE	90 FTE	90 FTE
100K per day	75K per day	90K per day	110K per day
Act and Determine Next Steps			
Was goal met?			NO: What changes can be made to action plan(s). What is the impact?
Was goal met?	Yes: Evaluate why successful. How will it be maintaned?		

Figure 9.9 A depiction of PDCA. (Courtesy of Wil Limp, Member, HIMSS Emerging Healthcare Leaders Task Force).

The 2008 version of ISO 9000 added the following guidelines:

- Monitor processes for effectiveness.
- Keep adequate records.
- Correct any found defects, if possible.
- Regularly review the quality system itself for effectiveness.
- Implement continuous improvement.[27]

The latest version of ISO 9000 also borrows the following key principles from TQM:

- Customer focus
- Leadership
- Involvement of people
- Process approach
- System approach
- Continual improvement
- Factual approach
- Mutually beneficial supplier relationships[28]

To be designated as an ISO 9000 organization, an organization must comply with the following standards and achieve certification:

- Develop a quality manual
- Document procedures
- Exhibit evidence of management commitment
- Ensure that customer requirements are met
- Allow periodic accredited registrar audits
- Conduct internal audits

ISO 9000 standards aim to establish and monitor product development and maintenance processes. They outline how managers can effectively communicate their commitment to quality standards and how organizations can provide resources to support the sustained implementation of the standards. Quality must be monitored from the initial concept through the final implementation of all products and processes. Importantly, ISO 9000 also instructs organizations on how to best leverage data in their quality management plans. These focus areas of ISO 9000 are represented in Figure 9.10.

Figure 9.10 Focus areas of ISO 9000.

Source: CC-BY by Travis Nimmo.

Despite the similarities, it is important to note that ISO 9000 and TQM are two different things, though they should not be seen as competing methodologies. They are not interchangeable, though ISO 9000 can be thought of as a subset of TQM. ISO 9000 is often implemented in situations that are not necessarily appropriate for TQM. For example, small-scale initiatives or traditional organizations can effectively apply ISO 9000 without needing the full TQM package with its emphasis on the entire enterprise and the people side of the organization. On the flip side, ISO 9000 would likely be redundant in an organization that is experienced in effectively implementing TQM.

Effectively managing quality is greatly facilitated through the use of specific tools, methods and standards. Whichever tools, methods and standards are applied, they should all be identified in a quality management plan that can be used to support a quality culture in which all employees are committed to achieving a high level of quality.

Summary

As in many industries, the desire to provide excellent customer service is a driving factor in the healthcare sector. The end user should be kept at the center of all improvement initiatives. Do we improve quality, do we minimize risk or do we help reduce costs? These are at the heart of health IT decisions. Naturally, the primary customer is the patient, but as the importance of electronic data continues to grow throughout HCO and across organizations, few healthcare professionals are going to be expected to deliver good customer service to more customers than health IT managers and staff members.

Consequently, whether or not a department is presently undertaking a health IT implementation project, or are involved with some form of system upgrade or taking part in a merger, managers must be fully versed in the use and leadership of teams, the importance of monitoring quality of service on an ongoing basis and how to work continually to ensure that health IT departments are meeting the needs and desires of the full range of health IT customers which includes patients and their families, providers, nursing, administration, ancillary staff, external healthcare professionals for continuity of care as well as the general public.

Among the skills critical to this effort are communication, team building, critical thinking, project management, adaptability, ethical leadership and QA and performance improvement.

References

1. Bradberry, T. (2014). Emotional Intelligence—EQ. www.forbes.com/sites/ travisbradberry/2014/01/09/emotional-intelligence/ (accessed 10 December 2014).
2. Goleman, D. (2000). *Emotional Intelligence and Social Intelligence: The New Science of Human Relationships*. New York, NY: Bantam Books.
3. Health IT Workforce Curriculum, Version 3.0. (2012). Component 12, Quality Improvement. Unit 7b, HIT Design to Support Teamwork and Communication. This material, Comp12_Unit7b, was developed by Johns Hopkins University, funded by the Department of Health and Human Services, Office of the National Coordinator for Health Information Technology under Award Number IU24OC000013. www.onc-ntdc.info/units/12.
4. Ibid.
5. Katzenbach, J. R., & Smith, D. K. (2005). The discipline of teams. *Harvard Business Review*. http://hbr.org/2005/07/the-discipline-of-teams/ar/1.
6. Salas, I. (2007). *Team Building*. World Health Organization. www.who.int/cancer/ modules/Team%20building.pdf.
7. Health IT Workforce Curriculum, Version 3.0. (2012). *Component 17, Working in Teams. Unit 1a, Health IT Teams: Examples and Characteristics*. This material, Comp17_Unit1a, was developed by Johns Hopkins University, funded by the Department of Health and Human Services, Office of the National Coordinator for Health Information Technology under Award Number IU24OC000013. www. onc-ntdc.info/units/17.
8. Health IT Workforce Curriculum, Version 3.0. (2012). *Component 16, Professionalism and Customer Service in the Healthcare Environment. Unit 6a, Teams and Small Groups*. This material, Comp16_Unit6a, was developed by The University of Alabama at Birmingham, funded by the Department of Health and Human Services, Office of the National Coordinator for Health Information Technology under Award Number IU24OC000023. www.onc-ntdc.info/units/17.
9. Ibid.
10. Ibid.
11. Wheelan's Four Stages of Team Development. http://en.wikipedia.org/wiki/ Group_development.

12. Health IT Workforce Curriculum, Version 3.0. (2012). *Component 16, Professionalism and Customer Service in the Healthcare Environment. Unit 6b, Managing Teams.* This material, Comp16_Unit6b, was developed by The University of Alabama at Birmingham, funded by the Department of Health and Human Services, Office of the National Coordinator for Health Information Technology under Award Number IU24OC000023. www.onc-ntdc.info/units/16.
13. European Council of Medical Orders. http://www.ceom-ecmo.eu/en/home.
14. International Medical Informatics Association. (2011). The IMIA Code of Ethics for Health Information Professionals. www.imia-medinfo.org/new2/node/39.
15. Agency for Healthcare Research and Quality (AHRQ). (2012). National Healthcare Quality Report (Publication No. 13-0002). www.ahrq.gov/research/findings/ nhqrdr/nhqr12/ (accessed 10 December 2014).
16. Agency for Healthcare Research and Quality (AHRQ). (2012). National Healthcare Disparities Report (Publication No. 13-0003). http://nhqrnet.ahrq.gov/inhqrdr/ reports/nhdr (accessed 12 December 2014).
17. James, J. T. (2013). A new, evidence-based estimate of patient harms associated with hospital care. *J Patient Safety,* 9(3), 122–128.
18. Institute of Medicine, Committee on Quality of Health Care in America. (2001). *Crossing the Quality Chasm: A New Health System for the 21st Century.* Washington, DC: The National Academies Press.
19. Health IT Workforce Curriculum, Version 3.0. (2012). Component 19, Quality Management. Unit 10a, Measuring Quality. This material, Comp 19_Unit 10a, was developed by Johns Hopkins University, funded by the Department of Health and Human Services, Office of the National Coordinator for Health Information Technology under Award Number IU24OC000013. www.onc-ntdc.info/units/18.
20. Ibid.
21. Ibid.
22. Ibid.
23. Ibid.
24. Ibid.
25. Griffith, John R., & White, Kenneth R. (2007). *The Well-Managed Healthcare Organization* (6th ed., p.52).
26. Snedaker, Susan. (2017). *Leading Healthcare IT: Managing to Succeed.* Boca Raton, FL: Taylor & Francis, pp. 7–8
27. Hoyle, D. (2009). *ISO 9000 Quality Systems Handbook: Using the Standards as a Framework for Business Improvement* (6th ed.). Burlington, MA: Elsevier.
28. Ibid.

Questions

For answers to the questions in this section, see the Answer Key beginning on page 175.

Section I. Healthcare and Technology Environments

Chapter 1: Healthcare Environment

Question 1

Patients who engage with their healthcare provider:

A. Experience better clinical outcomes
B. Have less expensive medical bills
C. Have fewer hospital visits
D. Live longer

Question 2

Outpatient providers include:

A. Ambulatory Surgery Centers
B. Emergency Departments
C. Community Health Clinics
D. All of the above

Question 3

The European healthcare system ensures that:

A. All citizens pay the same amount for healthcare coverage
B. All citizens may only receive healthcare in their country of origin
C. All citizens have access to basic healthcare
D. All citizens follow government healthcare guidelines

Question 4

Which plan is NOT part of Managed Care Plans?

A. Health Maintenance Organization
B. Medicaid
C. Preferred Provider Organization
D. Point of Service

Question 5

The cost of health insurance is influenced by:

A. Prescription costs
B. Technology costs
C. The prevalence of chronic conditions
D. All of the above

Question 6

Private insurance is regulated by ________.

A. State and Federal laws
B. Insurance and claims companies
C. Hospital and provider guidelines
D. State laws

Question 7

Coding is part of the ________ cycle.

A. Software design
B. Standardization
C. Authorization for service
D. Medical billing

Question 8

The ____ code determines what the hospital will be paid for all acute care services associated with the patient's case.

A. APC
B. DRG
C. Capitation
D. Self-pay

Chapter 2: Technology Environment

Question 1

There are two types of software: application and ______ software.

A. System
B. Multimedia
C. Process
D. Utility

Question 2

Knowledge management is a strategy that concentrates on:

A. Obtaining knowledge
B. Creating knowledge
C. Disseminating knowledge
D. All of the above

■ Question 3

CPOE helps medical practitioners ________________.

A. Track their patients' locations
B. Schedule patient appointments
C. Create and manage orders for medications and medical services
D. All of the above

■ Question 4

The data repository of a hospital's data warehouse system gathers data from the hospital's ________________.

A. Healthcare systems
B. Administration systems
C. Ancillary systems
D. All of the above

■ Question 5

Programming languages have ____________, just like natural languages.

A. Code
B. Syntax
C. Meaning
D. Greetings

■ Question 6

Which is NOT a factor to improve the use of technology in the delivery of care worldwide?

A. Rising healthcare costs
B. Aging populations
C. Patient data
D. Labor shortages

■ Question 7

To address the exchange of health data across borders in Europe, the eHealth Digital Service Infrastructure was developed; similar to __________ in the states.

A. HIE
B. FIHR
C. EHR
D. BI

■ Question 8

ePrescribing usually refers to ________________.

A. Hospital medication prescribing
B. Telehealth medicine
C. Outpatient prescribing
D. Diabetes medication

Section II. Clinical Informatics

Chapter 3: Clinical Informatics

Question 1

The Messaging Standard used for imaging is:

A. IEEE
B. HL7
C. DICOM
D. X12N

Question 2

The HITECH Act in the United States (U.S.) was intended to do what?

A. Encourage the implementation of electronic health records
B. Push for improved financial status
C. Include children <12 years old in the electronic health record
D. None of the above

Question 3

A solid-state drive is defined as:

A. An optional storage device
B. A data storage device with no moving mechanical components
C. A graphics card
D. The working memory of a computer

Question 4

The difference between hardware and software is:

A. Hardware is unbreakable and software is moveable and soft to the touch
B. Hardware is an internal programming and software is responsible for storing data
C. Hardware consists of several items, including interface equipment, and software consists of applications such as ones that can start and run a computer
D. Hardware is the computer's operating system and software is items such as keyboards and screens

Question 5

The Graphical User Interface (GUI) can be defined as:

A. A program that operates the various devices on a computer
B. A graphics display with user-friendly point-and-click capability
C. Software that helps analyze, configure, optimize or maintain the computer
D. A small program that loads and executes the command to "boot up" the computer

■ Question 6

The common measure in healthcare used for reflection of a clinical guideline and key interventions that impact clinical outcome is:

A. Outcome measure
B. Process measure
C. Balancing measure
D. Corrosion measure

■ Question 7

Some common data visualization techniques include:

A. Tables, charts and graphs
B. Handouts
C. Video recordings
D. Social media postings

■ Question 8

Which of the following is NOT one of the Five Rights of CDS?

A. Who
B. What
C. Where
D. How much

■ Section III. Healthcare Information and Systems Management

Chapter 4: Analysis

■ Question 1

What is the correct order of steps for process analysis?

1. Create process inventory
2. Report analysis findings
3. Identify variations and exceptions
4. Identify needed EHR functionality

A. 1, 2, 3, 4
B. 3, 1, 2, 4
C. 1, 3, 4, 2
D. 4, 1, 3, 2

■ Question 2

Choose the answer that best describes a process inventory:

A. Counting and tracking available stock
B. Objectifying and measuring processes
C. Analyzing and improving stock processes
D. Identifying and recording processes

Question 3

The benefit of completing an as-is workflow include:

1. Creates a better understanding of roles and responsibilities
2. Helps employees and staff understand problems with current workflow
3. If the implementation fails, there is a documented process that can quickly be redeployed
4. Provides a point of reference from which the employees can approach the new system

A. 1 and 2
B. 1, 2 and 3
C. 2, 3 and 4
D. 1, 2 and 4

Question 4

Health IT projects can be focused on:

A. Selection of new capability
B. Enhancing existing systems
C. Meeting reporting/analysis requests from the end-user community
D. All of the above

Question 5

Physician champions can act as leaders within the clinical community by:

A. Sharing information about the benefit of EHRs
B. Determining which EHR is best for the organization
C. Deciding whether a new EHR is actually necessary
D. Being an authority figure and telling everyone what they need to do

Question 6

The project management plan involves a collaborative effort between:

A. The project manager
B. Team members
C. Executive sponsor(s)
D. All of the above

Question 7

In the requirements gathering process, naturalistic observation involves:

A. Observing staff interactions to determine the best mix of personalities
B. Developing process scenarios in the event of an EHR system failure
C. Observing people at work to understand workflow and communication processes
D. B and C

Question 8

Functional requirements describe:

A. The electric power needs for a new EHR
B. The capabilities of the system and what the user should be able to do with it
C. The necessary backup system
D. A and B

Chapter 5: Design

Question 1

A medical center is evaluating Pharmacy Information Management Systems to replace their current solution. The evaluation committee has determined that the following system characteristics will be used to evaluate and compare the different vendor solutions:

- System availability
- Allowance for maintainability and enhancements
- Recovery from failure
- Reliability
- Response time
- Throughput

These are examples of ______________________________

A. Industry standard evaluation criteria
B. Functional requirements
C. Nonfunctional requirements
D. Global regulatory requirements

Question 2

Some of the activities that take place during project planning include:

1. Developing a communications plan including training for end users
2. Developing methods for users to accomplish a task when the usual or planned method does not work
3. Collecting and validating requirements
4. Developing a plan to reconstruct the project architecture to determine whether it is still valid

A. 1 and 4
B. 1 and 3
C. 1, 2 and 3
D. All of the above

Question 3

A hospital has decided that their new Radiology Information System design will be shaped by an understanding of the capabilities, as well as the limitations of the user. This is an example of ______________.

A. System design by area of focus
B. A swift user development plan
C. User-centered design
D. Universal Radiology system recommendations

Question 4

When users have to log into several disparate systems, forcing them to have to know how to use multiple systems and remember numerous logins and passwords, creating overly complex workflows, ultimately increasing the chance of error, the system suffers from a problem with ________________.

A. Connectivity
B. Usability
C. Reliability
D. ROI

Question 5

An EHR implementation team has decided that requirements for the new system may be gathered by observing people at work in order to understand workflow and communication processes. This is an example of ________________.

A. Deductive observation
B. Inductive observation
C. Work processes observation
D. Naturalistic observation

Question 6

Once the functional and nonfunctional requirements for a new system are identified, they should be ranked in order of importance and classified as ____________________.

A. Costly
B. Controversial
C. Not criticals
D. Patient care related

Question 7

The Certification Commission for Healthcare Information Technology (CCHIT) in the U.S., the European Institute for Health Records (EuroRec), the international Integrating the Healthcare Enterprise (IHE) organization and the European open EHR foundation are a few of the organizations defining functional characteristics of EHRs. According to the chapter, what are the organizations using to develop their functional characteristic lists?

1. Digital workplace experience
2. Joy and inclusive design
3. National preferences
4. Associated quality indicators

A. 1 and 3
B. 3
C. 2 and 4
D. 3 and 4

■ Question 8

While the last decade of health information technology's focus has been on the implementation and optimization of electronic health records the capture and sharing of data our efforts are shifting now to ____________________.

A. Using that data to improve individual healthcare quality
B. Diversity, equity and inclusion in healthcare
C. Meeting the digital realities of today's world
D. Collaborating on a roadmap for the future of healthcare

Chapter 6: Selection, Implementation, Support and Maintenance

■ Question 1

The support team for a production EHR system should do all of the following EXCEPT:

A. Manage user requests for access to the system
B. Review daily interface error logs for problems with the system
C. Develop software and new environments to respond to customer needs
D. Provide rapid response to customer issues

■ Question 2

Triage is an important step in:

A. Baseline testing
B. Help desk activity
C. Creating the production support team
D. Upgrading the EHR application

■ Question 3

Certification of EHR systems:

A. Reduces the financial risks to investment in EHR systems by providing additional assurance that the system is worthwhile
B. Facilitates interoperability between EHR systems, as each system would adhere to the same set of standards
C. Establishes a prerequisite for Medicare and Medicaid incentive payments, among other stimulus incentives
D. All of the above

■ Question 4

Performance baseline testing is also referred to as ____________________.

A. Critical testing
B. Operating system testing
C. Benchmark testing
D. Parameters testing

■ Question 5

To narrow the choice when selecting an EHR, implementation teams can determine a system's relevance by asking:

A. Does the vendor offer the best price?
B. Will the software interface with other systems in the HIS environment, and what is the vendor's experience in exchanging patient data with other systems, including a HIE or a RHIO?
C. Is the EHR currently under consideration typically marketed to practices similar to the healthcare organization that is looking to purchase a new one?
D. B and C.

■ Question 6

Contextual Implementation Models, in which implementation teams examine how one should approach health IT implementations, include taking into consideration:

A. Organizational context
B. Clinical unit context
C. Individual process context
D. All of the above

■ Question 7

Important consideration for the system selection process includes all the following EXCEPT:

A. Organizational change readiness
B. System supports the strategic direction of the organization
C. System improves limitations and expands inefficiencies
D. Key stakeholders are involved in the decision-making process

■ Question 8

Training for end users is critical to successful system implementation. Pre-implementation training should be:

A. Focused on expected clinical workflows
B. Customized to specific end-user group
C. Focused on current clinical workflows
D. Both A and B

Chapter 7: Testing and Evaluation

■ Question 1

Which of the following is NOT an important step in creating a testing strategy?

A. Identify testing environment
B. Create test scenarios and scripts
C. Identify participants
D. Identify required equipment

■ Question 2

The user acceptance testing phase of a project usually occurs immediately before:

A. Rollout
B. Project description
C. System backup
D. Project sign-off

■ Question 3

Designing the test scenarios is best performed by:

A. Less-experienced staff
B. Program experts
C. Workflow experts
D. B and C

■ Question 4

The ________________ is a centralized resource staffed by IT professionals who provide user support.

A. Systems maintenance
B. User trainers
C. Help desk
D. Database

■ Question 5

________________ maintenance diagnoses and fixes errors in an operational system.

A. Corrective
B. Adaptive
C. Perfective
D. Preventive

■ Question 6

Systems performance is measured with ________________.

A. Fault management
B. Benchmark testing
C. System faults
D. Capacity planning

■ Question 7

________________ testing focuses on the system as a whole

A. Unit
B. Integration
C. Module
D. System

Question 8

All of the following should be considered in selection of the pilot group EXCEPT:

A. Advice of the steering committee
B. Representativeness of a cross section of the user community
C. Readiness for the technology
D. Age

Chapter 8: Privacy and Security

Question 1

Which of the following implies right of an individual to keep his or her personal information secret?

A. Safety
B. Privacy
C. Security
D. Confidentiality

Question 2

Which of the following type of security measure encrypts data?

A. Physical
B. Application
C. User
D. Network

Question 3

As network administrator which method of *Access Control* would you use for minimal network administration but still ensure that the users have the necessary resources to perform their specific tasks?

A. Mandatory Access Control (MAC)
B. Role-Based Access Control (RBAC)
C. Discretionary Access Control (DAC)
D. Rule-Based access Control (RBC)

Question 4

As network administrator you want to ensure that the Internet users cannot access resources inside the organization. Which device would use for this purpose?

A. Router
B. Firewall
C. Switch
D. Bridge

Question 5

As network administrator, you want to ensure that the data both in stationery and transit forms cannot be read by unauthorized users. Which of the following technology will you choose?

A. Hashing
B. Encryption
C. Scrambling
D. Ciphering

Question 6

Which of the following HIPAA Security Rule Safeguards requires the organization to frame and implement policies and procedures to ensure privacy and security of health information?

A. Physical
B. Administrative
C. Technical
D. Virtual

Question 7

Your organization allows remote users to access your organization's sensitive health information. Which of the following technology would you implement to ensure the security of the connection?

A. PKI
B. VPN
C. Certificates
D. Hashes

Question 8

The hacking method in which the hacker impersonates another device or user on a network to steal data, spread malware or bypass access controls is termed.

A. Eavesdropping
B. Identity Spoofing
C. Brute Force
D. Phishing

Section IV. Management and Leadership

Chapter 9: Management and Leadership

Question 1

Which leadership style is characterized as better at engaging diverse and creative teams, but the process is more time intensive?

A. Autocratic or authoritarian
B. Laissez-faire
C. Participative or democratic
D. Emotional intelligence

Question 2

Self-awareness, social-awareness, empathy, self-management and social skills are all key components of what?

A. Autocratic or authoritarian
B. Laissez-faire
C. Participative or democratic
D. Emotional intelligence

Question 3

Leaders or individuals who are able to use their ability to pursue and build collaborative teams by reaching outside of their own team to include others is demonstrating which emotional intelligence skill?

A. Social skills
B. Self-management or internal motivation
C. Social awareness or empathy
D. Self-awareness

Question 4

This type of communication is important for exchanges that are meant to build interpersonal relationships, when decisions need to be made quickly, or when tone may otherwise be misinterpreted, such as in negotiation:

A. Synchronous communication
B. Asynchronous communication
C. Wheelan model
D. Collaborative model

Question 5

During this stage, team members are reluctant to challenge or express opposing viewpoints while they are still learning how the team operates:

A. Stage 1 – Dependency and inclusion
B. Stage 2 – Counter-dependency and flight
C. Stage 3 – Trust and structure
D. Stage 4 – Work

Question 6

Communication patterns, processes and procedures are all determined, and conflict is minimal at this stage:

A. Stage 1 – Dependency and inclusion
B. Stage 2 – Counter-dependency and flight
C. Stage 3 – Trust and structure
D. Stage 4 – Work

■ Question 7

You are helping to define where your organization wants to be in the future, but you are not mapping out the necessary details of how to actually get there. You are taking part in developing which of the following?

A. Strategic plan
B. Tactical plan
C. Alignment process
D. Governance structure

■ Question 8

This principle simply means that healthcare providers should do things that benefit the patient. This includes both actions meant to prevent problems and actions to address problems the patient is already experiencing.

A. Principle of autonomy
B. Principle of beneficence
C. Principle of non-maleficence
D. Principle of justice

■ Question 9

The following is an example of which? In many workplaces, informatics professionals work with doctors, nurses and other healthcare providers who are their coworkers, not their employers. According to the IMIA code of ethics, healthcare providers have a right to depend on the technological skills of health informatics professionals to help them meet their own professional obligations to patients:

A. Duties owed to coworkers
B. Responding to unethical practices
C. Whistleblowers
D. Conflicts of interest

■ Question 10

Defining quality healthcare depends to some extent on the point of view. Broadly speaking, there are four entities that define quality healthcare. This is an example of which set standards that define quality healthcare in terms of how well providers meet those standards:

A. Professional and regulatory bodies
B. Payers
C. Patients and families
D. Healthcare providers

■ Question 11

These activities are aimed at making sure that the process achieves target objectives during the development and maintenance cycles:

A. Quality control
B. Quality assurance
C. Total quality management (TQM)
D. Ethics

Question 12

Fully implementing these strategies is crucial in creating a quality culture. These activities entail both planning and improvement:

A. Quality control
B. Quality assurance
C. Total quality management (TQM)
D. Ethics

Question 13

Displaying drug alerts at time of order entry is far more efficient than reordering a different prescription upon realizing that the initial prescription will not work for the patient is an example of what?

A. Provide the right information to users at the right time
B. Provide the right amount of right information to users
C. Provide the right information to users in the right place
D. Total quality management (TQM)

Question 14

Overuse of system alerts and reminders that directly results in alert fatigue is an example of what?

A. Provide the right information to users at the right time
B. Provide the right amount of right information to users
C. Provide the right information to users in the right place
D. Total quality management (TQM)

Question 15

You are at what point in the PDCA cycle when you execute implementation plans for future state?

A. Plan
B. Do
C. Check
D. Act

Question 16

You are at what point in the PDCA cycle when you evaluate and measure results for corrective and preventative actions?

A. Plan
B. Do
C. Check
D. Act

Answer Key

Section I. Healthcare and Technology Environment

Chapter 1: Healthcare Environment

Question 1

Patients who engage with their healthcare provider:

Correct answer: A. Experience better clinical outcomes

Question 2

Outpatient providers include:

Correct answer: D. All of the above

Question 3

The European healthcare system ensures that:

Correct answer: C. All citizens have access to basic healthcare

Question 4

Which plan is NOT part of Managed Care Plans?

Correct answer: B. Medicaid

Question 5

The cost of health insurance is influenced by:

Correct answer: D. All of the above

Question 6

Private insurance is regulated by ______________.

Correct answer: A. State and Federal laws.

■ Question 7

Coding is part of the ______________ cycle.

Correct answer: D. Medical billing

■ Question 8

The _____ code determines what the hospital will be paid for all acute care services associated with the patient's case.

Correct answer: B. DRG

Chapter 2: Technology Environment

■ Question 1

There are two types of software: application and ______________ software.

Correct answer: A. System

■ Question 2

Knowledge management is a strategy that concentrates on:

Correct answer: D. All of the above

■ Question 3

CPOE helps medical practitioners ______________.

Correct answer: C. Create and manage orders for medications and medical services

■ Question 4

The data repository of a hospital's data warehouse system gathers data from the hospital's ______________.

Correct answer: D. All of the above

■ Question 5

Programming languages have ______________, just like natural languages.

Correct answer: B. Syntax.

■ Question 6

Which is NOT a factor to improve the use of technology in the delivery of care worldwide?

Correct answer: B. Aging populations

■ Question 7

To address the exchange of health data across borders in Europe, the eHealth Digital Service Infrastructure was developed; similar to __________ in the states.

Correct answer: A. HIE

■ Question 8

ePrescribing usually refers to ______________

Correct answer: C. Outpatient prescribing

■ Section II. Clinical Informatics

Chapter 3: Clinical Informatics

■ Question 1

The Messaging Standard used for imaging is

Correct answer: C. DICOM

■ Question 2

The HITECH Act in the United States (U.S.) was intended to do what?

Correct answer: A. Encourage the implementation of electronic health records

■ Question 3

A solid-state drive is defined as:

Correct answer: B. A data storage device with no moving mechanical components

■ Question 4

The difference between hardware and software is:

Correct answer: C. Hardware consists of several items, including interface equipment, and software consists of applications such as ones that can start and run a computer

■ Question 5

The Graphical User Interface (GUI) can be define as:

Correct answer: B. A graphics display with user-friendly point-and-click capability

■ Question 6

The common measure in healthcare used for reflection of a clinical guideline and key interventions that impact clinical outcome, is:

Correct answer: B. Process measure

■ Question 7

Some common data visualization techniques include:

Correct answer: A. Tables, charts and graphs

■ Question 8

Which of the following is NOT one of the Five Rights of CDS?

Correct answer: D. How much

■ Section III. Healthcare Information and Systems Management

Chapter 4: Analysis

■ Question 1

What is the correct order of steps for process analysis?

Correct answer: C. 1, 3, 4, 2

■ Question 2

Choose the answer that best describes a process inventory.

Correct answer: D. Identifying and recording processes

■ Question 3

The benefit of completing an as-is workflow includes:

Correct answer: D. 1, 2 and 4

■ Question 4

Health IT projects can be focused on:

Correct answer: D. All of the above

■ Question 5

Physician champions can act as leaders within the clinical community by:

Correct answer: A. Sharing information about the benefit of EHRs

■ Question 6

The project management plan involves a collaborative effort between:

Correct answer: D. All of the above

■ Question 7

In the requirements gathering process, naturalistic observation involves:

Correct answer: C. Observing people at work in order to understand workflow and communication processes

■ Question 8

Functional requirements describe:

Correct answer: B. The capabilities of the system and what the user should be able to do with it

Chapter 5: Design

■ Question 1

A medical center is evaluating Pharmacy Information Management Systems to replace their current solution. These are examples of ______________________.

Correct answer: C. Nonfunctional requirements

■ Question 2

Some of the activities that take place during project planning include:

Correct answer: B. 1 and 3

■ Question 3

A hospital has decided that their new Radiology Information System design will be shaped by an understanding of the capabilities, as well as the limitations of the user. This is an example of ______________.

Correct answer: C. User-centered design

■ Question 4

When users have to log into several disparate systems, forcing them to have to know how to use multiple systems and remember numerous logins and passwords, creating overly complex workflows, ultimately increasing the chance of error, the system suffers from a problem with ______________.

Correct answer: B. Usability

■ Question 5

An EHR implementation team has decided that requirements for the new system may be gathered by observing people at work in order to understand workflow and communication processes. This is an example of ______________.

Correct answer: D. Naturalistic observation

■ Question 6

Once the functional and nonfunctional requirements for a new system are identified, they should be ranked in order of importance and classified as ____________________.

Correct answer: C. Not criticals

■ Question 7

The Certification Commission for Healthcare Information Technology (CCHIT) in the U.S., the European Institute for Health Records (EuroRec), the international Integrating the Healthcare Enterprise (IHE) organization and the European open EHR foundation are a few of the organizations defining functional characteristics of EHRs. According to the chapter, what are the organizations using to develop their functional characteristic lists?

Correct answer: D. 3 and 4

■ Question 8

While the last decade of health information technology's focus has been on the implementation and optimization of electronic health records the capture and sharing of data our efforts are shifting now to ____________________.

Correct answer: A. Using that data to improve individual healthcare quality

Chapter 6: Selection, Implementation, Support and Maintenance

■ Question 1

The support team for a production EHR system should do all of the following EXCEPT:

Correct answer: C. Develop software and new environments to respond to customer needs

■ Question 2

Triage is an important step in:

Correct answer: B. Help desk activity

■ Question 3

Certification of EHR systems:

Correct answer: D. All of the above

■ Question 4

Performance baseline testing is also referred to as ____________.

Correct answer: C. Benchmark testing

■ Question 5

To narrow the choice when selecting an EHR, implementation teams can determine a system's relevance by asking:

Correct answer: D. B and C

■ Question 6

Contextual Implementation Models, in which implementation teams examine how one should approach health IT implementations, include taking into consideration:

Correct answer: D. All of the above

■ Question 7

Important consideration for the system selection process includes all the following EXCEPT:

Correct answer: C. System improves limitations and expands inefficiencies

■ Question 8

Training for end users is critical to successful system implementation. Pre-implementation training should be:

Correct answer: D. A and B

Chapter 7: Testing and Evaluation

■ Question 1

Which of the following is NOT an important step in creating a testing strategy?

Correct answer: B. Create test scenarios and scripts

■ Question 2

The user acceptance testing phase of a project usually occurs immediately before:

Correct answer: A. Rollout

■ Question 3

Designing the test scenarios is best performed by:

Correct answer: D. B and C

■ Question 4

The ________________ is a centralized resource staffed by IT professionals who provide user support.

Correct answer: C. Help desk

■ Question 5

________________ maintenance diagnoses and fixes errors in an operational system.

Correct answer: A. Corrective

■ Question 6

Systems performance is measured with ________________.

Correct answer: B. Benchmark testing

■ Question 7

________________ testing focuses on the system as a whole.

Correct answer: D. System

■ Question 8

All of the following should be considered in selection of the pilot group EXCEPT:

Correct answer: D. Age

Chapter 8: Privacy and Security

■ Question 1

Which of the following implies right of an individual to keep his or her personal information secret?

Correct answer: B. Privacy

■ Question 2

Which of the following type of security measure encrypts data?

Correct answer: D. Network

■ Question 3

As network administrator which method of *Access Control* would you use for minimal network administration but still ensure that the users have the necessary resource to perform their specific tasks?

Correct answer: B. Role-Based Access Control (RBAC)

■ Question 4

As network administrator you want to ensure that the Internet users cannot access resources inside the organization. Which device would you use for this purpose?

Correct answer: B. Firewall

■ Question 5

As network administrator, you want to ensure that the data both in stationery and transit forms cannot be read by unauthorized users. Which of the following technology will you choose?

Correct answer: B. Encryption

■ Question 6

Which of the following HIPAA Security Rule Safeguards requires the organization to frame and implement policies and procedures to ensure privacy and security of health information?

Correct answer: B. Administrative

■ Question 7

Your organization allows remote users to access your organization's sensitive health information. Which of the following technology would you implement to ensure the security of the connection?

Correct answer: B. VPN

■ Question 8

The hacking method in which the hacker impersonates another device or user on a network to steal data, spread malware or bypass access controls is termed ________.

Correct answer: B. Identity Spoofing

■ Section IV. Management and Leadership

Chapter 9: Management and Leadership

■ Question 1

Which leadership style is characterized as better at engaging diverse and creative teams, but the process is more time intensive?

Correct answer: C. Participative or democratic

■ Question 2

Self-awareness, social-awareness, empathy, self-management and social skills are all key components of what?

Correct answer: D. Emotional intelligence

■ Question 3

Leaders or individuals who are able to use their ability to pursue and build collaborative teams by reaching outside of their own team to include others is demonstrating which emotional intelligence skill?

Correct answer: A. Social skills

■ Question 4

This type of communication is important for exchanges that are meant to build interpersonal relationships, when decisions need to be made quickly or when tone may otherwise be misinterpreted, such as in negotiation.

Correct answer: A. Synchronous communication

■ Question 5

During this stage, team members are reluctant to challenge or express opposing viewpoints while they are still learning how the team operates.

Correct answer: A. Stage 1 – Dependency and inclusion

■ Question 6

Communication patterns, processes and procedures are all determined, and conflict is minimal at this stage.

Correct answer: D. Stage 4 – Work

■ Question 7

You are helping to define where your organization wants to be in the future, but you are not mapping out the necessary details of how to actually get there. You are taking part in developing which of the following?

Correct answer: A. Strategic plan

■ Question 8

This principle simply means that healthcare providers should do things that benefit the patient. This includes both actions meant to prevent problems and actions to address problems the patient is already experiencing.

Correct answer: B. Principle of beneficence

■ Question 9

The following is an example of which? In many workplaces, informatics professionals work with doctors, nurses and other healthcare providers who are their coworkers, not their employers. According to the IMIA code of ethics, healthcare providers have a right to depend on the technological skills of health informatics professionals to help them meet their own professional obligations to patients.

Correct answer: A. Duties owed to coworkers

■ Question 10

Defining quality healthcare depends to some extent on the point of view. Broadly speaking, there are four entities that define quality healthcare. This is an example of which set standards that define quality healthcare in terms of how well providers meet those standards.

Correct answer: A. Professional and regulatory bodies

■ Question 11

These activities are aimed at making sure that the process achieves target objectives during the development and maintenance cycles.

Correct answer: B. Quality assurance

■ Question 12

Fully implementing these strategies is crucial in creating a quality culture. These activities entail both planning and improvement.

Correct answer: C. Total quality management (TQM)

■ Question 13

Displaying drug alerts at time of order entry is far more efficient than reordering a different prescription upon realizing that the initial prescription will not work for the patient is an example of what?

Correct answer: A. Provide the right information to users at the right time

■ Question 14

Overuse of system alerts and reminders that directly results in alert fatigue is an example of what?

Correct answer: B. Provide the right amount of right information to users

■ Question 15

You are at what point in the PDCA cycle when you execute implementation plans for future state?

Correct answer: B. Do

■ Question 16

You are at what point in the PDCA cycle when you evaluate and measure results for corrective and preventative actions?

Correct answer: C. Check

Index

Note: Locators in *italics* represent figures and **bold** indicate tables in the text.

R

S

T

U

V

W

X